MASS ENLIGHTENMENT

SUNY SERIES IN SOCIAL
AND POLITICAL THOUGHT

KENNETH BAYNES, EDITOR

MASS ENLIGHTENMENT

Critical Studies
in
Rousseau and Diderot

Julia Simon

State University of New York Press

Published by
State University of New York Press, Albany

For information, address State University of New York
Press, State University Plaza, Albany, N.Y., 12246

Production by E. Moore
Marketing by Bernadette LaManna

Library of Congress Cataloging-in-Publication Data

Simon, Julia, 1961-
    Mass enlightenment : critical studies in Rousseau and Diderot /
Julia Simon.
        p.   cm. — (SUNY series in social and political thought)
    Includes bibliographical references and index.
    ISBN 0-7914-2637-8 (acid-free paper). — ISBN 0-7914-2638-6 (pbk.
: acid-free paper)
    1. Rousseau, Jean-Jacques, 1712-1778. 2. Diderot, Denis,
1713-1784. 3. Enlightenment—France. 4. France—Intellectual
life—18th century. I. Title. II. Series.
B2137.S55 1995
194—dc20   94-23757
                                                                CIP

10 9 8 7 6 5 4 3 2 1

TO SABINA

Contents

Preface

Interdisciplinary work such as the present study runs a certain number of risks. In attempting to combine the fields of literary criticism, philosophy, history of ideas, and political theory, I found myself faced with interesting conflicts between and among the disciplines. While literary critics never stray far from the text at hand, philosophers construct arguments, which may or may not follow the exact wording of the texts under analysis, and historians of ideas and political theorists seem to use the texts under study as a point of departure rather than as a court of last appeal.

Since my own training is in literary criticism, those who are expecting a work that strays far from the texts analyzed will be disappointed. For although the ultimate questions that this book raises concerning the rise of mass culture during the second half of the eighteenth century in France (and all its attendant anxieties) seemingly wander far afield of the terrain of literary criticism, my governing assumption in this inquiry has been that literature, like other cultural artifacts, has much to say about the conditions under which it is produced. This book, thus, belongs to the broadly defined field of cultural studies, which takes texts—be they literary, philosophical, political, economic, personal, or whatever—as a reflection of and agent in the production of history in the most general sense.

The argument concerning the emergence of mass culture is a complex one. I will not rehearse here the case made in the introduction for a critical frame inspired by the writers of the Frankfurt School to explore this question. But I would like to clarify the relationship between the general thesis of this book concerning the emergence of mass culture and the individual analyses. As I argue in the introduction, the phenomenon of mass culture signifies a *qualitative* rather than a *quantitative* shift. To diagnose the appearance of mass culture does not require counting numbers of periodicals and books. It does involve identifying the perception on the part of writers—and therefore their readers as well—of a change in the conditions of life. These include the conditions of production of literary and philosophical works. But even within these works, I hope to argue that the diagnosis of certain social tendencies by writers and intellectuals indicates the extent to which mass culture had already emerged. Concerns over alienated social relations, individual identity and autonomy, one's position in the public and private spheres, a crisis in ethics and the commodification of culture—all point to the more general trends that we now identify with modern mass societies. In other words, writers like Rousseau and Diderot are concerned about these issues because the individual's relation to the social order has changed and continues to change. It is my contention that their concerns reflect the emergence of the phenomenon of mass culture, indeed, that the Enlightenment inaugurates the mass culture of modernity.

Thus, in the following chapters, I have focused on specific issues that feed into a general argument about the emergence of mass culture. This argument has many facets that bridge several disciplines. The interdisciplinary approach is necessitated in some measure by the nature of writing during the Enlightenment period. Rousseau and Diderot did not adhere to the strict disciplinary boundaries that we know today. With the reader's patience, I hope that this multifaceted, interdisciplinary argument will offer a fresh perspective on the culture of late eighteenth-century France, and thus, of "modernity" itself.

Acknowledgments

The process of production of *Mass Enlightenment* coincided with the process of reproduction. Pregnancy, childbirth, and motherhood punctuated the creation of this work. But giving birth to my second child does not seem any easier for having had the biological experience. Indeed, both "productions" still bear the traces of the ongoing, dialectical struggle of becoming, in which *process* means everything. Thus, in keeping with Diderot's dialectical hermeneutics, I would like first of all to thank my readers who will infuse this text with life by critically engaging with the ideas that I have put down, thereby setting this "product" back into the motion of process.

Throughout the long, gestational process, numerous individuals contributed in various ways to helping my thoughts to take shape. To my family, I owe a tremendous debt of gratitude for their support, encouragement, and most especially for instilling in me a profound belief in the value of academic endeavors. I would like to thank Dick Terdiman for the care and patience he puts into the difficult task of being my mentor. His example sets a high standard both for academic work and for the personal side of a professional relationship. I would like to thank my graduate students at the University of California at Santa Cruz and at Washington University for challenging me to see new things in familiar texts. To the anonymous readers of the manuscript I would also like to express my gratitude for the significant contributions that their careful readings made. I would like to thank my colleagues and friends, Harriet Stone, Vaheed Ramazani, and Zilla Goodman, for their kind support and encouragement. Thanks is also due to the Department of Romance Languages and Literatures at Washington University for financial assistance. Special thanks go to my sister, Lisa Simon, for the cover design and illustration. Thank you also to Nancy Durbin and Melisa Shepley for help in proofreading the mansucript.

The interdisciplinary nature of this project is inspired and enabled by ongoing dialogues with people who question the limits and possibilities of their respective "disciplines." I am grateful for their restless minds, which prod mine when the "process" gets bogged down. I would like to thank David Ingram for years of inspirational conversations and for his careful readings of my work in progress. To him I owe my interest in the Frankfurt School, without which this book would not have been possible. Finally, I would like to express my deepest gratitude to Roxanne Lin and Charles Oriel for reminding me of the pleasures of academic pursuits. Their commitment to asking difficult questions and not settling for easy answers spurs me to push at the boundaries of the disciplines. Without their care and understanding the "process" would never have become a "product."

Acknowledgment is also made to other publishers for the kind permission to reprint materials:

Negative Dialectics by Theodor Adorno, copyright 1994 by the Continuum Publishing Company, reprinted by permission of the Continuum Publishing Company.

Dialectic of Enlightenment by Max Horkheimer and Theodor W. Adorno, copyright © 1993 by the Continuum Publishing Company, reprinted by permission of the Continuum Publishing Company.

Denis Diderot, *Rameau's Nephew/D'Alembert's Dream*, trans. Leonard Tancock, London: Penguin Classics, 1966, copyright © L.W. Tancock, 1966, reprinted by permission of Penguin Books Ltd.

Georg Wilhelm Friedrich Hegel, *Phenomenology of Spirit*, trans. A.V. Miller, Oxford: Oxford University Press, 1977, reprinted by permission of Oxford University Press.

Jean-Jacques Rousseau, *Reveries of the Solitary Walker*, trans. Peter France, London: Penguin Classics, 1979, reprinted by permission of Penguin Books Ltd.

Jean-Jacques Rousseau, *The Social Contract and Discourse on the Origin of Inequality*, copyright © 1967 by Washington Square Press, reprinted by permission of Pocket Books, a division of Simon & Schuster, Inc.

Chapter 1 first appeared as "Alienation, Individuation and Enlightenment in Rousseau's Social Theory," in *Eighteenth-Century Studies*, volume 24, no. 3, spring 1991.

Critical Introduction

Describing the conditions of modern literary production in *Just Gaming*, Jean-François Lyotard contrasts the writing practices of the seventeenth and eighteenth centuries. Lyotard distinguishes between the classical author who knew his audience and therefore could address its tastes and expectations, and the "modern" author who has no particular destinatee in mind:

> JFL: I believe that it is not true that one writes for someone. One can say afterwards: it is a book made for this type of person or that type of people. Or rather, this is what Butor does, one can dedicate a book to the provincials, another to the Indians. But it is an act of donation, which is part of the book, it is not a destination of writing. I think that it is important that there is no destinatee. When you throw bottles into the sea, you do not know to whom they are going, and it is very good this way. That must be part of modernity, I think.
>
> JLT: What do you mean by modernity?
>
> JFL: When someone like Corneille analyzes his tragedies, his analyses are intended for a public, for a set of readers, a precise, cultural group. He justifies, he defends what he does, in the name of a system of values which are the values accepted by his public. And in the end, that is what I would call classicism: that an author would be able to write by placing himself at the same time in the position of the reader. By being capable of substituting himself for his own reader, and of judging what he does and sorting out what he does, from the point of view of the reader whom he also is. The writer knows the demand that is being addressed to him, and shares it as a reader, he responds to it as an author. Whereas in what is called modernity, he no longer knows for whom he writes, because there is no more taste, no more system of internalized rules that permits him to sort out, eliminate certain things, to make others appear, all

this through anticipation in writing. One is without an inter-
locutor. The book goes off in distribution networks which are
not at all the reception networks, they are economic networks,
of sales. [20-21]

While Molière, Corneille, and Racine wrote under conditions that
largely dictated the form and content of their works, "modern" writers are compared by Lyotard to the sender of a message in a bottle:
they do not address their texts to anyone in particular. Less constrained by the exigencies of patronage and the attendant well-defined
expectations of a very select audience than seventeenth-century writers, writers of the eighteenth century like Diderot and Rousseau
found themselves addressing an everwidening reading public.[1] Compared to the seventeenth century, the readership of the eighteenth
century represented tremendous diversity in terms of age, level of
education, cultural background, and economic position. Thus, a work
like the *Encyclopédie* included articles on subjects ranging from philosophy and religion to stockings and their manufacture.

As the subject matter of literature changed and expanded to
meet the needs of the changing "literary" public, so too did the production of books. To continue with the *Encyclopédie* as a prime
example of the changes in literary production and dissemination
during the eighteenth century, Robert Darnton explains in *The Business of Enlightenment* that format and price shrank while print-
runs grew to meet the demands of the "new" public:

> The *Encyclopédie* became smaller in size and cheaper in price
> as it progressed from edition to edition. While the format
> shrank from folio to quarto and octavo, the subscription price
> fell from 980 to 840, 384 and 225 livres. At the same time, the
> size of the pressruns increased—from 4,225 and 2,200 in the
> case of the two folio editions, to more than 8,000 quartos and
> 6,000 octavos. Having satisfied the "quality market," the pub-
> lishers tried to reach a broader public by producing in quan-
> tity. [273]

Darnton's studies demonstrate the extent to which the book market
began to cater to the needs of the less well-off in the latter part of the
eighteenth century. Books became affordable for the middle class as
well as for some skilled artisans and tradespeople.[2]

Although the growth of the reading public in terms of numbers does not perhaps justify the use of the term "mass," the changes

in the production and dissemination of literature indicate that a fundamental *qualitative* shift took place during the eighteenth century.[3] This shift is responsible for a change in the perception of writing as an occupation and in the writer's relation to the public.[4] Increasingly distanced and alienated from their public, writers set their "message in a bottle" adrift into a sea of anonymous readers.[5]

These changes in the production and dissemination of literature anticipate the appearance of mass culture in the nineteenth and twentieth centuries, because they necessitate the same types of changes in the authors' attitudes with respect to both their work and audience. As Elizabeth Eisenstein has pointed out in her study of the printing press, "The advent of an 'industrialized' society is too often made responsible for conditions that were shaped by an ongoing revolution in communications."[6] Industrialization only spurred a process that had already been set in motion by the advent of the printing press and significant changes in the composition of the reading public. Thus, in this sense, the writers of the Enlightenment are part of the beginning of the phenomenon of mass culture and it is in this sense that I use the term *mass enlightenment.*

Ultimately, mass culture is always only a possibility—even in the twentieth century there are no guarantees of reaching millions or even thousands.[7] But reaching out to a mass audience—no matter how large or small—entails creating a cultural space for a certain type of reception. The gesture itself indeed creates the space, for texts not only reflect "the real," but also produce it. Returning to Lyotard's metaphor, it is more important that the author toss his message into the sea than that it actually reach its public. The production of mass culture, then, does not require actually reaching a "magic number" of people, it requires creating a space for a cultural possibility.

The following study focuses on the appearance of "mass culture"—with all of its attendant anxieties—as it is manifested in the works of Rousseau and Diderot. It reads back into their texts the development of industrial societies, mass consumer markets, and the crisis tendencies of late capitalism. In other words, it looks at the late eighteenth century in light of late twentieth-century problems and preoccupations. In a sense, it does an injustice to the eighteenth century. It bends and distorts its texts and representations as they are refracted through the prism of twentieth-century theory. But the distortions of hindsight are inevitable.[8] Rather than focus on these distortions, I would like to suggest that my study of the late eighteenth century sheds light on twentieth-century dilemmas by offering insight into the "roots" of our problems. Reading eighteenth-century texts through twentieth-century theory foregrounds the problems of "modernity" as they were already articulated during the Enlightenment. It is my hope that this history of early "modernity" will provide insight into late twentieth-century problems and vice versa.

———————

Tracing the emergence of mass culture in the texts of Rousseau and Diderot requires a critical approach that takes into account social, historical, and economic factors as they affect literature. To this end, I have relied upon the writers of the Frankfurt School and the tradition that informs their work to explore the connections between the rise of capitalism, the spread of a consumer market, changes in social relations, changes in the public and private spheres, and the production and reception of literature. The work of Adorno, Horkheimer, and Habermas focuses on the tensions and contradictions of capitalism as they play themselves out in twentieth-century culture. I have used their analyses to look back at the eighteenth century and the beginning of capitalism to diagnose the same tensions and contradictions that they see at work in late capitalism. In particular, I have borrowed their use of dialectical method to critique bourgeois ideology in its nascent form.

Horkheimer and Adorno's analysis of the dialectic of enlightenment illustrates their method. *Dialectic of Enlightenment* begins by noting that, "in the most general sense of progressive thought, the Enlightenment has always aimed at liberating men from fear and establishing their sovereignty. Yet the fully enlightened earth radiates disaster triumphant" (3). From this grim opening Horkheimer and Adorno develop the thesis that there is a price to be paid for "enlightenment"—that enlightenment leads to its opposite—domination. They maintain that the spread of reason and knowledge entails the "enslavement of men," because "technology is the essence of this knowledge" (4).

As Horkheimer and Adorno see it, the negative side of enlightenment is a result of the conception of reason as domination, which developed from the seventeenth century on. Building on Weber's theory of rationalization, Horkheimer and Adorno interpret the birth of science as the beginning of reason's domination of nature.[9] The scientific-analytical gaze cuts and classifies in order to understand and use nature. Diderot's *Encyclopédie* illustrates this attempt to circumscribe and thus contain nature within knowledge.[10] Coupled with the rise of capitalism, disenchanted nature becomes the raw material for the capitalist/scientist to exploit. In the context of the eighteenth century, scientific rationality encourages means-ends calculation in order to turn a profit. Not only nature but human beings as well are seen as tools and resources to be skillfully manipulated by the capitalist.

Rationality in the service of capitalism undermined the religious-metaphysical worldview that pervaded in Europe well into the seventeenth century. On the positive side, the claims of universal reason helped to undermine aristocratic privilege and the abuses of the church, and thus are responsible for the destruction of the ancien régime. On the negative side, reason conceived as domination was also responsible for undermining the foundations for ethical life. As means-ends calculation replaced respect for nature and other human beings grounded in religious belief, exploitation and colonization were justified in the name of the free market. Human beings became simply another commodity to be exploited. The work of the Marquis de Sade represents the most exaggerated example of this phenomenon from French literature. In Sade's work, libertines justify every kind of excess and abuse in the name of rationality and utility.

In the eyes of Horkheimer and Adorno, the spread of Enlightenment rationality led to the alienation of modern life under capitalism. Following Marx, they believe that human beings became alienated from both the products of their labor and from each other as the capitalist market dictated the forms of social relations. Moreover, political life was also influenced by the needs and interests of capitalism. As the bourgeois individual increasingly experienced alienation in the public sphere, the private sphere gained in importance as a haven of domestic bliss and fulfillment. In bourgeois ideology, the private sphere promised the moral values and sense of wholeness that were found to be lacking in the public sphere.

But the private sphere could offer no haven from the rigors of alienated public life. Instead, the domestic sphere merely replicated the problems and tensions of capitalism as they were played out in the family. Ultimately, the dialectical relation between the public and private spheres requires that they represent different instances of the same set of problems. Due to alienation and commodification, bourgeois individuals find that they are just as isolated and secluded in the private sphere as they are in the public sphere.

New art forms appeared during the eighteenth century that testify to the growing importance of the private sphere despite its ultimate inability to shield against the alienation of public life. The domestic novel, genre paintings, and portraiture, as well as bourgeois drama, all suggest the increasing emphasis being placed on activities within the home. But these art forms also suggest that the public sphere easily penetrates into the private sphere. The novels in particular tend to have a homogenizing effect on the "culture" of the domestic space. Readers of Rousseau and Richardson were moved to tears because of their bourgeois sensibilities, but also imitated these authors and named their children after their characters.[11] Thus, the private sphere becomes merely the mirror image of the public sphere, alienated and commodified by the capitalist market.

In *Dialectic of Enlightenment*, Horkheimer and Adorno link the appearance of the "culture industry" to the same dialectic of enlightenment, which they hold responsible for the spread of domination in other political and social forms. In spite of technological advances, Horkheimer and Adorno find that culture bears the mark of homogeneity:

> The sociological theory that the loss of the support of objectively established religion, the dissolution of the last remnants of precapitalism, together with technological and social differentiation or specialization, have led to cultural chaos is disproved every day: for culture now impresses the same stamp on everything. [120]

Their analysis highlights repetition and conformity in cultural productions—characteristic effects of reason's efforts at domination. Culture ultimately replicates reason's alienating effects in the private sphere where it is consumed. In the eighteenth-century context, I will argue that these same forces—although not on the same scale as in the twentieth century—are at work in early bourgeois culture, which most often represents the domestic space with homogenizing effects.

The eighteenth-century public sphere also bears the stamp of the market in its cultural productions. While the culture industry does not yet exist in the form recognized by Horkheimer and Adorno, the market is nonetheless already having a palpable effect on culture.[12] As Habermas's genetic account of the public sphere makes clear, this social space emerges historically as part of an effort to protect private property against tyrannical intervention by the state (74). Habermas sees the bourgeois public sphere as an outgrowth of the creation of an autonomous market for capitalist trade. In this sense, the bourgeois public sphere and the mode of relations within it are shaped by their historical dependence on the capitalist market.[13]

This is not to say that all public culture in eighteenth-century France is commercially engineered for profit. Clearly, critical discussions are as integral a part of the bourgeois public sphere as are profit motives.[14] But I would like to suggest that the move from state-controlled culture toward public culture was historically linked to the appearance of a market, and that the effects of the market are already evident in Enlightenment cultural productions.

Rather than compare eighteenth-century culture to the culture industry of the twentieth century, it may be more useful to briefly recall the "public sphere" of seventeenth-century France. Thoroughly controlled by an absolutist monarchy, this public sphere produces representations and interpretations in order to consolidate power and authority, the most striking instance of which is the manufacture of the king himself. Peter Burke, Louis Marin, and others have analyzed the elaborate cultural production of Louis XIV.[15] They highlight the creation of his persona in the public realm through the coining of medals, portraiture, and the general pomp and ceremony of his reign. During this period, "public culture" is inseparable from either political or religious culture, and indeed Louis's attempts to consolidate his power represent efforts to eclipse the latter. Absolutism demands public representations that invite of no interpretation or uncertainty. The public culture of the Grand Siècle serves political aims in its efforts to secure reception and meaning.

As Lyotard's remarks cited in the opening of this introduction suggest, the control of culture is achieved in part through the restriction of the "market." Patronage constitutes a form of censorship in seventeenth-century France. By contrast, eighteenth-century public culture is relatively freer of the restrictions of patronage. In fact, the increase in state censorship in the eighteenth century may be attributed in part to the development of a "free" market for culture. In any event, the public culture of the Enlightenment is addressed to a wider audience and subject to broader interpretation because of its break from court control and the restrictions of patronage.

The growth and expansion of the capitalist market, however, caused a redistribution of power consistent with economic changes.[16] Already during the seventeenth century, the nobility was relatively weakened both by Louis XIV's efforts to centralize political authority and by the increasing wealth of portions of the Third Estate.[17] The nascent bourgeoisie, although politically disenfranchised, nonetheless exerted their influence precisely in the creation of a public sphere separate from both the state and civil society. This site of critical debate was also clearly a *marketplace of ideas* structured by the forces of the market.[18]

In a sense, the culture of the French Enlightenment stands midway between the patronage of the seventeenth century and the marketplace of twentieth-century culture. Writers like Rousseau and Diderot obtained financial support from wealthy patrons—which they experienced as a restriction on their freedom—and at the same time, they sold their works to printers, thus feeling the pressures of a market economy. Both writers exhibit an awareness of the dual nature of the public sphere: on the one hand, it represents a liberation from state control of culture; on the other hand, it subjects culture to the forces of the market. Critical debate can only appear once state control of culture has abated, yet critical debate also signals that the exchange of ideas will be somewhat limited by financial considerations.

With the appearance of the bourgeois public sphere, the possibility of the culture industry was born. Although the printers and booksellers of eighteenth-century France could not engage in the kinds of marketing strategies devised today by Madison Avenue, they nonetheless sought to create everwidening markets of distribution. Sales of books promoted critical thinking but also helped industrious individuals turn a profit. This is not to say that all forms of public culture are necessarily determined to the same degree by market forces, but only a reminder that culture is never free from these constraints—this is as true today as it was two hundred years ago.[19] Under Louis XIV public culture served the political ends of the monarchy and toward the end of the old regime, public culture to varying degrees was marked by the mechanisms of capitalism.

From the above account of Horkheimer and Adorno's conception of the dialectic of enlightenment and Habermas's account of the public sphere, it becomes clear that using Frankfurt School ideology critique to analyze eighteenth-century French culture does present certain difficulties, in particular in the definition of certain key terms. While Horkheimer, Adorno, and Habermas use terms such as *bourgeoisie, capitalism*, and *public sphere* to rather unproblematically characterize certain aspects of modern society, the use of these terms in the eighteenth-century French context raises some important questions. I will address these definitional questions here in the introduction in order to better situate the critical relation between the Frankfurt School and the works of Diderot and

Rousseau that I analyze in the following chapters.[20]

Much recent historical work has centered on the problem of the "bourgeoisie" in eighteenth-century France. Since the late 1960s revisionist historians such as Alfred Cobban, Elizabeth Eisenstein, William Doyle, George V. Taylor, Colin Lucas, and Guy Chaussinand-Nogaret have debated Marxist historians about the existence of the bourgeoisie in France during the prerevolutionary period.[21] At stake in this debate is the conception of the revolution of 1789 as a bourgeois cultural revolution goaded by class antagonism between the aristocracy and the bourgeoisie. Many of these writers have correctly pointed out that the bourgeoisie was not economically distinguishable from the aristocracy either from the perspective of their professions or sources of income. George C. Comninel ably summarizes the revisionist position in his defense of Marxist theory:

> The bourgeoisie was certainly not a capitalist class. Lawyers and owners of non-noble state offices—notaries, bailiffs, lower-ranking magistrates, etc.—along with the far less numerous private professionals, together formed the largest group within the bourgeoisie. They may have been as much as 60 percent of the whole; they certainly were not much less than a majority. The next largest group, at about one-third of the total, were the rentiers, who lived off the income from their property. Of the remainder who were engaged in commerce or industry at all, the overwhelming majority were merchants, eager to acquire enough wealth to buy land and a dignified, and preferably ennobling office. [180]

As Comninel's description of the bourgeoisie under the ancien régime clearly shows, they were not a capitalist class in the classic Marxist sense. Their economic identity, to a large extent, was indistinguishable from the aristocracy. Complicating this problem further is the existence of noble titles available for purchase, some of which were a source of income (Comninel, 181). Thus, nobility itself was considerably watered down as a distinguishing class characteristic.

For the purposes of my analyses here, the difficulty of isolating the bourgeoisie as a capitalist economic class is immaterial. In Comninel's conclusion he remarks that thinking of the revolution as a definitive break from feudalism is simply an outdated conception of prerevolutionary society. Instead Comninel suggests that the aristocracy adopted bourgeois practices as much as the bourgeoisie emulated the practices of the landed gentry: "As for the need to break 'feudal fetters', it should be noted that 'bourgeois' patterns of efficient estate management had become widespread in the nobility, even among the great houses of 'ancient' nobility" (181).

In the end, what is important in characterizing the "bourgeoisie" of the old regime is less their relation to the means of production than their style of life. In other words, I am more concerned with documenting and critiquing the appearance of a bourgeois sensibility than I am with individual capitalists.[22] In keeping with Sarah Maza's recent call for "a historical dynamic definition of French 'bourgeois culture'" in reply to critiques of Habermas, the notion of bourgeois sensibility allows for flexibility and subtlety in examining a wide range of cultural practices.[23]

As the work of both revisionist and Marxist historians has clearly shown, aristocrats as well as wealthy artisans share sentiments, concerns, and interests that will later be identified with the bourgeoisie. Thus, for the purposes of my analysis, I take the Frankfurt School definition of the bourgeoisie to indicate an ideological set of values that may be held by members of other economic classes as those classes are defined in terms of their relationship to the mode of production. I would also suggest that bourgeois ideology borrows freely from and adapts aristocratic ideology to suit its needs. Thus, the line of demarcation between the two classes is necessarily blurred.

In the eighteenth-century French context this means that I consider to be "bourgeois" all those who read Richardson and Rousseau and identify with their "family values,"[24] those who have relatively fewer children than typical aristocratic families, spend time with their children, plan their children's futures according to an inheritance plan that includes dividing the family wealth, those who believe in marriages based on love rather than on the consolidation of wealth and property.[25] In other words, aristocrats, titled professionals, wealthy artisans, merchants, shopkeepers, and tradespeople are included in this "bourgeoisie" conceived as a group sharing a certain sensibility that runs counter to aristocratic assumptions about the family and society. Even valets and other domestic servants who identify with their employers to the extent that they emulate them in their dress, or send their children to school in the interest of social mobility, may be considered "bourgeois" in their sensibilities.[26] Many of these "bourgeois values" are directly inspired by practices stemming from a growing capitalist market and the attendant techniques of money management that it produced, even if many who share them are only indirectly involved in capitalist pursuits. The effects of the market were experienced by a wide segment of the population in the form of growing consumerism, commodification, and means-ends rationality as these market-related phenomena had a social impact.

Thus, talk about the bourgeoisie and bourgeois ideology in the eighteenth-century context signals the emergence of a counter-ideology to the dominant one of aristocratic privilege. It includes liberal political discourse, but more importantly inaugurates a conception of family and private life that continues to be valued and influential today.[27]

It may be objected that it is anachronistic and wholly inappropriate to use the term 'bourgeois' to characterize aspects of old regime society. Why not simply eliminate the term altogether in the interests of historical accuracy? I would argue that there are several good reasons for continuing to use the term in the eighteenth-century French context. First, to believe that any late twentieth-century account of life under the old regime would not contain "anachronisms" seems to me to be unrealistic. At best, cultural history attempts a reconstruction that necessarily bears the traces of temporal distance. Given this "barrier," it would seem most useful to openly acknowledge conceptual debts to the twentieth century. Second, and this is related to the previous point, no historical account is free from interpretation that necessarily entails theoretical assumptions. To foreground these theoretical assumptions allows for critical discussions around points of dispute that are highlighted by theory. Third, my effort here is not limited to cultural history, but rather takes its cue from Frankfurt School theory and attempts cultural critique. The use of theoretical language that originally described the culture of late capitalism to analyze eighteenth-century culture allows for a critical perspective that links the past to the present. Some of the trends of bourgeois society are more apparent in their nascent forms, while others appear clearly only under late capitalism. A careful comparison of the two periods allows for critical insight into various aspects of both early and late capitalist society.

Finally, turning to the specific question of the use of the term 'bourgeois' in the eighteenth-century French context, it seems apparent that early bourgeois ideology exhibits many of the traits that continue to characterize it today. The bourgeois sensibility encompasses various social, political, and cultural assumptions that are still associated with the bourgeoisie. But even eighteenth-century usage of the term 'bourgeois' reveals similarities between the understanding of the term under the old regime and its connotations today. Darnton's research has revealed that the conception of 'bourgeois' as indicative of a way of life as opposed to an economic class was accepted and used during the eighteenth century. Contemporary definitions taken from dictionaries and encyclopedias indicate that 'bourgeois' meant far more than the restricted Marxist definition of "capitalist." Darnton cites examples from Louis Savary's *Dictionnaire universel de commerce, d'histoire naturelle, et des arts et métiers* of 1759 and from the *Dictionnaire universel françois et latin, vulgairement appelé Dictionnaire de Trévoux* of 1771 to demonstrate both contemporary senses of the term "bourgeois":

> Savary places the bourgeois squarely between the nobility and the common people, but in a favorable light: "Bourgeois. It is generally applied to a citizen who inhabits a city. More particularly, it denotes those citizens who are not counted among the clergy nor the nobility; and more particularly still those who, although not occupying the highest positions in the courts or other distinguished offices, nonetheless are far above the artisans and the common people, owing to their wealth, their honorable profession, or their commerce. It is in this sense that one says of a man one wants to praise that he is a good bourgeois." Finally, the dictionaries show how the word evoked a style of life. Thus the *Dictionnaire de Trévoux*: "A bourgeois house is a house built simply and without magnificence but in a comfortable and liveable fashion. It is opposed equally to a palace or mansion and to a cabin or cottage of the sort inhabited by peasants and artisans. . . . One also says in ordinary conversation, a bourgeois soup, meaning a good soup. . . . A bourgeois wine [is] . . . wine that has not been doctored, that one keeps in one's cellar, as opposed to cabaret wine."[28]

If the first definition from Savary describes an economic class, it does so without reference to capitalism. Indeed, contemporary usage indicates that "bourgeois" meant "middle-class." The second definition cited by Darnton, however, suggests a "bourgeois sensibility," which I have been describing. Clearly motivated initially by economic factors, the bourgeois lifestyle soon became independent of those economic concerns. Thus, one could live in a "bourgeois house" and eat "bourgeois soup" without necessarily meeting the Marxist criteria for being "bourgeois."

In effect, this conception of the bourgeoisie is more consistent with a Marxist conception of ideology than with a notion of class consciousness. Historically, bourgeois ideology developed around a class that was economically independent and reflected its interests, but it quickly extended beyond that class to include members of other classes. This notion of bourgeois ideology is consistent with both Marx's and Frankfurt School theorists' conceptions of ascendant class ideology. Ideology inevitably extends beyond particular class interests in becoming dominant.

Marx and Engels assert in reference to bourgeois ideology that ascendant class ideology makes its appeals seem universal in contrast to the dominant class ideology:

> Each new class which puts itself in the place of one ruling before it, is compelled, merely in order to carry through its aim, to represent its interests as the common interest of all the members of society, that is, expressed in ideal form: it has to give its ideas the form of universality, and represent them as the only rational, universally valid ones. The class making a revolution appears from the very start, if only because it is opposed to a *class*, not as a class but as the representative of the whole of society; it appears as the whole mass of society confronting the one ruling class. [*The German Ideology*, 65-66]

Putting aside the static and rigid economic class stratification issue in the eighteenth-century French context, it seems clear that bourgeois *ideology* appealed to a large portion of the population, which saw its interests being represented against the interests of either the nobility or the clergy. The eighteenth-century French context provides an example of ascendant bourgeois class ideology being shared by not only the petty bourgeoisie, but members of the laboring classes and the aristocracy as well.[29] In the final analysis, my point in using Frankfurt School terminology is to demonstrate the extent to which bourgeois ideology's negative effects are apparent to Rousseau and Diderot, a point that also shows to what extent it has already become the ascendant ideology.

The fact that bourgeois ideology extended beyond the middle class to include the aristocracy and the members of the lower classes in late eighteenth-century France suggests that Frankfurt School critique of bourgeois ideology in this context will be applicable to a large portion of society. Marx and Engel's use of the term "whole mass of society" is significant in this context. To understand the "bourgeoisie" as all those who accept certain values that dictate a style of life explains how market relations stemming from the growth of capitalism can come to determine social relations in spite of the lack of "capitalists" in eighteenth-century France. The ideology clearly spread faster than the actual economic mode of relation that gave rise to it.

The extension of bourgeois ideology throughout eighteenth-century French society and its claims to universal applicability lend credence to the use of the term "mass culture" in this historical context. Although, as I have already suggested, the numbers may not indicate that a major quantitative shift has occurred in the consumption of culture by the population, nonetheless, a *qualitative* change has taken place that justifies the use of the term "mass culture." Indeed, the "bourgeoisie" represent themselves to be the whole of society and as such inaugurate "mass culture" as a trend toward homogenization and a new consumer attitude, both of which are reflected in the work of Diderot and Rousseau.[30] In the following analyses I will show that these authors were able to diagnose from contemporary trends toward alienation the course of bourgeois development toward true mass culture in the twentieth century.

Any discussion of "mass culture" during the prerevolutionary period cannot ignore the peculiar conditions of literary production under which these authors worked. Turning now to the question of literary output, I will first consider the state of publishing in general during the eighteenth century before turning to the issue of censorship and attempted government control of literary-philosophical production.

There is no disputing the fact that the eighteenth century saw a dramatic rise in the number of periodicals in circulation. The authors of the comprehensive study, *Histoire générale de la presse française*, cite 1720 as an approximate date for the turning point in periodical production:

> One can hardly assign a precise date to the birth of a large press [*grande presse*]. It seems nonetheless that around 1720 general conditions became favorable to the multiplication and diversification of papers [*feuilles*]. Beginning in 1700, Peter Bayle maintains in his *Réponse aux Questions d'un Provincial* "the numbers of *mercures* or works that would merit this name has

so multiplied that it is time to give a history of it. . . . The number of gazettes published in all of Europe is prodigious." In 1723, the very important *Code de la Librairie* appears; in 1724, the *Journal des Savants* and the *Mercure* are reorganized. One could choose this date to mark, in this periodization of the history of journalism, the beginning of this "century of journals," of which a Dutchman speaks in a letter to the abbot Bignon, in 1708. [I:159]

Significantly, these gazettes, *mercures*, and journals often contained in addition to news, reviews, and critical discussions, lengthy citations of recent works in science, philosophy, and literature. They enabled a larger portion of the population to be familiar with recent works published than could have otherwise actually read all the recent works. In some sense, this periodical literature was the eighteenth-century equivalent of *Apostrophes*.[31] It fostered the critical discussion that was the hallmark of the bourgeois public sphere as defined by Habermas.

Consistent with this reading, Claude Labrosse maintains that the periodical literature of eighteenth-century France anticipates the mass communication of the twentieth century:

> As tools of production of cultural conduits, the periodicals of this time anticipate the great functions of modern media. Their organized analysis would enable a better understanding of the processes that have led us to the "age of communication." This instrument also allows us to follow, in the proceeding of communication, the putting into place of "average readers," . . . tied to the appearance of masses of poorly differentiated readers (publics) and to estimate in relation to these phenomena the correct resonance of certain literary events (for example the *New Heloise*). [127]

The growing importance of printing and publishing can be measured not only in terms of numbers of publications, but also in the government's increasing concern with controlling the printed word. As I maintained above, the creation of the possibility of mass culture is more significant than the actual number of people reached. Consistent with this line of argument, the government's attempts at censorship testify to the emergence of an important cultural space. Many of the writers of the Enlightenment were under police surveillance and risked being thrown into prison for what they wrote.[32] In cases in which the government was unable to physically punish the authors of the banned works, the works themselves were ceremoniously punished as part of the spectacle of royal authority.

According to Foucault's analysis of the rise of the penal system, the eighteenth century marks a turning point between the spectacular displays of monarchical authority, which characterize juridical power, and the authority to incarcerate and normalize, which characterizes managerial power. The spectacle of the scaffold was gradually replaced by the mysterious power to control all aspects of life inside the walls of the prison.[33] The power to censor publications represents an odd combination of the two types of power identified by Foucault. On the one hand, reaching into the private sphere and determining what may be read clearly indicates a normalizing function of censorship, which makes it a form of managerial power. However, in practice, publications were ceremoniously condemned and destroyed as part of a display of monarchical authority similar to the torture of convicts. The French Revolutionary Collection of the Newberry Library contains pamphlets that condemn other pamphlets and describe the censorship practices of the period.

In a "*Sentence de Police*" from May 30, 1788, two libelous pamphlets are condemned for among other things being "secret and hidden arms" under the authority of an ordinance from 1786. They are "sentenced" to be lacerated and burned in front of the city hall of Rennes:

> THE SEAT, acceding to the request of the Remonstrances and Conclusions of the King's counsel, issued to him the act of his complaint and his denunciation; acceding to it, *commands that the said two Manuscripts, will be immediately lacerated and burned, by the executor of the High Court, at the entry door of City Hall, as seditious and injurious to the very Person of the King;* commissioned the King's counsel, to investigate through all types of proof, those who wrote or posted the said two Manuscripts. *Commands that the Declaration of the 31 October 1786, relative to secret and hidden arms be well and duly executed, as well as the Sentence of the Seat of the 27 September 1782, approved by decree, also relative to the carrying of arms, canes and sticks;* that Edict of the month of July 1561, the Declaration of September 1567, that of the 27 May 1610, and the Ordinance of 1629, relative to the illicit assemblies and mobs, as also the Laws, Decrees and regulations relative to good order and public safety, will be well and duly executed,

under the penalties that apply: *commands moreover that the present sentence be printed, read, published and posted everywhere that need be;* mandates the Police Commissioners, and enjoins the Patrol, to see to its execution. The four mandated Police Commissioners, soliciting the King's counsel, the Seat had them read the above Sentence and repeated to them the injunctions contained within it.[34]

The sentence maintains that the pamphlets are hazardous to the "person of the king," citing them as forms of weapons. They are to be punished in lieu of their authors in a public spectacle. That is to say, that the textual bodies are to be inscribed with the mark of royal authority in place of authors' bodies. In this display of power the king exercises his "right to put his subjects to death"; in this case the right is modified to include putting texts "to death."[35]

The pamphlet of sentencing also dictates that it be read, published, and posted "everywhere as need be" as part of the display of royal authority. In this way, the government mimics and attempts to coopt the main avenue of social criticism—namely, the printed pamphlet. This aspect of the exercise of royal authority marshals managerial power in its attempt to dictate what is read by removing offensive material and supplying its own propaganda in its stead.

In another censorship pamphlet, also from Rennes, the government explains the necessity of punishing and destroying libelous and seditious pamphlets:

> Vile and mercenary Writers present themselves, and would like to weaken, extinguish, destroy the confidence and hope, the only sentiments that today, in the hearts of faithful Subjects and good Citizens, can sweeten the bitterness of the evils that one feels, and make the idea of the future bearable, confidence and hope, the only good that remains to us, the guarantor and the pledge of our devotion to the Monarch whom his People have not stopped blessing.[36]

The banned pamphlets are cited as undermining "confidence and hope" during troubled times. In other words, they stir up trouble when the public is already disgruntled about social conditions. Thus, the censorship practices are aimed at controlling the influences on public opinion and incorporate juridical power displays to this end. The censorship practices also tacitly acknowledge the power of the written word and its normative function in their replication of the practices they seek to condemn: if the pamphlet was published, a government pamphlet replaces it in circulation. If the pamphlet was read, so was a government pamphlet, and so on.

The censorship practices on the eve of the French Revolution indicate the extent to which the government was aware of the dangers of the printed word. They also indicate that significant changes have taken place in the production and dissemination of literature. The government feels the need to control the production and dissemination of the printed word because more people have access to it than ever before. Censorship practices indicate the perception on the part of the government of an increasingly wider dissemination of literature into a "mass market." Most importantly for my argument here, the censorship practices contribute to the alienating effects of the *literary* market. Writers and also readers are subject to possible disciplinary action under royal authority—a condition that no doubt exacerbated the sense of alienation on both ends.

The following study focuses on the effects of the appearance of mass culture during the eighteenth century in France as they are manifested in the work of Diderot and Rousseau. I have chosen to focus on Rousseau and Diderot for numerous reasons. First, they reacted in opposite ways to the spread of Enlightenment and the attendant changes in cultural practices. Rousseau saw the corruption of humankind in the development of the arts and sciences, while Diderot capitalized on enlightenment as editor of the *Encyclopédie*. Thus, in their work, one finds positive and negative reactions to the changes taking place in literary production.

Related to this first point, I have chosen to analyze the work of Rousseau and Diderot because they are both dialectical thinkers who anticipate the critical tradition that followed them. Rousseau thinks dialectically "in spite of himself." He never quite harnasses dialectical logic to his advantage and seems to get tangled in a web of contradictions. Diderot, on the other hand, enjoys the philosophical challenge of paradox and uses paradoxes as the foundation for most of his work.

Finally, Rousseau and Diderot are in some sense representative of the French Enlightenment. In the breadth and scope of their work they touch on most of the major themes of the day, and do so with philosophical insight and sensitivity. From social and political philosophy to ethics, epistemology and aesthetics, Diderot and Rousseau come the closest to developing philosophical systems. This makes their work easier to analyze because their positions are carefully developed with respect to other positions. It also places them at the beginning of a philosophical tradition that extends through Kant, Hegel, and Marx to the Frankfurt School. But the importance of these two thinkers in their own right cannot be stressed enough. Although at times my analyses seem highly critical of ideological aspects of their positions, I would like to state here in the introduction that my admiration and respect for their work facilitates and even necessitates this criticism. It is in recognition of our indebtedness to them that I offer critical studies of their philosophical contributions.

The first half of *Mass Enlightenment* is dedicated to the work of Rousseau. Beginning with his social philosophy, chapter 1 explores the tensions and contradictions in Rousseau's conception of the individual in the state of nature. A close reading of the *Discourse on the Origin of Inequality* suggests that Rousseau's emphasis on individual independence is designed to check the domination of the public sphere. However, Rousseau's attempt to secure the private realm for individual expression ultimately leads to totalitarian implications.[37] As Horkheimer and Adorno's analysis of the relation between the public and private spheres in *Dialectic of Enlightenment* would suggest, Rousseau's overemphasis on the individual leads to a form of isolationism that fails to provide for meaningful contact between individuals and families. Rather his vision of utopia leads to social conformism, which I read as a form of totalitarian social control.

Rousseau has often been charged with totalitarianism, but the dialectical critique of his privileging of individualism differs significantly from earlier charges. The totalitarianism that I diagnose in the *Second Discourse* involves the effect his isolationism has on the private lives of individuals. Consistent with Horkheimer and Adorno's claims about the homogenizing effects of the culture industry in the twentieth century, Rousseau ironically shields his individuals from technological development only to imprison them in isolated and identical lives concerned almost exclusively with their own subsistence. In a paradoxical sense, Rousseau replicates the effects of the culture industry because his efforts to protect the private sphere only lead to its ultimate impoverishment.

Chapter 2 raises the more classic question of totalitarianism in relation to the problem of community in Rousseau's political philosophy. While chapter 1 focuses on the isolationism inherent in Rousseau's conception of the private sphere, chapter 2 analyzes specific political programs proposed for achieving these ends. Readings of *On Political Economy*, *The Project of Constitution for Corsica*, and *The Considerations on the Government of Poland* underscore

not only Rousseau's attempt to protect the private sphere from technological domination, but also the totalitarian implications of his
efforts to instill a sense of community among the citizenry. According to a more classic definition of totalitarianism as a collapse of
the distinction between the state and civil society, I demonstrate
that the connections between Rousseau's emphasis on civic virtue,
his attempt to impose an agrarian economy and prohibit trade, combined with his call to nationalism, bear a striking resemblance to fascism. Using Adorno's Freudian analysis of fascist propaganda to read
these texts highlights their protototalitarian character and indicates
that Rousseau responded to the beginning of modernity in a way
that anticipated twentieth-century political ills.

In light of the growing influence of capitalist modes of relation
in the public sphere, Rousseau's reponses in both his social and political theory, although contradictory, are not surprising. On the one
hand, his social theory attempts to protect individual autonomy by
privileging the private sphere at the expense of developing communal
ties. On the other hand, his political programs eradicate the distinction between the state and civil society, making the question of alienated social relations a moot point. All relations are both social and
political relations in Poland and Corsica because the state mediates
all aspects of its citizens' lives. Rousseau's nostalgia for classical
republics, combined with his interest in preserving individual autonomy, culminates in political programs that resemble the mass engineered domination of totalitarian regimes. Thus, Rousseau's vision of
modernity anticipates many developments of mass industrial societies, yet seeks to remedy these trends in paradoxical ways.

The final chapter on Rousseau focuses on his autobiographical works—*The Confessions, Rousseau Judge of Jean-Jacques*, and
The Reveries of the Solitary Walker—in light of the changes occurring in the public sphere. My reading maintains that the autobiographical works are aimed at correcting Rousseau's "public image"
and are designed to resist the commodification and alienation of the
public sphere. Critiquing Rousseau from the perspective of Adorno's
analysis of subject/object relations in *Negative Dialectics*, I argue
against the possibility of writing the "private self." Thus, I maintain
that the project of autobiography as Rousseau understands it can
never be realized.

In comparison to the social and political theory, Rousseau's
autobiographical works offer insight into a more personal response to
the changes in the public sphere. Rousseau's ambivalence toward
the public sphere and his efforts to shield the private sphere in the

autobiographical works echo the same tensions and contradictions present in his theoretical writings. They also testify to one individual's experience of his changing relation to social formations. Thus, the reading of the autobiographies interrogates the relationship between the public and private spheres from the perspective of one exemplary individual.

The second half of *Mass Enlightenment* focuses on Diderot and raises questions concerning epistemology, ethics, and aesthetics in his work. Beginning with *D'Alembert's Dream* in chapter 4, I analyze in detail the implications of Diderot's materialism for his epistemology. Comparing Diderot to Marx and Adorno, I maintain that Diderot's dynamic materialism requires a hermeneutics that incorporates a negative dialectic. Ultimately, I contend that Diderot's use of literary forms must be read as an attempt to resist identitarian thinking.

The analysis of Diderot's epistemology in chapter 4 highlights a significant shift in theory from a static to a dynamic form of materialism. I argue that Diderot's philosophical position enables theorizing change over time. From the standpoint of both epistemology and metaphysics, this development is important in preparing the way for dialectical materialism. With respect to the historical context in which it developed, Diderot's dynamic materialism is important because it signals the need for a way of understanding social and political change. In other words, Diderot's conception of an everchanging universe and thus everchanging knowledge reflect the overall perspective that the world is subject to sometimes radical forms of change. In the eighteenth-century context, Diderot's theory provides an explanatory model for understanding changing social dynamics at the same time that it reflects the changes occurring in the social world.

Chapter 5 addresses the ways in which changes in social relations affected ethical life during the second half of the eighteenth century. Reading Diderot in conjunction with Hegel's reading of *Rameau's Nephew* in the *Phenomenology of Spirit*, I trace the breakdown of the religious foundation for ethical conduct and the growing influence of means-ends calculation encouraged by capitalism represented in the dialogue. My reading highlights the agreement between Hegel and Diderot concerning the changes wrought by the Enlightenment. I maintain that Diderot diagnoses the same problems that Hegel sees in eighteenth-century culture.

Ultimately, these are the same problems attendant upon changing social relations identified by Rousseau. But, whereas Rousseau attempts to protect the individual from alienated social relations by isolating him/her in the private sphere, Diderot's dialectical under-standing of the interconnection between the public and private spheres provides a cynical commentary on bourgeois society. In sharp contrast to Rousseau's nostalgia for a simpler time, Diderot's ironic dialogue anticipates the skepticism and pessimism of twenti-eth-century theorists.

Concluding the readings of Diderot, chapter 6 returns explicitly to the question of the dialectical relation between the public and private spheres as it is articulated in Diderot's *Salons*. Close readings of the *Salons* of 1765, 1767, and 1769 demonstrate the growing influ-ence of the capitalist market on the art world. Collectors began to invest in art for its economic value, consequently holding a deter-mining power over the production, dissemination, and reception of art. This raises both aesthetic and moral questions in the context of the eighteenth century, and again highlights the implications of the development of a consumer market.

The interplay between the bourgeois public and private spheres is recast in Diderot's aesthetic theory as the competing interests of connoisseurs and antirococo critics. While connoisseurs view art as a financial investment, critics like Diderot wish to preserve a space for aesthetic reception that is directly tied to the appreciation of the moral worth of art. Diderot's turn toward an aesthetic of judgment—which anticipates Kant's *Third Critique*—locates aesthetic experi-ence within the private realm of the subject. In this sense, his aes-thetics prepares the way for modern aesthetics of judgment. Diderot's art criticism illustrates the connections between the bour-geois conception of the private sphere as a haven from the alienating effects of the market in the public sphere, and also as a site of sub-jective experience impervious to considerations of interest.

If my readings of Rousseau and Diderot in light of analyses of crisis tendencies in capitalism by members of the Frankfurt School underscore the negative side of enlightenment, it is also necessary to point out that these eighteenth-century thinkers share with Adorno, Horkheimer, and Habermas a belief in the values of the Enlighten-ment to shape a more just vision for the future. Far from abandoning the goal of enlightenment, the Frankfurt School attempts a form of rescue criticism to bring the power of reason to bear on itself and thereby eradicate the social ills that are a result of domination. As Adorno and Horkheimer maintain in *Dialectic of Enlightenment*, the Enlightenment became unrealizable when reason ceased reflect-ing on itself, "with the abandonment of thought, which in its reified form of mathematics, machine, and organization avenges itself on the men who have forgotten it, enlightenment has relinquished its own realization" (41). For Horkheimer and Adorno the solution lies in a "true revolutionary practice [which] depends on the intransigence of theory in the face of the insensibility with which society allows thought to ossify" (ibid.). The critical project of enlightenment, which continues today in the work of Habermas, owes a tremendous debt to the dialectical questioning of progress in the work of Rousseau and Diderot. Both of these eighteenth-century theorists problematize the vision of progress they seek to realize. In so doing they inaugurate the field of critical theory.

1 Alienation, Individuation, and Enlightenment in Rousseau's Social Theory

In their landmark study *Dialectic of Enlightenment*, Horkheimer and Adorno put forth a strikingly pessimistic interpretation of reason and enlightenment. They maintain that despite the advantages gained through reason's capacity to explain and ultimately to control nature, there is a dark side to the process of enlightenment. The cost of this process, they argue, is in the growth of domination:

> Knowledge, which is power, knows no obstacles: neither in the enslavement of men nor in compliance with the world's rulers. . . . Technology is the essence of this knowledge. It does not work by concepts and images, by the fortunate insight, but refers to method, the exploitation of others' work, and capital. . . . What men want to learn from nature is how to use it in order wholly to dominate it and other men. . . . Power and knowledge are synonymous. [4]

Horkheimer and Adorno's portrait of the development of enlightenment stresses the emergence of bourgeois capitalist society and the concomitant emphasis upon equivalence and quantification (7). Their analysis of mass culture highlights the increasing alienation in even the private sphere (120-30). What was once reserved as the bourgeois individual's sphere for self-expression is seen as an extension of the domination and alienation that individuals experience in the capitalist marketplace. Bourgeois individuals only believe that they express their individuality by selecting *customized* cars from Detroit or by seeing the latest film. In actuality, their consumer needs and desires are dictated by Madison Avenue, so that these desires may be "fulfilled" by General Motors or the Hollywood film industry.[1]

Horkheimer and Adorno's analysis in *Dialectic of Enlightenment* ultimately points to the similarities between bourgeois ideology

and totalitarianism. In defining enlightenment as increased technological domination, they draw frightening parallels between late industrial capitalism and fascism. Paradoxically, because of the emphasis on
the individual in capitalist ideology, the alienated and atomistic members of bourgeois society are easily manipulated and dominated as a
collectivity. Ideology permeates every aspect of their lives to the point
that they "willfully" participate in their own domination. Individuality becomes "an illusion" perpetrated by the culture industry (154).

Much of Horkheimer and Adorno's critique thus focuses on the
relationship between bourgeois conceptions of individuation and the
forces of domination. They contend that in bourgeois society the
ideal of equality and the constraints of the capitalist marketplace
converge to produce an emphasis upon quantification. Following
Marx and Weber, they maintain that everything becomes reducible to
exchange value: "Bourgeois society is ruled by equivalence. It makes
the dissimilar comparable by reducing it to abstract quantities" (7). In
this way the demands of capitalism combine with the power of
instrumental reason to reduce bourgeois individuals to mere means to
the end of production. Ironically, the bourgeois notion of the self—tes-
timony to the importance of individual freedom in bourgeois society—aids in the domination and suppression of the very individuals it
would seem to safeguard. Horkheimer and Adorno argue that the
highly ideological bourgeois notion of the self relies upon domination:

> Man's domination over himself, which grounds his selfhood, is
> almost always the destruction of the subject in whose service it
> is undertaken; for the substance which is dominated, sup-
> pressed, and dissolved by virtue of self-preservation is none
> other than that very life as functions of which the achieve-
> ments of self-preservation find their sole definition and deter-
> mination: it is, in fact, what is to be preserved. The irrational-
> ism of totalitarian capitalism, whose way of satisfying needs
> has an objectified form determined by domination which
> makes the satisfaction of needs impossible and tends toward
> the extermination of mankind, has its prototype in the hero
> who escapes from sacrifice by sacrificing himself. The history
> of civilization is the history of the introversion of sacrifice. In
> other words: the history of renunciation. [54-55]

Bourgeois subjects dominate their desires by renouncing their own
satisfaction. Industrious bourgeois work either for others (family, co-
workers) or for the future (capital to reinvest). In either case, whatever

satisfaction they derive from work, they believe to be generated by the system. In other words, their needs are met because they believe that the system satisfies their needs. Ultimately, the system demands that they satisfy their needs with what is available to them:[2]

> The principle dictates that he should be shown all his needs as capable of fulfillment, but that those needs should be so predetermined that he feels himself to be the eternal consumer, the object of the culture industry. Not only does it make him believe that the deception it practices is satisfaction, but it goes further and implies that, whatever the state of affairs, he must put up with what is offered. [142]

In the final analysis, bourgeois ideology promotes domination under the guise of rationality. Rather than protect individual freedom, the emphasis upon equality and self-preservation ultimately ensures the self-domination of each individual. Thus, "enlightened" bourgeois rationality culminates in extreme alienation.

This dystopia bordering on totalitarianism, which Horkheimer and Adorno describe as a result of the dialectic of enlightenment, bears a certain resemblance to the dystopic effects of enlightenment on civil society envisaged by Rousseau. Both Rousseau and, some two centuries later, Horkheimer and Adorno interpret the advance of civilization and particularly the growth of enlightenment dialectically. Their analyses focus on the negative implications for the advancement of "reason." Closely analyzing the *Discours sur l'origine et les fondements de l'inégalité parmi les hommes*, I will demonstrate Rousseau's attempt to anticipate and avoid the difficulties presented by the dialectic of enlightenment. I will conclude with an examination of his proposed solution to the problem of alienated society and a critique of his highly ideological emphasis on individuation.[3]

Individuation and the State of Nature

In the *Discourse on the Origin of Inequality*, Rousseau posits the fictive state of nature as necessary for any understanding of civil society, or more precisely for understanding the human being as it ought to be. Rousseau writes:

> For it is no such easy task to distinguish between what is original and what is artificial in the present nature of man, and to make oneself well acquainted with a state which, if it ever did,

does not now, and in all probability never will exist, and of which, notwithstanding, it is absolutely necessary to have just notions to judge properly of our present state. [*123*, 168-69, translation altered][4]

Whether or not the state of nature ever existed for Rousseau is an insignificant detail. What does matter is conceiving of *natural man* so that he may gain an understanding of natural law and natural right. Once he has a conception of natural law and natural right, he will have established grounds for criticizing contemporary society, "after having removed the dust and sand which surround the edifice, we can perceive the unshakable basis upon which it stands" (*127*, 173, translation altered).

But the state of nature as conceived by Rousseau is far from utopian. First of all, man in the state of nature finds himself already in a state of inequality.[5] Rousseau maintains that there are natural, physical inequalities that already distinguish men in the state of nature. These inequalities consist of "the difference of age, health, bodily strength, and the qualities of the mind, or of the soul" (*131*, 175). But these *natural* inequalities are inconsequential as long as men lead isolated existences in the state of nature. It is not until men live together in a collectivity that inequality poses any difficulty.

Rousseau's *hypothetical* state of nature already reveals certain biases that will become apparent in his diagnosis of the ills of contemporary society. Most prominent among them is his insistence upon the isolated existence of individuals in the state of nature. Collective existence, although responsible for the greatest joy imaginable for Rousseau—family life—also introduces the greatest obstacle to the attainment of happiness—property. Isolation in the state of nature ensures individuation and independence, but at the price of not testing that individuation. To maintain that isolated individuals are independent from one another is a tautology.

The isolation of the state of nature does, however, ensure individuation without requiring alienation in the form of self-objectification or reflection. Rousseau maintains that "the state of reflection is a state against nature, and that man who meditates is a degenerate animal" (*138*, 183, translation altered). Thus, the isolationism of the state of nature guarantees independence without resorting to *dangerous* reflection. For Rousseau, reflection entails a doubling of consciousness or a folding back of thought on itself (*155-56*, 203). He maintains that this kind of reflection is dangerous because it leads man to see himself as others see him. In other words, it engenders *amour propre. Amour propre* in turn is responsible for introducing vice (pride, greed, vanity, deception) into the otherwise innocent and happy life of man (*169-70*, 218-19). Thus, any form of self-consciousness that entails reflection is dangerous because of its alienating effects. Self-conscious man judges himself on the basis of what others think and inevitably finds himself to be deficient in some way.[6] Reflection of this kind leads to alienating self-objectification. Rather than experience himself as whole and sufficient to his own happiness, alienated man experiences himself as inadequate and insufficient. Thus, the negative evaluation of reflection does not imply a kind of antirationalism on the part of Rousseau. It may be read as distinguishing between alienating and nonalienating forms of rationality. As I shall demonstrate, in addition to isolationism two other essential aspects of the state of nature—namely, the self-preservation instinct and *amour de soi*—also serve as a basis for individual identity without recourse to alienating reflection.

As Rousseau describes man in the state of nature, he is barely distinguishable from an animal, which is nothing more than an "ingenious machine" (*141*, 186). "Natural" man spends most of his time attempting to remain alive:

> Alone, idle and always surrounded by danger, savage man must be fond of sleep and sleep lightly like other animals, who think but little, and may, in a manner, be said to sleep all the time they do not think: *self-preservation being almost his only concern*, he must exercise those faculties which are most serviceable in attacking and in defending, whether to subdue his prey, or to prevent his becoming that of other animals . . . such is the animal state in general, and accordingly, if we may believe travelers, it is that of most savage peoples. [*140-1*, 185-86, translation altered, my emphasis]

But the self-preservation instinct of man in the state of nature, although it precedes reason (*126*, 171), does differ from that of other animals. Rousseau distinguishes man in the state of nature from animals by granting him a certain degree of freedom:

> I see nothing in any animal but an ingenious machine, to which nature has given sense to wind itself up, and guard, to a certain degree, against everything that might destroy or disorder it. I perceive the very same things in the human machine, with *this difference, that nature alone operates in all the operations*

of the beast, whereas man, as a free agent, has a share in his. One chooses or rejects by instinct; the other by an act of liberty. [*141*, 186, translation altered, my emphasis]

Man's choice either to follow his instincts or not demonstrates his freedom, while at the same time indicating that man in the state of nature has a prereflective understanding of himself as a free agent. His freedom is not dependent upon self-domination, which would entail self-objectification and alienation. On the contrary, the freedom that Rousseau ascribes to natural man acts as a principle of individuation and identity constitution without the alienating effects of reflection. Natural man's free will, although prerational, allows nonetheless for at least a glimmer of self-consciousness:

Nature commands all animals, and beasts obey her voice. Man feels the same impulse, but he perceives himself to be free to resist or to acquiesce; and it is above all in *the consciousness of this liberty, that the spirituality of his soul chiefly appears*: for natural philosophy [*la Physique*] explains, in some measure, the mechanism of the senses and the formation of ideas; *but in the power of willing, or rather choosing* [*dans la puissance de vouloir ou plutôt de choisir*], and in the feeling of this power, nothing can be discovered but acts, that are purely spiritual, and cannot be accounted for by the laws of mechanics. [*141-42*, 187, translation altered, my emphasis]

Like the isolationism of the state of nature, the self-preservation instinct enables the formation of individual identity without running the risk of self-objectification. Rousseau's self-correction from "the power of willing" to "or rather choosing" indicates the difficulty of articulating a conception of freedom that does not engage at least some notion of the will.' I will return to this problematic conception of freedom in my discussion of pity in the state of nature. Suffice it to say that the self-preservation instinct provides for a rudimentary conception of self as free agent.

Finally, the distinction between *amour de soi* and *amour propre* also distinguishes between degrees of self-objectification in principles of individuation. The "natural" *amour de soi*, Rousseau maintains, is nothing more than an extension of the self-preservation instinct. "Self-love is a natural sentiment, which inclines every animal to look to his own preservation" (*219, note XV*, 256, note o). This *natural* love of self is also prereflective. Because man is ostensibly alone in the state of nature, he cannot compare his actions to the actions of others and judge himself based on these comparisons:

> I say that selfishness does not exist in our primitive state, in the true state of nature; for every man in particular regarding himself as the only spectator who observes him, as the only being in the universe which takes an interest in him, as the only judge of his own merit, it is impossible that a sentiment arising from comparisons, which he is not in a condition to make, should spring up in his mind. [*219, note XV*, 256, note o]

His love of self allows him to see himself [the only spectator who observes him], and to judge himself [the only judge of his merit], without running the risk of feeling inadequate in comparison to others. He experiences nothing but "grief at his failure, or joy at his good success" [*la douleur ou la joye d'un bon ou mauvais succès*] (*220, note XV*, 256, note o). But these feelings of pain or joy differ significantly from simple sense data. They are produced by the love of self, which functions as a *primitive* form of self-consciousness. Isolated and guided by the self-preservation instinct, man in the state of nature does experience himself as a free agent capable of good and bad actions.[8] In other words, Rousseau provides the rudiments of moral consciousness in the state of nature. He does not, however, conceive of moral consciousness as necessarily repressive and alienating. I would suggest that such a conception of *natural* man attempts to avoid the dominating effects of reason as diagnosed by Horkheimer and Adorno. Rousseau provides a prereflective conception of self-consciousness, and perhaps in so doing provides the grounds for a different conception of rational society.

Pity and the Progression to Social Life

So far, my discussion of Rousseau's account of the state of nature has highlighted man's isolation, his self-preservation instinct, and his *amour de soi*, but has not touched on the other of the two principles anterior to reason—namely, pity. Rousseau writes:

> Laying aside therefore all the scientific treatises, which teach us merely to consider men such as they have made themselves, and confining myself to the first and most simple operations of the human soul, I think I can perceive in it two principles prior to reason [*deux principes antérieurs à la raison*]; one of them interests

us deeply in our own preservation and welfare, the other inspires us with a natural aversion to seeing any other being [*tout être sensible*], but especially any being like ourselves [*principalement nos semblables*], suffer or perish. [*125-6*, 171, translation altered]

The *natural* feeling of pity serves as a prereflective principle of moral consciousness similar to the *amour de soi*. Man feels compelled to act "morally," (in accordance with *natural law*), not because of his capacity to reason, but because of his capacity to suffer and his awareness that other beings suffer:

In fact, it seems that, if I am obliged not to injure any being like myself, it is not so much because he is a reasonable being, as because he is a feeling being [*être sensible*]; and this quality, by being common to men and beasts, ought to give to the one the right not to be unnecessarily mistreated by the other. [*126*, 172, translation altered]

At first glance, the feeling of pity seems superfluous, given Rousseau's account of the state of nature. If, as Rousseau maintains, man leads an isolated life concerned primarily with his own preservation, and if, as Rousseau also maintains, man is not naturally prone to combat, but on the contrary is generally timid and fearful (*136*, 181), why is the feeling of pity necessary?

Isolationism guarantees that men seldom run across one another. The self-preservation instinct ensures that they are fearful of one another when they do meet. The *amour de soi* provides a rudimentary self-concept without resorting to an alienating form of reflection such as self-objectification. So why does Rousseau include pity in his account of the state of nature?

Pity would seem to run counter to many of the principles established by Rousseau in the state of nature.[9] In fact, pity suggests a capacity requisite for social life, rather than a capacity necessary for independent and free individuals living in a state of relative isolation. Moreover, pity also points to a capacity for identification with another being, which would entail more reflection, and therefore a greater degree of self-objectification, than either the self-preservation instinct or the *amour de soi*. Ironically, Rousseau cites an example taken from literature to illustrate what he means by this *natural* feeling of pity:[10]

It is with pleasure we see the author of the Fable of the Bees, forced to acknowledge man a compassionate and sensitive being; and lay aside, in the example he offers to confirm it, his cold and subtle style, to place before us the pathetic picture of a man confined [*enfermé*], who is obliged to behold outside a ferocious beast tear a child from the breast of its mother, and then with its murderous teeth break the feeble limbs, and with its claws rip the throbbing entrails of this child. What horrible emotions must not such a witness experience at the sight of an event which does not personally concern him? What anguish must he not suffer at his not being able to assist the fainting mother or the expiring infant?

Such is the pure impulse of nature, anterior to all manner of reflection: such is the force of natural pity. [*154-55*, 202, translation altered]

Anterior to reflection and purely natural, the feeling of pity nonetheless requires a physical separation between the spectator who feels pity and the victim whom he pities. What does this feeling of pity entail if not a certain degree of identification with the victim or the overcoming of this distance? Both pity and the natural law that arises from it based on the common capacity for suffering require projection on the part of the one who pities. Identification with the victim based on projection, in turn, necessitates a degree of self-alienation.[11] But Rousseau maintains that this identification remains distinct from the alienating effects of reason:

Though it were true that commiseration is no more than a sentiment, which puts us in the place of him who suffers, a sentiment obscure but active in the savage, developed but weak in civilized man, how could this notion affect the truth of what I advance, but to make it more evident? In fact, *commiseration must be so much the more energetic, the more intimately the animal, that beholds any kind of distress [l'animal Spectateur], identifies with the suffering animal. Now it is evident that this identification must have been infinitely closer [étroite] in the state of nature, than in the state of reason.* It is reason that engenders self-love [*amour-propre*], and reflection that strengthens it; it is reason that makes man shrink into himself [*replie l'homme sur lui-même*]; it is reason that separates him from everything that can trouble or affect him; it is philosophy that isolates him; it is in consequence of her that he secretly says at the sight of human suffering [*l'homme souffrant*], Perish if you will, I am safe. [*155-56*, 203, translation altered, my emphasis]

Identification with the suffering victim, although it does require a certain distance from the victim, paradoxically seems to entail the bridging of this distance. The feeling of pity produces a form of close identification that approaches the effacement of self-consciousness. Reason, by contrast, produces a more alienating experience involving self-objectification.

Rousseau's account thus seeks to avoid the interference of reason in the *natural* feeling of pity by sidestepping the issue of moral obligation.[12] The example of pity given by Rousseau distances the viewer from the scene in such a way as to highlight his feeling of pity without requiring his intervention. This distinction between the subjective feeling of pity and the intersubjective, moral obligation to act suggests that Rousseau's conception of pity, although it entails the degree of self-alienation necessary to identify with the object of pity, does not entail the alienation necessary for moral agency. In other words, Rousseau does not go so far as to maintain that pity requires the subject to compel itself to act. This distinction between the alienation requisite for identification and the alienation required for moral compulsion seemingly avoids the trap of defining freedom in terms of domination and repression for which Horkheimer and Adorno fault Kant. Adorno specifically maintains that the linking of identification with a notion of the will leads to a conception of freedom defined paradoxically as a form of determinism:

> The identity of the self and its alienation are companions from the beginning; this is why the concept of self-alienation is poorly romanticist. Identity, the condition of freedom, is immediately and simultaneously the principle of determinism. There is a will insofar as a man objectified himself into a character. Toward himself—whatever that may be—he thus becomes something external, after the model of the outward world of things that is subjected to causality. [*Negative Dialectics*, 216-17]

Rousseau's conception of pity does not require self-objectification in the form Adorno describes and consequently does not lead to a moral consciousness based on self-domination. By keeping his spectator *confined* [*enfermé*], distanced from the spectacle he witnesses, Rousseau attributes a mere *feeling* of pity to man in the state of nature, and not a rational idea compelling him to act. Rousseau's *natural* man experiences himself as a feeling being and nothing more. In fact, the *subject* even momentarily loses himself in the feeling of pity because of his close identification with the victim.

Returning to the passage cited above concerning the self-preservation instinct, the self-correction, "the power of willing, or rather of choosing" (*142*, 187) further underscores Rousseau's attempt to avoid the paradox described by Adorno. Defining freedom as an act of choice as opposed to an act of will evades the paradox of understanding freedom as a form of determinism.[13] In other words, Rousseau's man in the state of nature chooses to perform certain actions in order to prolong his existence. For example, he chooses to eat berries as opposed to roots, and in so doing he demonstrates his freedom. He does not, however, compel himself through an act of will to perform certain actions. Thus, Rousseau, in his attempt to establish forms of both freedom and moral consciousness distinct from any conception of obligation, seems to anticipate the problematic aspect of the bourgeois conception of freedom, based on a notion of rationality conceived as domination. The feeling of pity contributes to his development of a conception of a prereflective, independent consciousness capable of experiencing itself as a free agent, but without recourse to the alienating rational function of self-objectification.

But the feeling of pity clearly serves another function in Rousseau's theory. Pity is only really necessary if men live in a collectivity. In effect, Rousseau also describes pity as a limit to individual *amour de soi* in its function as a self-preservation instinct of the species: "It is therefore certain that pity is a natural sentiment, which, by moderating in every individual the activity of self-love [*l'amour de soi même*], contributes to the mutual preservation of the species" (*156*, 204). Rousseau's hypothetical state of nature in some sense presupposes a social existence for his independent and free natural men. But it is precisely in this social existence as Rousseau conceives it that inequality becomes problematic.

Perhaps the most paradoxical aspect of Rousseau's account of the development of civil society out of the state of nature in the *Second Discourse* is the simultaneous appearance of both the greatest evil and the greatest good known to man in what he terms the *first revolution* (*167*, 216). Property and love appear together in the first of a series of dialectical arguments that highlight the dark side of the "progress" of civilization. Close examination of Rousseau's dialectical critique of civil society reveals its similarity to the ideology critique of Horkheimer and Adorno. Specifically, the emphasis on increased dependence as a result of technological *progress* leads to a vision of *modern* alienated society, which stresses the illusory nature of freedom and autonomy. Read together with the *Discourse on the Arts and Sciences*, the *Discourse on the Origin of Inequality* reveals a concern with the spread of enlightenment and with it the growth of technological domination, which threatens to produce a form of social life that borders on social totalitarianism.

At the moment Rousseau terms the *first revolution*, the introduction of property enables cohabitation of males and females, which in turn fosters the first feelings of love:

> The first developments of the heart were the effects of a new situation, which united husbands and wives, fathers and children, under one roof; the habit of living together gave birth to the sweetest sentiments known to man, conjugal and paternal love. [168, 216, translation altered]

But Rousseau seems unable to conceive of cohabitation without simultaneously envisaging a form of dependence characterized by a division of labor.[14] He continues:

> Each family became a little society, so much the more firmly united, as reciprocal attachment and liberty were its only bonds; *and it was then that the sexes, whose way of life had been hitherto the same, began to adopt different ways. The women became more sedentary, and accustomed themselves to stay at home and look after the children, while the men went out to seek subsistence for the whole family [la subsistance commune].* [168, 216, translation altered, emphasis added]

Seemingly in contradiction with his first assertion that "reciprocal attachment and liberty were its only bonds," he goes on to maintain that male and female lose some of their ferocity and vigor, but that "if on the one hand each individual became less able to fight separately with wild beasts, they on the other hand were more easily got together to make a common resistance against them" (168, 216, translation altered). The loss of a certain degree of "savagery" due to cohabitation suggests that reciprocal attachment and freedom are not the only ties that bind the small community represented by the family. The man, woman, and child are also bound together, and thus dependent on one another, for their common survival.

Rousseau would attribute this *bad* form of dependence not to the feelings of love but to the advent of property and the concomitant appearance of a division of labor. As he continually stresses, the appearance of property throws into relief the natural inequalities that were inconsequential in the state of nature. It also tends to lead to innovations that paradoxically complicate rather than simplify men's lives. Although appearing to *free* some individuals for leisure activities, the division of labor in actuality becomes another hindrance to *true* freedom. So-called labor-saving devices become indispensable commodities, which require all the more work for their production and/or purchase:

> In this new state of things, with a simple and solitary life, very limited needs, and the instruments which he had invented to satisfy them, man enjoyed a great deal of leisure, he employed it to supply himself with several kinds of commodities unknown to his ancestors; *and this was the first yoke he inadvertently imposed upon himself, and the first source of evils which he prepared for his descendants*; for besides continuing in this manner to soften both body and mind, these commodities through use lost almost all their ability to please, and having at the same time degenerated into real needs, the privation of them became far more cruel than the possession of them had been agreeable; to lose them was a misfortune, to possess them no happiness. [168, 216-17, translation altered, my emphasis]

Rather than free men and women from toil, the invention of new *commodities* further enslaves them by increasing their dependence on material goods. Whereas for Rousseau, hunter-gatherers are relatively independent because they require few tools for their self-preservation, agricultural societies create forms of dependence through the expansion of needs and an increasingly complicated division of labor. Specific duties are isolated, defined, and assigned as subsistence requires more and more complex forms of labor.

As civilization advances, so the chains that bind men increase. In a series of dialectical reversals, commodities and leisure become a yoke; love produces jealousy and hatred (169-70, 218-19); agriculture and metallurgy introduce new forms of slavery and dependence (171, 220). Ultimately, the mastery of new forms of knowledge forces men into a form of servitude to this knowledge (174-75, 223-24). Men lose all their former independence until "domination becomes dearer to them than independence" (188, 239, translation altered).

Rousseau's account parallels in large measure Horkheimer and Adorno's assessment of the effects of the dialectic of enlightenment. While technological advances seemingly simplify men's and women's lives in one sense, they in fact lead to forms of life characterized by greater dependence and domination. The expansion of needs generates increasingly complex social configurations able to meet those needs. In turn, rationality in the form of domination aids in the progressive development of a more complex division of labor.[15]

As Rousseau and the critical tradition that follows him remark, the twin aims of efficiency and productivity spark alienated forms of labor for human subsistence. Thus, increased rationality fuels an expansion of needs and also encourages a division of labor that eventually leads to alienated labor in the service of capitalism. Humans become increasingly dependent on one another due to their increased dependence on commodities. Their work entails the performance of menial tasks, which isolates them from one another. Dependence on commodities also involves dependence on other people, seemingly bringing them together. Yet the division of labor and increased rationalization isolate and alienate individuals from each other. Hence, Rousseau's paradoxical conclusion that social life ultimately leads to jealousy, hatred, competition, and domination.

Like Rousseau, Horkheimer and Adorno also stress the bourgeois individual's increasing feeling of isolation and helplessness as the domination of nature leads to a form of self-domination characterized by objectification and alienation. Even self-preservation serves to constrain the bourgeois individual to perform a function assigned by the technico-economic system:

> It is not merely that domination is paid for by the alienation of men from the objects dominated: with the objectification of spirit, the very relations of men—even those of the individual to himself—were bewitched. The individual is reduced to the nodal point of the conventional responses and modes of operation expected of him. . . . Automatically, the economic apparatus . . . equips commodities with the values which decide human behavior. . . . Through the countless agencies of mass production and its culture the conventionalized modes of behavior are impressed on the individual as the only natural, respectable, and rational ones. He defines himself only as a thing, as a static element, as success or failure. His yardstick is self-preservation, successful or unsuccessful approximation to the objectivity of his function and the models established for it. . . . The more the process of self-preservation is effected by the bourgeois division of labor, the more it requires the self-alienation of the individuals who must model their body and soul according to the technical apparatus. [28-30][16]

The advance of technological domination spurred by enlightenment rationality ultimately enslaves the society that sought freedom from endless toil. Instead, "for the profit of a few ambitious individuals all of mankind was henceforth subjected to perpetual labor, servitude and misery" (*Inequality*, 178, 228, translation altered).

From Alienation to Social Totalitarianism

If Rousseau's account of the rise of inequality in some sense antici- pates much of Horkheimer and Adorno's critique of bourgeois ratio- nality with its reliance upon domination, in combination with his other works it also provides the basis for a conception of utopia. Presumably, this utopia would be immune from many of the ills that he diagnoses in the two *Discourses*. But his utopian model does not anticipate all the negative effects of the dialectic of enlighten- ment. In particular, in an effort to avoid the problem of alienation, Rousseau's emphasis on individual autonomy protected by the pri- vate sphere leads to a conception of civil society that borders on totalitarianism.[17] Using Adorno's critique of bourgeois individual- ism in *Negative Dialectics*, I will demonstrate how Rousseau's model of the ideal society, although protected from the threat of technological domination, nonetheless falls prey to domination based on an ideological conception of individuation.

Rousseau's vision of the ideal community necessarily adheres to the principles of natural law as he develops them in the state of nature. As I have already outlined, his conception of the state of nature stresses the independence and freedom of individuals due to their iso- lation, self-preservation instinct, *amour de soi*, and to a certain extent their capacity for pity. As I have also pointed out, Rousseau's account attempts to ground individual self-consciousness and freedom without resorting to self-alienation and objectification based on a dominating conception of reason. In addition, his claim that, despite the evils that property introduces, the period of the *first revolution* represents mankind's happiest moment (171, 216), suggesting that the ideal soci- ety would encourage the development of familial love. From these claims one must infer that Rousseau's ideal community would be composed of small family groups living in relative isolation from one another. They would be self-sufficient units, producing nearly all that is required for their subsistence.[18] In this way, their independence and freedom are ensured in an atmosphere that still enables them to cul- tivate their "natural" capacity for pity toward its ultimate moral end.

They would be loving, moral agents protected from the alienating effects of too much social contact or too much knowledge, which both would lead to the development of *amour propre*.

Certain aspects of the political structure described in *On the Social Contract* reinforce this vision of Rousseau's ideal community. In particular, his insistence on little to no contact between citizens in order to ensure the functioning of the general will, highlights the crucial role isolation plays in his conception of the ideal state: "If, when the people being sufficiently informed deliberate, *if the citizens have no communication between themselves, from the great number of little differences between them the general will will always result*" (371, 31, translation altered, my emphasis). Moreover, his emphasis on the need for social unanimity (439, 111), and his preference for a small state (386, 49), both suggest that ideally the isolated and autonomous families would all resemble one another as closely as possible in order to foster the smooth functioning of legitimate government.[19] As we will see in the following chapter, Rousseau's practical advice for Poland and Corsica attempts to forge social cohesion through the imposition of an agrarian lifestyle aimed at fostering a unified vision of citizenship in these states.

More and more, Rousseau's utopia approaches a nightmarish state in which social conformity is reinforced by the isolation of families. Rather than cultivate their "individuality" in the private sphere, families spend all their time working to stay alive in the only *sphere* they know. When they do come together to discuss matters pertaining to government, their unanimity is guaranteed by their identical interests. Paradoxically, each individual is subsumed under the *general will* of common, identical interests. Rousseau's account fails to recognize, as Adorno following Hegel correctly points out, that the principle of individuation is dependent upon a universal. "The universal by which every individual is determined at all, as one of his particular kind, that universal is borrowed from what is extraneous and therefore heteronomous to the individual as anything once said to have been ordained for him by demons" (*Negative Dialectics*, 315).[20] Adorno continues:

> Guiding Hegel is the picture of the individual in individualist society. It is adequate, because the principle of the barter society was realized only through the individuation of the several contracting parties—because, in other words, the *principium individuationis* literally was the principle of that society, its universal. *And the picture is inadequate because, in the total functional context which requires the form of*

*individuation, individuals are relegated to the role of mere
executive organs of the universal.* [342-43, my emphasis]

In an attempt to avoid severe alienation in the form of technological domination, Rousseau's emphasis upon the principle of individuation paradoxically produces an "ideal" community in which the *individual* becomes no more than an exemplum of the rule. Completely
independent in one sense (they are self-sufficient), the units are wholly
dependent on one another in another sense (for their *identities*). Their
very isolation is necessarily mediated by their collective existence:

> The general principle is that of isolation. To the isolated, iso-
> lation seems an indubitable certainty; they are bewitched, on
> pain of losing their existence, not to perceive how mediated
> their isolation is. . . . Stubbornly the monads balk at their real
> dependence as a species as well as at the collective aspect of all
> forms and contents of their consciousness—of the forms,
> although they are that universal which nominalism denies,
> and of the contents, though the individual has no experience,
> nor any so-called empirical material, that the universe has not
> predigested and supplied. [*Negative Dialectics*, 312-13]

In the final analysis, Rousseau's utopia bears a striking resemblance to one of Horkheimer and Adorno's descriptions of city hous-
ing projects:

> Yet the city housing projects designed to perpetuate the indi-
> vidual as a supposedly independent unit in a small hygienic
> dwelling make him all the more subservient to his adversary—
> the absolute power of capitalism. Because the inhabitants, as
> producers and as consumers, are drawn into the center of work
> and pleasure, all the living units crystallize in well-organized
> complexes. The striking unity of microcosm and macrocosm
> presents men with a model of their culture: the false identity of
> the general and the particular. Under monopoly all mass cul-
> ture is identical, and the lines of its artificial framework begin
> to show through. [120-21]

The isolated individual believes that his *individuality* is protected by his
own "independent unit," in other words his family life. But isolationism
serves to reinforce the power of the system to dominate these same
individuals. The highly abstract political and social life, described by
Adorno and Horkheimer as "well-organized complexes," is in constant

tension with the almost primitive conditions of daily life as Rousseau understands it. The tension between social interaction, which would be characterized by highly abstract and generalized, almost anonymous relations between citizens, and the particular, need-fulfilling, but also extremely *simple* quotidian existence, would inevitably pull the whole social fabric apart at the seams. The end result of the emphasis on individuation could only be extreme alienation.[21]

Rousseau's independent and free individuals are destined to spend their lives in an endless process of reproduction: not only will they reproduce themselves and the necessary commodities for the satisfaction of their needs, they will also reproduce one another in a society composed ironically of identical, unique individuals. Free in one sense to pursue their immediate interests, their isolation and lack of social contact limit the scope of these interests as well as the possibility for their development. In an effort to avoid totalitarianism arising as a result of technological domination, Rousseau produces a vision of society where conformity is enforced by the principle of individuation. Ironically, instead of preserving individual identity and freedom, individuation serves to dominate and alienate the very bourgeois individuals it was designed to protect.

In effect, although avoiding the homogenizing effects of mass culture imposed by a highly developed social and political apparatus, Rousseau's utopia produces nearly identical results. For these isolated individuals are not dominated by a mass culture imposed from without, but rather are complicit in their own domination of themselves by a culture that effaces difference through its inability to allow for change and development. The form of life of the isolated bourgeois family units is dictated by their limited needs and interests, and the system's inability to assume responsibility for those needs. They are locked into identical, isolated lives in this primitive system as effectively as Horkheimer and Adorno's analysis suggests that the modern bourgeois family is. Rousseau has duplicated the effects of mass culture by homogenizing difference in spite of his careful efforts to protect the individual.

Rousseau's effort to steer clear of the technico-economic domination that he sees as the result of enlightenment—although it fails to secure a form of life free from other forms of domination— nonetheless signals the degree to which he is aware of the dialectical workings of enlightenment rationality. His anticipation of Horkheimer and Adorno's reading of the dialectic of enlightenment indicates that the process of rationalization had already made its effects felt by the mid-eighteenth century in France. In particular, it seems that the appearance of commodity fetishism may have been largely responsible for Rousseau's critical analysis of the fate of bourgeois society. His accounts in both the *First* and *Second Discourses* equate enlightenment with the spread of dependence, or what Horkheimer and Adorno would characterize as domination. Moreover, he identifies this form of dependence with the appearance of property, the division of labor, and the expansion of needs.

Insofar as Rousseau is aware of the dangers of a form of rationality characterized by domination and the ease with which it may be used to serve the interests of capitalism, his work represents a significant step toward critical theory. But insofar as his solution to the problem of technico-economic domination caused by enlightenment rationality falls into another of the traps of bourgeois ideology—namely, overemphasis on the individual—he represents a clear example of a theoretical articulation of this ideology.

Protecting the individual only becomes a concern historically at a moment marked by increasing social conformity. It is this conformity that Rousseau rails against in the *Discourse on the Arts and Sciences*,[22] and identifies as an aspect of the problem of inequality in his critical exploration of the sources of domination in the *Second Discourse*. As we have seen, Rousseau's "solution" also relies on social conformity, but conformity that does not issue from rational domination from without. Rousseau's attempts to preserve individual autonomy mark the historical appearance of mass culture, specifically in his measures to guard against the homogenization of identity through a manipulatable mass market. His attempts to avoid the division of labor, the expansion of needs and commodity fetishism signal his anticipation of forms of domination available under more advanced forms of capitalism analyzed in detail by Horkheimer and Adorno. Notwithstanding, Rousseau already seems to see the potential for manipulating desire and therewith individual identity through the creation of material and psychological dependence on commodities. In this respect his analysis pinpoints some of the dangers of mass culture in relation to the dialectic of enlightenment, in spite of his own failure to avoid some of the same results.

As we will see in the following chapter, given Rousseau's antipathy toward dependence and domination, the problem of social cohesion resurfaces to create problems for his political theory. Protecting the individual's freedom and autonomy in the face of the division of labor and commodity fetishism, requires elaborate social engineering on Rousseau's part. How can one retain a sense of community without encouraging dependence and domination, while at the same time safeguarding individual identity? The following chapter explores these questions in Rousseau's political programs for Corsica and Poland.

2 Rousseau and the Problem of Community: Nationalism, Civic Virtue, Totalitarianism

In the preceding chapter I argued that Rousseau's *Discourse on the Origin of Inequality*, while anticipating many of the negative effects of the dialectic of enlightenment diagnosed by Horkheimer and Adorno, nonetheless overemphasizes individualism to the point of advocating a form of social life bordering on totalitarianism. I maintained that Rousseau's ideological emphasis on the individual culminates in radical alienation by separating individuals from one another. While avoiding the alienation and domination of technological reason, nonetheless Rousseau's theory produces a form of social existence in which nearly all aspects of individuals' *private* lives are determined for them.

While this reading of Rousseau highlights many of the tensions and contradictions inherent in his conception of the individual, and in particular focuses on his efforts to steer clear of the dialectical effects of reason, it does not address the question of totalitarianism in the more traditional sense of the term. In this chapter, I would like to address this issue in Rousseau's political theory, specifically with respect to his more practically oriented works.

Rather than rely upon Horkheimer and Adorno's definition of totalitarianism in *Dialectic of Enlightenment*, in the following analysis I will examine passages of Rousseau's *De l'économie politique*, *Projet de constitution pour la Corse* and *Considérations sur le gouvernement de Pologne*, which advocate political practices that breakdown the distinction between civil society and the state. Totalitarian regimes inevitably blur or abolish this distinction in their attempts to exercise power over virtually all aspects of citizens' lives.[1] Although it is evident that Rousseau's problematic conception of the individual and individual identity clearly contributes to the difficulties in the broader issue of community in these works, here I will focus on the specific political remedies offered by Rousseau to promote social cohesion and combat social disintegration that tend toward totalitarianism. In the final section of this chapter, I will return to the problem of individuation in Rousseau, examining the relation between the bourgeois conception of the self, liberal political theory, and totalitarianism.

It may seem anachronistic to attempt to pinpoint totalitarian or protototalitarian impulses in Rousseau's political theory. For many political theorists, this term designates a specific set of historical, social, and political circumstances characterized by the breakup of a democratic regime, the desire for global conquest, anti-Semitism or racism, or, at the very least, the presence of a mass society.[2] To identify certain tendencies in Rousseau as totalitarian seems to deny historical fact. How is it possible for a political theorist writing before the emergence of mass democracies to be totalitarian?

First, I would argue that much of Rousseau's theory anticipates the phenomenon of mass culture or mass society. In particular, his extreme aversion to Paris and French society in general sensitizes him to many of the social trends toward mass society that do not become widely recognized until the nineteenth century. For example, in the *Discourse on the Arts and Sciences*, he bemoans the conformism of French society, while in the *Considerations on the Government of Poland* he claims that there are no more national characters, only Europeans who have adopted French tastes and customs.[3] Thus, his distaste for conformism and city life in general anticipates the homogenization characteristic of modern mass culture, while at the same time indicating that certain of these trends were already identifiable during the Enlightenment.

Second, as a political theorist, even Rousseau's *practical* works contain a hypothetical dimension. That is to say, that he is able to anticipate political developments or at least hypothesize them in a theoretical way. Thus, I would argue that, although in the case of both Corsica and Poland no direct parallels may be drawn either to Mussolini's Italy, Hitler's Germany, or Stalin's Russia, Rousseau's texts nonetheless exhibit an idealist concern with social disintegration and anarchy that prefigures a totalitarian concern.[4] In both of these texts Rousseau's *solution* to the problem of social disintegration imposes unity at the cost of near total social control. Thus, my analysis will focus on several issues central to the problem of community in view of locating common ground between Rousseau's liberal political theory and totalitarian regimes.

In a sense, Rousseau's totalitarian tendencies issue directly from his combination of classical political formations with a modern, liberal notion of the abstract individual. While it may be argued that insofar as Rousseau simply copies the models of Sparta, Plato's Republic, and the Roman Republic, his theory is not totalitarian or fascist, he nonetheless integrates his interest in protecting individual freedom into these models, thus rendering them problematic.[5] The following analysis will focus on specific aspects of his reform programs for Corsica and Poland, which highlight his nostalgic attempt to replicate classicism while at the same time preserving individual autonomy consistent with liberalism.

The General Will As Abstract Community

The problem of the origin of community, and therefore of the nature of the social bond (according to the genetic logic of the eighteenth century), is never fully accounted for in Rousseau's works.[6] Rousseau purports to trace society back to its origins in the *Discourse on the Origin of Inequality*. In fact, he only includes a brief description of the development of "some gross idea of mutual engagements" between men, which he hastily qualifies with "but this only insofar as *their present and obvious interest required*" (*166*, 215, translation altered, emphasis added).[7] He implies that the first social bonds were inspired by the need for cooperation in performing certain tasks necessary for survival. Almost in spite of himself he thus attributes to man in the state of nature instrumental calculation as the motive for social existence.[8] Two paragraphs later he introduces both property and the family, seemingly begging the question as to the origin of communal life. Likewise, in *On the Social Contract*, he invokes the family as the most ancient form of society (*352*, 8). But tracing back to the family as a *natural* form of society ultimately prevents Rousseau from commenting on the nature of or motives behind the social bond. Using the family as precursor and model temporarily silences questions concerning the nature of community.

The problem of community resurfaces, however, in *On the Social Contract*. In Chapter VI of Book 1, in which he explains the social pact, one could argue that community in some sense already exists. Rousseau writes:

> I assume that men have reached the point at which the obstacles that endanger their preservation in the state of nature overcome,

by their resistance, the forces which each individual can exert with a view to maintaining himself in that state [*l'emportent par leur résistance sur les forces que chaque individu peut employer pour se maintenir dans cet état*]. Then this primitive condition can no longer subsist, and the human race would perish unless it changed its mode of existence. [*360*, 17, translation altered]

As Althusser has shown, not only is the state that precedes the social contract a state of war, but this in turn implies that some form of society—albeit a disadvantageous one—already exists.[9] Rousseau's formulation of the dilemma of finding a form of association that will bind men to each other while at the same time preserving their individual liberty indicates that some type of community *precedes* the social contract:

> Now, as men cannot create any new forces, but only combine and direct those that exist, they have no other means of self-preservation than *to form by aggregation a sum of forces which may overcome resistance, to put them in action by a single motive, and to make them work in concert.*
>
> *This sum of forces can be produced only by the combination of many;* but the strength and freedom of each man being the first instruments of his preservation, how can he pledge them without injuring himself, and without neglecting the cares which he owes himself? [*360*, 17, translation altered]

The united forces that overcome resistance, in order to form a community united behind a single motive, clearly exist *before* the contract is established. In other words, Rousseau's account of the social contract begs the question of the origin of community because it constitutes a tautology: a group must be formed in order to form the group.

Furthermore, as Althusser points out, Rousseau's version of the contract is paradoxical: the two parties to the contract are in fact the same group of individuals (95-96).[10] Indeed, in order for the pact to work, some form of community must precede the pact presumably constitutive of society itself. This prior *community* then contracts with itself in order to form the *true* community:

> *Each of us puts in common his person and his whole power* [puissance] *under the supreme direction of the general will; and in return we receive every member as an indivisible part of the whole.* [*361*, 18-19, translation altered]

Although on one reading—embraced by Althusser, among others—it would seem that each *individual* enters the contract separately, the "us" in "each of us" indicates, on the contrary, that some form of social association exists prior to the *execution* of the contract. Each individual member of a preexisting *us* submits his/her person and power to the common authority of the general will.[11] Thus, the first party of the contract constitutes a community prior to and necessary for society itself.

In exchange for submitting their persons and power to the general will, the group receives itself in return—transformed by the contract into an indivisible social body. In point of fact, there is no exchange between parties to this contract, since the first party existed prior to entering the contract and contracted with the second party—the same group transformed by the contract (Althusser, 97).

I would argue that rather than a contract in the sense of an exchange between parties, Rousseau's formulation constitutes a productive transformation. The preexisting social group is transformed into a group bound by the newly created general will. Thus, the general will emerges as the force that unites the individuals of this community as a direct result of the contract. Despite the fact that a community of sorts pre-existed the contract, it seems evident that in Rousseau's formulation the general will constitutes the significant difference between community and lack thereof. Since there really is no contract, the general will as product of the *social contract*, represents at least a necessary if not a sufficient condition for community.

What then is the general will? There seem to be two conflicting conceptions of the general will that traverse *On the Social Contract*. In the most concrete terms used to describe it, Rousseau suggests that the general will is the common interest behind all particular interests within society: it is the public good (368, 30-31). In this sense, Rousseau uses the term to distinguish between private, particular interests and the interest that ought to be the true guiding force behind the state—public interest. Thus, the community itself seemingly embodies the general will—gives it a concrete form— when it reaches agreement concerning the public good either unanimously or by giving voice to all interested parties (369, *note*, 31, note). Consistent with this reading of the general will in *On the Social Contract*, is Rousseau's conception of the general will in *On Political Economy*, which he summarizes by stating, "The most general will is always the most just, and . . . the voice of the people is in effect the voice of God" (246, 213). But Rousseau at times suggests a more abstract conception of the general will. In II, iii of the *Social*

Contract, he cautions that the general will is not merely the will of all: "There is often a great deal of difference between the will of all and the general will; the latter regards only the common interest, while the former has regard to private interests, and is merely the sum of particular wills" (*371*, 30-31). In the most abstract sense, the general will seems to serve as a regulative ideal shaping the political process, but which itself can never be completely realized. It functions as a *sensus communis* that makes political deliberations virtually unnecessary because of a tacit agreement among citizens of the state (*SC, 372, 31*). Consistent with this more abstract conception of the general will is the role Rousseau attributes to it in shaping the collective identity of the community. The general will gives to society its character as a *public person* because it unites it behind the collective goal of the public good:

> Forthwith, instead of the individual personalities of all the contracting parties, this act of association produces a moral and collective body, which is composed of as many members as the assembly has voices, and which receives from this same act its unity, its common *self* [*moi commun*], its life and its will. This public person, which is thus formed by the union of all the individual members, formerly took the name of *city*. (*361*, 19)[12]

Thus, in the abstract sense, the general will confers upon the community its identity by uniting it behind the communal, moral self of public interest.

Returning to the earlier question concerning the nature of the social bond, it would seem that only the second more abstract definition of the general will provides any insight into Rousseau's conception of community. For if we take the concrete definition of the general will—that is to say, we define it as the manifestation of public interest in actual political process—then we have no basis from which to distinguish the general will from the will of all. Furthermore, the conception of community that ensues from this concrete definition provides no basis for distinguishing between a community founded upon just principles and a community driven by commonly held private interests that do not further the public good. Only the abstract definition of the general will—because it is a regulative ideal—provides grounds for distinguishing between just and unjust political practices and ultimately, between true communities and associations founded on private interests. Paradoxically then, it is the abstract and not the concrete conception of the general will that provides insight into the nature of the social bond in Rousseau's work.

Using the abstract conception of the general will conceived as either regulative ideal or *sensus communis* in the Kantian sense, however, leads to further difficulties in establishing a conception of the communal bond.[13] If the concrete conception of the general will leaves no foundation for evaluating political practices and communities, then the general will taken as *ideal community* in a normative sense requires further elaboration. Exactly what constitutes an "ideal community" for Rousseau? How does one distinguish between true and false public interest? In other words, how does one determine when a community is founded upon and acting in accordance with the public good?

In *On Political Economy*, Rousseau explicitly states that general assemblies are not necessary for determining the general will. Although consulting the general will is the first duty of the good legislator—who must ensure that all laws conform to the general will—he is not required to assemble the people and listen to them. Consulting the general will simply entails acting in a just manner:

> Therefore, I conclude that just as the legislator's first duty is to make the laws conform to the general will, the first rule of public *economy* is for the administration to be in conformity with the laws. . . . How, I will be asked, can the general will be known in cases where it has not expressed itself [*elle ne s'est point expliquée*]? Must the whole nation be assembled at each unforeseen event? *Such an assembly is all the less necessary because it is not certain that its decision would be the expression of the general will [Il faudra d'autant moins l'assembler, qu'il n'est pas sûr que sa décision fût l'expression de la volonté générale]*; for this means is impractical for a large people; and because it is rarely necessary when the government is well-intentioned. *For the leaders know very well that the general will is always for the party most favorable to the public interest*, that is to say, for the most equitable; *so that it is only necessary to be just and one is assured of following the general will.* [251, 216 emphasis added, translation altered]

How then does the legislator know what is in the public interest? How does he know what course of action is most favorable to the public good? On what basis does he determine what the needs of the community are?

Determining the Public Interest: The Case of Corsica

Both the *Project of Constitution for Corsica* and the *Considerations on the Government of Poland* offer concrete examples of how the legislator, guided by Rousseau, is to determine and pursue the public interest. In both cases the overriding concern of the two nations regards preserving their newly won independence. Paralleling his concern for individual autonomy that we saw in chapter 1, Rousseau replaces the individual with the state and attempts to preserve its autonomy. Thus, at the most basic and unproblematic level, the public interest lies in protecting political liberty from outside domination. But this seemingly legitimate goal leads to rather disturbing consequences in its shaping of Rousseau's suggestions for political practices in the two nations. The need to preserve political independence inspires the inculcation of certain nationalistic values and an emphasis on civic virtue, which resemble practices of totalitarian regimes.

According to Rousseau, in the case of Corsica, preserving national independence necessitates eliminating all ties and treaties between it and other nations:

> For whatever reason the Corsican nation wishes to police itself, the first thing that it must do is to give to itself all the stability that it can have. Whoever depends on another and does not have his own resources in himself, will never be free. Alliances, treaties, the word of men, all that can tie the weak to the strong, but never ties the strong to the weak. [903]

This includes commercial ties as well as political treaties, and thus necessitates pursuing an agricultural economy as the strongest guarantee against Corsica's dependence on other nations:

> The only means of maintaining the independence [*l'indépendance des autres*] of a State is agriculture. Had you all the riches in the world, if you do not have something to eat you are dependent on another. Your neighbors can give to your money the value that suits them because they can wait. But that bread that we need has for us a price that we are not able to haggle over, and in all types of commerce it is always the one who is least hurried who makes the law for the other. I admit that in a system of finance it would be necessary to operate according to other views. Everything depends on the final goal. *Commerce produces riches but agriculture assures liberty.* [905, emphasis added]

The emphasis upon agriculture to ensure both economic and political independence in the *Project for Corsica*, however, leads to some paradoxical positions concerning the public interest and the nature of community.

In particular, rather than attempt to foster the growth of cities to increase contact between citizens and thus strengthen intersubjective ties—as the above cited passage from the *Social Contract* (*361*, 19) suggests he might—Rousseau instead advocates preventing cities from developing. He advises the Corsican legislator to adopt and promote a rural, agrarian existence for the Corsican people. Not only will this aid Corsica in establishing and maintaining economic and political independence from its neighbors, but agrarian life will help to inculcate a patriotic attachment to the land. Rousseau writes:

> Peasants are a lot more attached to their soil than are city dwellers to their cities. The equality, the simplicity of rustic life has for those who know no other an attraction that does not make them want to change. From there the contentment with one's condition that makes man peaceful, from there the love of mother country [*patrie*] that attaches him to his constitution. [*905*][14]

By contrast, city life, according to Rousseau, tends to inculcate noxious habits and vices that diminish civic virtue and threaten the independence of the state:

> Cities are useful in a country in proportion to the degree to which commerce and the arts are cultivated there, but they are harmful to the system that we have adopted. Their inhabitants are farmers or idle. Now, cultivation [*culture*] is always better when made by husbandmen rather than urbanites, and it is from idleness that all the vices that have devastated Corsica up until now have come. The stupid pride of the bourgeois only degrades and discourages the laborer. Indulging in indolence, in the passions that it excites, they plunge themselves into debauchery and sell themselves for satisfaction; interest renders them servile, and laziness makes them anxious, they are either slaves or mutineers, never free. This difference really made itself felt during the present war, and since the nation has broken its chains. . . . The cities, populated by mercenary men, have sold their nation in order to preserve some small privileges . . . and justly punished for their cowardess, they remain

nests of tyranny, while already the Corsican people enjoys the glory of liberty that it acquired for itself at the price of its own blood. [*911*]

Not surprisingly, cities only promote the kind of corruption Rousseau diagnoses as a result of enlightenment in the *First Discourse*. Luxuries and other cultural diversions—products of commerce—enslave men to their passions and worse still, make them lose all sense of value.[15] Given his preference for individualism safeguarded by isolation as we saw in chapter 1, he believes that city life alienates individuals from each other, because it enhances private interests and diminishes both feelings of love for the country and a sense of the importance of liberty. Rousseau warns Corsica not to make the same mistake as Switzerland:

> Poverty only made itself felt in Switzerland when money began to circulate. . . . Commercial and manufacturing establishments multiplied. The arts removed a multitude of hands from agriculture. . . . The population diminished appreciably, and while people multiplied in the cities, the cultivation of lands was neglected even more; the necessities of life became more onerous making foreign staples more necessary; this put the country in a state of great dependence on its neighbors. The idle way of life introduced corruption and multiplied the state pensioners [*pensionnaires des puissances*]. *Love of the mother country [la patrie] extinguished in all hearts gave way to the sole love of money.* [*916*, emphasis added]

By encouraging agrarian life and discouraging the development of cities—and therewith the growth of commerce—Rousseau sees the possibility of strengthening civic pride and nationalism in view of safeguarding Corsica's independence.[16]

But what is the price paid for instilling national, political independence as the overriding public interest? How is the legislator to ensure that the Corsicans remain a patriotic, agrarian people, and thus protect them from domination from without? In an above cited passage, one sentence indicates that ignorance of other possibilities keeps the people content in their rustic lives: "The equality, the simplicity of rustic life has *for those who know no other* an attraction that does not make them want to change" (*905*, emphasis added). In other words, the Corsicans will value their agrarian lifestyle—and therefore their independence from other nations—as long as they are not aware that other possibilities exist. In fact, ideally they will identify their agrarian values with the fact that they are Corsican, thus achieving the twin goals of instilling a spirit of patriotism in the citizenry and promoting a particular system of values.

The *public interest* in political independence hence necessitates both establishing and maintaining an agrarian economy, and inculcating patriotic values: two convergent projects. In a passage startling for its conscious attempt at manipulating national character, Rousseau maintains that by imposing an agrarian lifestyle on the Corsican people, not only will the legislator be able to correct the Corsican penchant for murder and theft, but as a result the Corsicans will also internalize the civic pride and work ethic of rural farmers:

> Let the Corsicans returned to a laborious life lose the habit of roaming the island like bandits, let their equal and simple occupations keep them concentrated on their families leaving them little interest in fighting amongst themselves! Let their work easily furnish them with the means of subsistence, them and their families! Let those who have all the necessities of life not be obliged to have cash [*argent en espéces*] either for paying taxes and other impositions or for furnishing the needs of fantasy and luxury that without contributing to the well-being of the one who displays them only excite the envy and hatred of others! [*918*]

But Rousseau does not advocate giving to the Corsican people a free choice in the matter. It is up to the legislator to *determine* the public interest and to "force the Corsican people to be free":[17]

> One easily sees how the system to which we have given preference leads to these advantages, but that does not suffice. It is a question of making the people adopt the practice of this system, *of making them love the occupation that we want to give them, of fixing their pleasures, their desires, their tastes, of generally making it their life's happiness, and limiting their projects and ambitions to it [de lui faire aimer l'occupation que nous voulons lui donner, d'y fixer ses plaisirs, ses desirs, ses gouts, d'en faire généralement le bonheur de la vie, et d'y borner les projets de l'ambition].* [*918*, emphasis added][18]

Thus, the public interest—that which guides the general will—is ultimately determined by the legislator for the people. The general will amounts to the will of Rousseau/the Legislator to infuse the Corsican people with a *good* (read agrarian) national character.[19]

It is no longer surprising that one of the functions of the general will is to establish the *moi commun* for the social group. In the Corsican example, it is evident that Rousseau uses the concept of the general will to establish nationalism and patriotism as essential to the public good. In other words, it is always in the interest of a people to share a common identity, to mark itself by specific national characteristics that set it apart from other nations.[20] This *national character* aids in maintaining the independence of the state, because it sparks citizens to fight for their country. But the Corsican example also demonstrates that *national character*, for Rousseau, is by no means *natural*. It is inculcated in a people; it is imposed and maintained by the legislator.[21]

Rousseau's advice to Corsica signals prototatotalitarian traits in his conception of the general will.[22] Although one could interpret his advice to Corsica in the banal sense that the legislator ought to ensure that the people are bound to one another by a common identity—a national identity—in order to preserve independence, it is evident that another reading is also possible. Because the legislator's job entails "fixing the pleasures, desires and tastes" (918) of the Corsican people by imposing an agrarian lifestyle on them and preventing them from knowing that any other possibilities exist, Rousseau's advice is nothing less than totalitarian. The inculcation of patriotic zeal in conjunction with the determination of civic values testifies to the extent to which the distinction between the state and civil society has collapsed.[23]

Rousseau's project for Corsica involves engineering a set of values, tastes, and mores that will come to be identified as the Corsican *national character*.[24] Ideally, the people will identify with these values to such an extent that they will be willing to fight to maintain them at all costs. This ideological indoctrination involves determining the general will in such a way that the people believe that they freely pursue their interests in an independent and democratic nation. In point of fact, their interests—the public interest—have been determined for them by Rousseau/the Legislator for optimum national security. Patriotic zeal will prevent domination from the outside, while ideological indoctrination will prevent revolution from within.[25]

Civic Virtue: The Case of Poland

In many respects Rousseau's advice to Poland resembles his project for Corsica: here again the overriding national concern involves preserving recently acquired political independence. But whereas in the case of Corsica Rousseau recommends instilling a distinct national character by imposing an agrarian economy and isolationist politics in order to form the basis for a sense of community, the case of Poland is more difficult. The situation in Poland exhibits signs of social disintegration and general anarchy, which make it ready prey for political takeovers (953-54, 972). In addition, Poland's geographical size and ethnic diversity prohibit the easy imposition of a unified national character (971). In short, inspiring patriotic zeal to preserve national independence will be more difficult in the case of Poland than it was in Corsica.

Simply providing a new constitution for Poland will not suffice. In his opening remarks in the *Considerations*, Rousseau underscores the importance of the *character* of law. It is not enough to create new laws, the laws must be inscribed in the hearts of the citizens:

> There will never be a good and solid constitution except the one in which *the law reigns over the hearts of citizens*. As long as legislative power does not go that far, laws will always be eluded. But how to reach hearts [*arriver aux coeurs*]? That is what our lawgivers, who only see force and punishments, hardly dream of, and for which material rewards will hardly be any better. Even the purest justice will not lead there, because justice, like good health, is something that people enjoy without feeling it. It does not inspire enthusiasm, and one only values it after it has been lost. [955]

Rousseau's insistence that the law "reign over the hearts of citizens" is consistent with his characterization of law in *On Political Economy*. In that work he maintains that laws draw their force not from the threat of punishment, but from the respect they inspire, "the first law is to repect laws. Severity of punishments is merely a vain expedient thought up by small minds in order to substitute terror for this respect that they cannot obtain" (249, 215, translation altered). This first law of law, the law of respect, resembles the Kantian law of reason, which demands respect before the moral law. For Kant all rational beings respect the moral law, because reason demands it. Thus, to lack respect for the law is not only to act immorally, but also irrationally.[26] In the Rousseauian version of the law of law, it is not entirely clear that it is *reason* that demands respect for the law. Although he maintains:

> it is to law alone that men owe justice and freedom; . . . it is *this celestial voice that tells each citizen the precepts of public reason, and teaches him to act according to the maxims of his own judgment* to not be in contradiction with himself. [*PE*, 248, 214]

The italicized phrase remains open to interpretation. If we take *public reason* to mean a faculty common to all human beings, a *sensus communis*, then Rousseau's position is consistent with Kant's. But we could read *public reason* as that which a particular public, in this case the Polish public, takes to be rational. On this second reading, it is no longer all human beings who must have respect before the law because of their common capacity to reason, it is the members of a particular community who share a common system of beliefs, and therefore hold their laws in respect.

Even the most charitable reading of the second conception of *public reason* suggests that not all human beings are necessarily rational. If *rational* is defined according to the customs and standards of a particular community, then at best all humans may be considered *potentially rational*. According to this reading of Rousseau, only if persons share and value the same customs and traditions can they be considered *rational* in the sense of having respect for the law(s) of the community.[27] Many aspects of Rousseau's advice to Poland are consistent with this second interpretation of *public reason*. In particular, his emphasis upon the need to instill respect for the law and love of the country through children's games suggests that *reason* is not *natural* or *innate*. The paragraph following the one cited above begins:

> How, then, to move men's hearts, and make them love the mother country [*la patrie*] and her laws? Dare I say it? through children's games, through institutions deemed pointless in the eyes of superficial men, but that form cherished habits and invincible attachments. [*955*]

Rousseau's emphasis upon education in the *Considerations* in fact indicates that reason must be guided, shaped, and nurtured in order to obtain the desired result.[28] Although one could maintain that reason is *natural* to all, but takes shape under the proper tutelage—a position consistent with *Emile*—this renders the concept of *untutored* reason problematic at best. Ultimately, *reason* seems to indicate both a natural disposition and the result of cultivation. Thus, the state must assume the responsibility of shaping reason in order to ensure the unanimity and *rectitude* of *public reason*.[29]

In order to instill a strong sense of Polish identity in the future citizens of the state, Rousseau specifically encourages the formation of a system of public education:[30]

> At the age of twenty, a Pole ought not be another kind of man, he must be a Pole. I want him to learn to read by reading things of his country, at ten I want him to know all that his country has produced, at twelve all the provinces, all the roads, all the cities, at fifteen he should know all of its history, at sixteen all the laws. There should not be in all of Poland a beautiful action or an illustrious man that does not fill his memory and heart, and of which he could not give an account at any moment. . . . The law must regulate the matter, the order and the form of their studies. [966]

But the system of education does more than instill a sense of Polish identity in future citizens; this education dialectically shapes the identity of both the citizens and the nation. While giving the children a *national identity*, at the same time it shapes the identity of the nation by instilling patriotic values in its future citizens:

> It is education that must give to souls a national force, and guide their opinions and tastes so that they will be patriotic out of inclination, out of passion, out of necessity. A baby first opening its eyes must see the mother country [*la patrie*] and until death must only see her. The true republican sucks love of his mother country [*la patrie*] with his mother's milk, that is to say, laws and liberty. This love makes up his entire existence, he sees only the mother country [*patrie*], he lives only for her, as soon as he is alone, he is nothing [*nul*]; as soon as he has no more mother country [*patrie*], he is no longer, and if he is not dead, he is worse. [966]

In *On Political Economy* he goes even further and explicitly equates the role of the state with that of the mother: "Let the mother country, then, prove to be the common mother of the citizens [*Que la patrie se montre donc la mere commune des citoyens]"* (258). These passages shed new light on what Rousseau means when he stipulates that the people receive a *moi commun* from the general will. It would seem that the state ideally functions as a mother who helps form the individual identities of her citizens. Thus, shaping *public reason* entails controlling identity formation from the earliest possible moment; it implies that the state assumes the role of parent with respect to each citizen.[31]

In addition, the system of public education promotes patriotic values in other ways. Rousseau maintains the importance of physical education in developing a sense of moral value:

> In all the schools [Colléges] a gymnasium or site for physical education for the children must be established. This item is too often neglected and in my opinion is the most important part of education, not only for forming robust and healthy temperaments, but even more for the *moral aim* [of education]. . . . Prevent vices from appearing, you will have done enough for virtue. [967-68, emphasis added]

Designed to encourage all the values associated with competitive sports, Rousseau holds that the proper emphasis on physical education will contribute to the shaping of civic virtues:

> [Children] must not be allowed to play separately according to their whims, but they must play all *together* and *in public*, so that there is always *a common goal to which all aspire and which excites competition and emulation*. Parents who prefer education at home, and who raise their children under their own eyes, must nonetheless send them to these exercises. Their instruction may be at home and private, but *their games must always be public and common to all*; for it is not only a question of keeping them busy, of forming robust constitutions and making them agile and muscular, *but of early on making them accustomed to rules, to equality, to fraternity, to competitions, to living under the gaze of their fellow citizens and of desiring public approbation*. [968, emphasis added]

Clearly, all aspects of these public exercises are designed to fit the interests of the state, but the importance of *public approbation* in particular cannot be overemphasized. Because the public judges the games and competitions, they will promote a sense of pride and civic virtue among children and adults alike. In fact, these public games—like the civic ceremonies and festivals he also recommends instituting—reinforce the formation of a *public* conceived as a patriotic group identity.[32]

Nationalism, Civic Virtue, Totalitarianism

Rousseau's linking of certain key elements in his recommendations for Poland suggests that the state will tend toward totalitarianism. In particular, the relation between respect for the law, public reason, and civic virtue suggests that the individual's relation to the state is determined wholly by the state. The state, in fact, serves a parental function with respect to the individual, which indicates that the distinction between state and civil society has all but disappeared. A comparison of Adorno's analysis of fascist propaganda from a Freudian perspective with Rousseau's suggestions for Poland will bring to light some of the prototatalitarian and even protofascist aspects of Rousseau's political theory.

It may be objected that the distinction between political theory and propaganda ought to be strictly maintained, that Adorno's study of fascist propaganda applies to the psychosocial mechanisms that enable it to be effective, while Rousseau's advice to Corsica in the form of political theory has a very different status. I would like to suggest that the psychosocial appeal of fascist propaganda that makes it so effective bears a strong resemblance to the mechanisms at work in Rousseau's practical advice for Poland. The similarities indicate that Rousseau's suggestions include attempts at social engineering not unlike those that support fascist propaganda. In other words, aspects of his political reform program—his educational program in particular—represent long-term, state engineered and maintained systems of propaganda, which work according to the psychosocial principles analyzed by Adorno following Freud.

In "Freudian Theory and the Pattern of Fascist Propaganda,"[33] Adorno argues that fascist propaganda demonstrates many traits consistent with Freud's analysis of mass psychology in *Group Psychology and the Analysis of the Ego*. Adorno, following Freud, points out that group psychology is dependent upon weak individuals who share a "willingness to yield unquestioningly to powerful outside, collective agencies" (85). These individuals are transformed into a group through a libidinal bond, usually with a father figure (86-87). In

Freud's account, he uses the analogy of the bond of the church to illustrate the sublimation of the libido that occurs in the group. Adorno explains:

> In organized groups such as the Army or the Church there is either no mention of love whatsoever between members, or it is expressed only in a sublimated and indirect way, through the mediation of some religious image in the love of whom the members unite and whose all-embracing love they are supposed to imitate in their attitude towards each other. [88]

Freud's analysis sheds light on the nature of the social bond in Rousseau's conception of community. In particular, Rousseau's equation of the state with the mother exemplifies the sort of sublimated libidinal bond that Freud describes in the church. In Rousseau's advice for Poland, it is love for the country that helps to sublimate and mediate the love of individuals for each other, and which also serves as a role model in its *all-embracing love* for them. The ideology proclaims: mother country loves you; you love your country; therefore, you should love your fellow citizens. Thus, the communal bond in Rousseau, like the bond identified by Adorno in fascist society, represents a sublimated libidinal bond mediated by the mother figure of the state.[34]

The mother state, in turn, serves an important function in the formation of the identities of the citizens. As we have already seen in the *Considerations*, the Polish citizens are supposed to identify so strongly with the state that love of their country becomes their whole existence (*"this love makes up his entire existence, he sees only the mother country" [cet amour fait toute son existence; il ne voit que la patrie]*). This role played by the state in the identity formation of its citizens corresponds to Freud's conception of a group. Freud defines a group as "a number of individuals who have substituted one and the same object for their ego ideal and have consequently identified themselves with one another in their ego" (80, cited in Adorno, 90). In the case of Poland, it is evident that it is the state that assumes the function of the object onto which the group cathects. The mother state serves as a mediator for the identity of the group. Consistent with this reading of the *Considerations*, Rousseau maintains in *On Political Economy*:

> If, for example, men are trained early enough *never to consider their persons except as related to the body of the State, and not*

to perceive their own existence, so to speak, except as part of
the State's, they will eventually come to identify themselves in
some way with this larger whole; to feel themselves to be
members of the mother country; to love her with that exquisite
feeling that any isolated man feels only for himself; to elevate
their soul perpetually to this great object; and thereby to trans-
form into a sublime virtue this dangerous disposition out of
which all our vices are born. [259-60, 222, translation altered,
emphasis added]

The last phrase of the passage indicates the psychic function assigned
to the state in its role as mediator: the state serves to inculcate moral
values in its citizens. Significantly, this is consistent with the
Freudian account. The mediating object in group identity is substituted for the superego in the individual psyches of members of the
group (Adorno, 98). Thus, Rousseau's emphasis upon respect for the
law, civic virtue, and the construction of identity in the *Considera-*
tions are all consistent with the Freudian reading. In Rousseau, it is
the state itself that stands in for parental authority.[35]

As long as the state plays the role of the parent—and in fact
prohibits the *resolution* of the oedipal complex—then the "children" of the state never internalize the superego. They remain as
children whose will must be externalized in the authority of the
state. Thus, their *group identity*—a national character that shapes
the *general will*—ensures the cohesion of the community. At the
same time, the *general will*—as externalization of each individual
will—inhibits the psychic and moral development of the citizens of
the state.

The *arrested* psychic development of individuals in fascist societies—produced by their substitution of an object for their supere-
gos—determines their narcissistic character. Following Freud,
Adorno maintains that the cohesion of fascist groups derives from
this narcissism. The narcissism, in turn, produces the in-group/out-
group mentality characteristic of fascism. The members of the in-
group identify strongly with each other because they have all
cathected onto the same ego ideal in the formation of their identities.
They then deny humanity to those who differ from themselves and
whom they consequently deem to be inferior. In Freud's example
he cites the Christian church to illustrate this phenomenon:

Even during the kingdom of Christ, those people who do not
belong to the community of believers, who do not love him,

and whom he does not love, stand outside this tie. Therefore, a religion, even if it calls itself the religion of love, must be hard and unloving to those who do not belong to it. [50, cited in Adorno, 92]

For Adorno, the genocidal project of the Nazi regime clearly exemplifies this fascist phenomenon. However, in the case of Rousseau, his abhorance of any act of violence committed by the state against any member of the community (*PE*, 256, 220) seemingly precludes the possibility of the persecution of out-groups. His constitution of the communal bond nonetheless is based on group narcissism consistent with Freud and Adorno's readings. Thus, one might imagine the systematic expulsion or banishment (in the ancient Greek style of scapegoating) of persons deemed unpatriotic or not rational. Given the narcissistic foundation for group identity in the Rousseauian state, persecution of out-groups is not inconceivable—and in fact sheds light on Robespierre's use of Rousseau to justify state terrorism.[36]

Other aspects of Adorno's Freudian reading of fascist propaganda signal further similarities between the state envisaged by Rousseau and fascism. In particular, Adorno highlights the importance of hierarchy in fascist societies: "The fascists down to the last smalltime demagogue, continuously emphasize ritualistic ceremonies and hierarchical differentiations" (92). In turn, Rousseau writes:

> Do not neglect a certain amount of *public decoration;* let it be noble, imposing and let the magnificence be in the men more than in the things. *One cannot believe to what degree the heart of the people follows its eyes and how much the majesty of ceremony impresses the people. It gives to authority the air of order and rule that inspires confidence and removes ideas of capriciousness and whim associated with arbitrary power.* [*Poland*, 964, emphasis added]. . . .
>
> All the active members of the Republic, I mean those who will participate in the administration, *will be divided into three classes, marked by the same number of distinct emblems that these classes will wear on their persons. . . . I would like the emblems of the three orders that I propose to be badges of different metals, whose value will be in inverse relation to the rank of the ones who wear them.* [*Poland*, 1020, emphasis added]

Significantly, Adorno relates the maintaining of a hierarchical structure with the persecution of out-groups. And, as we have already
seen, the in-group/out-group mentality appears to be highly motivated in the Rousseauian state.

Finally, Adorno maintains that the hierarchical structure and in-
group/out-group mentality of fascist mass psychology go hand in
hand with what he dubs "repressive egalitarianism." Adorno explains:

> They emphasize their being different from the outsider but
> play down such difference within their own group and tend to
> level out distinctive qualities among themselves with the
> exception of the hierarchical one. . . . The undercurrent of mali-
> cious egalitarianism, of the brotherhood of all-compromising
> humiliation, is a component of fascist propaganda and Fascism
> itself. . . . Repressive egalitarianism instead of realization of
> true equality through the abolition of repression, is part and
> parcel of the fascist mentality. [94]

Rousseau's advice for both Corsica and Poland exhibits traits of this
repressive egalitarianism, which was already evident to a great extent
in his social theory (chapter 1). The indoctrination of agrarian values
through the imposition of a rural, agrarian economy, the use of taxa-
tion as a deterrent to luxury items (*PE, 275-78*), and as a means to
redistribute wealth (*PE, 270-71*), sumptuary laws (*Corsica, 936*), and
finally, the emphasis upon patriotic brotherhood are all consistent
with Adorno's description of fascism. Although Rousseau does not
advocate genocide to ensure group identity, his projects for Corsica and
Poland employ many of the psychosocial appeals that encourage the
mass psychology characteristic of fascism. It is clear that Rousseau's
concern over inequality motivates not only these suggestions, but
also his general suspicion of money, wealth, and luxury. However,
one cannot disregard the end result because of the motivation. Egalitarian ends attained through repressive social controls resemble fascist
and totalitarian political practices more than they do democratic ones.

Ultimately, we must ask whether or not the same circumstances motivate Rousseau's projects for Corsica and Poland and the
fascist project to ensure social cohesion. One of Adorno's final obser-
vations concerning the *secret* appeal of fascism sheds light on the
similarities between the two:

> It may well be the secret of fascist propaganda that it simply
> takes men for what they are: the true children of today's stan-

dardized mass culture, largely robbed of autonomy and spontaneity, instead of setting goals the realization of which would transcend the psychological *status quo* no less than the social one. Fascist propaganda has only to *reproduce* the existent mentality for its own purposes—it need not induce a change—and the compulsive repetition which is one of its foremost characteristics will be at one with the necessity for this continuous reproduction. [97]

Rousseau's suggestions for Corsica and Poland rely upon an initial change to induce a static state of social conformity that ironically resembles a mass society. While Rousseau is largely motivated by his disdain for conformism—which he attributes to the growth of commerce and the concomitant alienation of individuals from their "true" selves—he ends up advocating conformism in the form of a mass culture for both Corsica and Poland. In short, his suggestions for both countries ironically amount to engineering a mass parochial community similar to the utopia outlined by the *Discourse on Inequality*. These mass societies, however, run a high risk of devolving into totalitarian or fascist societies.

In the preceding chapter I argued that Rousseau's conception of the individual contributes to the problem of alienation in his version of utopian social life. There I maintained that his attempt to steer clear of the alienating effects of reason went too far in the opposite direction: his individuals could never be fully autonomous, only independent in their isolation from one another. Likewise, in his political theory, the same individuals "largely robbed of autonomy and spontaneity" are shaped into a community bound by ties that are protototalitarian. This underlying resemblance between Rousseau's political theory and totalitarianism/fascism raises some key questions concerning the historical context of the eighteenth century.

While it is generally acknowledged that the eighteenth century saw the rise of the modern conception of the individual and in particular of the bourgeois notion of the self, the motivating force behind fascism is generally taken to be a crisis in individual autonomy. Thus, on the one hand, in the historical context of Rousseau's work, the individual appears to be relatively strong. While on the other hand, the end of the nineteenth century and the early twentieth century saw the undermining of the notion of the autonomous individual due to increased industrialization, war, imperialism, and the like. But my reading of the *Discourse on the Origin of Inequality* suggests that Rousseau anticipates many of the dominating effects of reason that did not become fully apparent until the nineteenth century. Furthermore, my analyses of *On Political Economy*, *Project for Corsica*, and the *Considerations* indicate that he perceives a level of social disintegration and alienation that requires political remedy. These texts suggest that Rousseau was aware of the development of a mass society during the Enlightenment—in fact, according to him, caused by the Enlightenment. Moreover, his texts also signal a crisis at the level of the individual.

Rather than read the development of the bourgeois conception of the self as indicative of the growing autonomy of the individual, I suggest that it in fact serves a mythic function: the myth of the bourgeois individual masks the loss of autonomy experienced in the birth of a new mass society.[37] On my reading, the appearance of the notion of the autonomous, bourgeois individual actually signals the relative weakness of individuals in Enlightenment society. The need for the representation of the individual as autonomous and individualistic stems from the same forces that reach a crisis level in the nineteenth century: capitalism, colonialist expansion, exploitation, the distinction between the public and the private. These forces, which are usually read as shaping and spurring the bourgeois faith in the individual, in fact necessitated the creation of the myth. Thus, read in this light, nineteenth-century romanticism signals the failure of eighteenth-century myth to hide the reality. By the late nineteenth and early twentieth centuries, these forces had produced social crises at many levels, which led to fascism among other things.

Produced in the historical context of capitalist expansion and colonialism driven by the desire to exploit persons and natural resources for economic gain, Rousseau's political theory and programs respond to certain crisis tendencies at the level of the individual already palpable during the eighteenth century. The attempt to respond to these crises plays itself out in a theory that promotes social cohesion at the cost of individual autonomy. Returning to my introductory analysis of the general will, his political theory engineers a general will for both Corsica and Poland *in the public interest*. Although his texts lack certain essential elements for true fascism—namely, imperialism, a racist element, and a strong father figure (although this latter is not necessarily absent)[38]—nonetheless, his advice may be deemed prototitalitarian or even protofascist.[39] Thus, I would argue that Rousseau's political theory responds to a crisis in individual autonomy similar to the one which motivated fascism's actual occurance in the twentieth century. *On Political*

Economy, Project for Corsica, and the *Considerations* constitute Rousseau's response to the mass society of the Enlightenment.

Ironically, Rousseau's concerns about dependence and domination as they affect both individuals and nations lead him to construct programs for political reform that suffer from the same faults as his social theory. While the *Second Discourse* uses individual autonomy to shield against the dangers of rationality as a form of domination, his political theory attempts to secure individual nations' autonomy through isolationist politics reinforced by state-engineered programs to increase nationalism and civic virtue. While he recognizes the dangers of certain Enlightenment tendencies toward social conformism at best and homogenizing mass culture at worst, he nonetheless employs some of the same mechanisms to prevent economic development and "progress." As in his social theory, Rousseau's political theory recognizes and critically analyzes dialectical tendencies, while at the same time he falls prey to others due to his bias in favor of independence.

Individualism as a goal on a national scale easily translates into socially engineered conformism in the service of national security. Thus, while Rousseau recognizes the potential political effects of the dialectic of enlightenment in his efforts to protect Corsica and Poland from being exploited by other nations, he fails to see the same mechanisms at work in national politics. His programs encourage ideological domination through the inculcation of civic virtue as both an individual and social identity. In this respect, his advice is not very different from fascist programs aimed at increasing social cohesion through civic celebrations, in-group/out-group politics, educational programs, and displays of patriotism.

From the standpoint of critical theory, his political reform programs and his social theory, insofar as they attempt to avoid technological "progress," identify potential ways in which mass markets can be exploited through the expansion of needs. In this respect he anticipates the possibility of manipulating the masses through channels only fully exploited in the twentieth century by the culture industry, and he attempts to shield against it. But like his social theory, his political programs also demonstrate an ideological blind spot where independence is concerned. This fault proves fatal for preventing the manipulation of mass societies for political ends.

Thus, Rousseau's *totalitarianism* combines the social engineering of Plato's Republic, the patriotism and civic virtue of Rome and Sparta, and the highly mediated and alienated relations of modern liberal societies. Though civic virtue could be defended as a means of combating totalitarian political practices—especially in the service of democracy, as it is articulated in the *Social Contract*—in the context of Rousseau's programs it takes on a militaristic character, given the interests in protecting both Poland and Corsica from outside domination. In particular, the system of rank and hierarchy recommended for Poland reinforces the militaristic flavor of both patriotism and civic virtue, and suggests the type of status system favored by totalitarian regimes. Likewise, the lack of political parties in Rousseau's schema—which would be an essential feature of fascism—nevertheless effectively precludes institutionally recognized forms of political dissent. Coupled with the tendency toward ingroup/out-group politics inherent in his engineered conception of community, the lack of political parties only reinforces the ruler's ability to dominate fully every aspect of citizens' lives. Finally, the lack of distinction between the state and civil society in these texts ironically allows for both the complete ideological domination and the alienating isolation of these societies. Rousseau's efforts to combine classical political formations with the liberal conception of the abstract individual culminate in a prefiguration of the engineered mass societies of totalitarianism and fascism.

The implications for diagnosing mass culture during the eighteenth century in Rousseau's political programs for Poland and Corsica are paradoxical. His concern over domination from without and, in particular, his efforts to combat it with socially engineered national identities, civic virtue, and patriotism indicate that the social disintegration characteristic of modern mass societies is already apparent to him. Individuals in modern mass societies are alienated from one another, and therefore do not pull together in the common interest in times of crisis.

As we have seen, Rousseau's programs attempt to use the state to mediate individual identity in such a way as to prevent social disintegration and alienation. Furthermore, Rousseau's attempts to stem the tide of technico-economic "progress" by encouraging agrarian economies and discouraging commerce and trade, again link technological advancement with alienation and domination as we saw in the *Discourse on Inequality*. In this context, the obstacle to technico-economic "progress" ensures that Poland and Corsica will not develop large pools of alienated laborers, self-interested capitalists, or an idle leisure class composed of aristocrats. Effectively, the obstacles to technological and economic development, like the socially engineered national identity, are designed to prohibit the appearance of a mass alienated society.

And yet, these social and political programs ironically encourage a mass society in much the same way that totalitarian and fascist programs do. Rousseau uses state-controlled mass culture in order to prevent the development of social disintegration and alienation issuing out of the mass culture of modernity. In effect, the pendulum swing in the opposite direction—away from alienating "progress," toward "integrating" agrarianism or patriotic militarism—replicates the end result.

In attempting to preclude the development of mass culture, Rousseau institutionalizes culture with the same hegemonic and homogenizing results he seeks to avoid. His individuals may not be alienated from one another because the state mediates all social and political relations. Nevertheless, there is little difference between the effects of state-engineered mass culture and mass culture determined by market forces. In the end, these individuals are as constrained, determined, and even dominated by the mass culture of the state as bourgeois individuals in a modern mass society.

3 The Public Sphere, Alienation and Commodification: Rousseau's Autobiographical Writings

The preceding chapters examined dialectical questions concerning the individual in relation to the social order in Rousseau's social and political theory. These analyses highlighted Rousseau's concern with maintaining individual identity and autonomy in view of the spread of enlightenment rationality. In particular, I focused on the problematic tension between individual expression and communal existence. In this chapter, I will recast this question in terms of the public/private distinction of bourgeois ideology. Taking as a test case Rousseau's autobiographical works, I wish to explore the tensions and contradictions inherent in such a distinction. My discussion will take as its point of departure Habermas's conception of the bourgeois public sphere in order to problematize the attendant notion of a private sphere. Ultimately, I will again raise questions concerning the assumptions underlying bourgeois ideology's claims to protect individual autonomy as exemplified in Rousseau.

In *The Structural Transformation of the Public Sphere*, Jürgen Habermas investigates "the structure and function of the *liberal* model of the bourgeois public sphere" (xviii). His analysis highlights certain key aspects of the public sphere, in particular, those which relate to *publicity*. In his discussion of feudal society of the High Middle Ages—although, as he points out, the distinction between "public" and "private" strictly speaking did not yet exist—he nonetheless signals the importance of representation in the feudal *public* realm:

> The *publicness* (or *publicity*) *of representation* was not constituted as a social realm, that is, as a public sphere; rather, it was something like a status attribute, if this term may be permitted. In itself the status of the manorial lord, on whatever

level, was neutral in relation to the criteria of "public" and "private"; but its incumbent represented it publicly. He displayed himself, presented himself as an embodiment of some sort of "higher" power. The concept of representation in this sense has been preserved down to the most recent constitutional doctrine, according to which representation can "occur only in public . . . there is no representation that would be a 'private' matter." For representation pretended to make something invisible visible through the public presence of the person of the lord. [7][1]

Habermas contrasts this complete reliance upon representation by the nobility with representation's diminished importance in bourgeois society. He contends that the bourgeois public sphere differs significantly from the feudal one in its barring of representation of this type. Citing Goethe's *Wilhelm Meister*, Habermas argues that the bourgeois public realm reflects the shift in emphasis from representation to production:

> In our context Goethe's observation that the bourgeoisie could no longer represent, that by its very nature it could no longer create for itself a representative publicness, is significant. The nobleman was what he represented; the bourgeois, what he produced: "If the nobleman, merely by his personal carriage, offers all that can be asked of him, the burgher by his personal carriage, offers nothing, and can offer nothing. The former has a right to *seem*: the latter is compelled to *be*, and what he aims at seeming becomes ludicrous and tasteless." [13]

This shift from representation to production, however, is more problematic than it would seem at first glance. Despite the increased emphasis upon monetary worth in bourgeois society as opposed to the representationally oriented focus on genealogy in feudal society, representation continues to play a key role in the constitution of the public realm, specifically with respect to public image. As Habermas's discussion of the rise of the bourgeois public realm demonstrates, the new "public" still engaged in practices involving "representation".

Ultimately, Habermas's socio-historical account of the rise of the bourgeois public sphere focuses on the emergence of a sphere in which citizens exercise their capacity to reason in a critical manner. Although the bourgeois public realm, broadly conceived, represents "the sphere of private people come together as a public" (27), Habermas also conceives of it as historically determined by the rise of the press during the eighteenth century, and the concomitant appearance of literary salons. In other words, he sees the rise of the bourgeois public sphere in large measure paralleling and being determined by the rise of a reading public (23-24). With the rise of this public, the possibility of persons coming together to discuss common concerns in a critical manner coincides with and aids the rise of liberal democracies (36).

If this rise of a critical reading public can be seen as having certain positive effects socially and politically, it also marks the splitting off of a separate realm of art and culture.[2] Whereas art and culture were previously integrally linked to the social institutions of the church and court, and as such maintained a certain *aura*, now divorced from these institutions, art and culture were subject to the laws and constraints of the capitalist market.[3] Although this separation suggests the liberation of art and culture in one sense, it also signals their commodification. Habermas argues that it is the rise of a critical reading public that necessitates this break:

> Discussion within such a public presupposed the problematization of areas that until then had not been questioned. The domain of "common concern" which was the object of public critical attention remained a preserve in which the church and state authorities had a monopoly of interpretation . . . even at a time when for specific social categories, the development of capitalism already demanded a behavior whose rational orientation required ever more information. To the degree, however, to which philosophical and literary works and works of art in general were produced for the market and distributed through it, these cultural products became similar to that type of information: as commodities they became in principle generally accessible. [36]

Art and literature were commodified, moving them out of the public realm of representation determined by the church and court, and into the bourgeois public realm of critical discussion and interpretation:

> [Cultural products] no longer remained components of the Church's and the court's publicity of representation; that is precisely what was meant by the loss of their aura of extraor-

dinariness and by the profaning of their once sacramental character. The private people for whom the cultural product became available as a commodity profaned it inasmuch as they had to determine its meaning on their own (by way of rational communication with one another), verbalize it, and thus state explicitly what precisely in its implicitness for so long could assert its authority. As Raymond Williams demonstrates, "art" and "culture" owe their modern meaning of spheres separate from the reproduction of social life to the eighteenth century.[4]

If Habermas sees the coincidence of the shift in emphasis from representation to production and the commodification of art and culture, it is because his account highlights the emergence of the public sphere as site of a critical gaze. That is to say, representation in the feudal context, for Habermas, implies that *interpretations* of representations are established and maintained institutionally by the church and the court. In some sense, both the church and the court claim authority from God, and thus guarantee the stability of the social order by founding it on divine authority. Through a circular process, culture helps to maintain the social order by reinforcing the religious-metaphysical worldview upon which the social order is founded. Culture also ceaselessly reestablishes this same religious-metaphysical worldview by inscribing it within cultural products. But culture also relies upon this same ideology (the religious-metaphysical worldview) for its own authority. Thus, the public realm in the feudal context appears as nothing more than the outward manifestation of the implicit link to God.

By contrast, in the bourgeois public sphere one finds representation again in the form of cultural products, but now subject to critical interpretation. The tie to divine authority has been severed, thus rendering the meaning of cultural products unstable.[5] These cultural products require interpretation by individuals to resecure their meaning(s). Interpretation, in turn, encourages the use of critical reason in a public arena that thus founds and maintains a public sphere.

The appearance of the public sphere and with it critical discussion as part of public culture distinct from the church and court nonetheless runs the risk of being influenced and ultimately controlled by market forces, because the commodification of culture is motivated by precisely the same forces that sparked the appearance of the public realm itself. Increased rationality in the public sphere prompts critical discussion, but also inspires capitalist ventures motivated by a desire for economic gain. Cultural products are easily commodified in such a context in which their break from certain public institutions increases their accessibility, which in turn encourages public interest in culture.

The possibility of exploiting these cultural commodities for economic profit occurred to more than a few Enlightenment hacks.[6] After all, the manipulation of cultural symbols in the service of political ends was raised to new heights during the reign of Louis XIV, a master in the art of cultivating power through "representation."[7] It does not require a tremendous leap in conceptualization to realize that public culture, which had long been used to consolidate political power, could be employed to amass large amounts of capital. However, the principal difference between the public spheres of the seventeenth and eighteenth centuries lies in the increased rationalization of the latter. Thus, culture's break from the court and church saw both positive and negative effects on the public realm: it encouraged critical discussion while at the same time it made cultural products more easily adaptable to capitalist exploitation.

Returning to Habermas's earlier distinction between representation and production in the public sphere, I would assert that the culture *producers* in the bourgeois public realm still engage in the practice of representation. The difference is that according to the religious-metaphysical worldview, the representations of the feudal period arise "naturally," as outward physical manifestations of the divine order of things, whereas the bourgeois *representations* are produced "artificially," and thus require interpretation. In other words, the commodification of culture helps to foreground the conventional or socially constructed nature of meaning. Commodified cultural products, thus, encourage individual interpretation on the part of consumer-critics. Commodification also fuels the expansion of the *public*, which further ignites the commodification of culture.

Clearly, the instantiation of a critical public that turns its discerning eye toward not only cultural products but also social institutions, serves the ends of enlightenment.[8] In order to produce such an *enlightened* society, the intellectual elite must train the reading public to use its rational capacities critically. Enlightenment entails conditioning the public to think independently and critically about precisely those social institutions such as the church and the court, which previously maintained the interpretations in the public realm. Enabled by the shift from representation to production, the cultivation of a heightened awareness of the artificiality of representation among the public is one of the goals of enlightenment. The more aware the public becomes of the artificiality of *produced* representations, the more apt it will be to use this knowledge critically to interpret social institutions, political practices, and the like. Ironically, this also implies that the public would eventually be able to critically analyze the very cultural products (art, literature, philosophy), which were designed to nurture the public's critical sensibilities. Theoretically, the new reading public would be able to interpret critically the *representations* proffered by the intellectual elite.

Thus, the process of enlightenment depends upon the commodification of culture, but necessitates exposing its *cultural elite* to the critical gaze of the public it aims to constitute. Artists, writers, and intellectuals of the enlightenment carry out the noble task of educating a "backward public," and are rewarded for their hard work with the criticisms of this same public. If the heightened awareness of the artificiality of representations signals the increased rational, critical capacity of the public, it also entails a parallel heightened awareness of the *production* aspect of representation among the intellectual-cultural elite themselves. Artists', writers', and intellectuals' engagement in the enlightenment project entails that they become conscious of their own participation in the production of culture.

I will argue that the case of Rousseau's autobiographical writings attests to the alienation and anxiety that attend the awareness of what it means to be a public figure in the newly constituted bourgeois public sphere. These autobiographical works suggest that it is not only culture that is commodified as a result of enlightenment, but the producers of culture as well.[9]

The Case of Rousseau Writing Rousseau

Rousseau's three autobiographical works—the *Confessions*, *Rousseau Judge of Jean-Jacques*, and the *Reveries of the Solitary Walker*—may all be read as corrective measures aimed at undoing what Rousseau perceived to be his undeserved reputation.[10] Rousseau writes in the opening explanation for *Rousseau Judge of Jean-Jacques* entitled, "Of the Subject and Form of This Writing," after citing as one of his reasons for writing, the fact that it enables him to think better of his contemporaries:

> That is not, however, the only motive which put a pen in my hand. Another even stronger and no less legitimate one will

make itself felt in this writing. But I protest that in these motives there is no longer either the hope or even the desire to finally obtain from those who have judged me the justice that they refuse me and that they are very determined to refuse me always. [661-62][11]

Despite the fact that he does not dare hope to receive justice at the hands of his persecutors, there can be no doubt that this hope and desire motivates his writing. He maintains—through his mouth-piece in the *Dialogues*, Rousseau—that *public utility* ought to be the writer's only motive for writing. "Some felicitous discovery to publish, some grand and beautiful truth to circulate [*répandre*], some general and pernicious error to combat, or finally some point of public utility to establish; these are the only motives which can make them take pen in hand" (673). Clearly, the "general and pernicious error" that needs to be combated in the *Dialogues* is Jean-Jacques's undeserved reputation. Likewise, in the "Sketch of the Confessions," he explains:

All things considered, it is not that I have something to com-plain about concerning the public discourse on my account; if they have sometimes torn me to pieces without a care, like-wise, they have often honored me. This depended upon the diverse dispositions in which the public found itself on my account, and according to its favorable or contrary prejudices, it was no more bounded in the good than in the bad. As long as I was judged only by my books, according to the interest or the taste of the readers, I was only made into an imaginary and fantastic being, who changed face with each writing that I pub-lished. Nothing was more different from me than that portrait: I wasn't better, if you will, but I was other. . . . *Here are not only the motives which made me undertake this entreprise, but the guarantors of my fidelity in executing it.* Since my name must endure among men, I didn't want it to carry a false reputation. [1152-53, my emphasis]

In a note added later to this same passage, Rousseau indicates that this earlier statement was naive in its underestimation of the ill will of the public. "I wrote this in 1764, already fifty-two years old, and very far from foreseeing the fate that awaited me at that age. I would now have too much to change on that account that I will not change anything at all" (1152).[12]

Despite Rousseau's repeated claim that he writes for himself, it is evident even in the *Reveries* that the work is aimed at a *public*, with the specific intent of gaining its sympathy:

> I wrote my first *Confessions* and my *Dialogues* in a continual anxiety over the means of concealing them from the rapacious hands of my persecutors, in order to transmit them, if it was possible, to other generations. The same worry no longer torments me for this writing, I know that it would be useless, and the desire to be better known by men having been extinguished in my heart only leaves profound indifference over the fate of my true writings and the monuments of my innocence, which perhaps have already all been destroyed forever. [*1001*]

Although he claims to have given up on the idea that the public will ever truly *know* either him or his works, one must seriously question what it would mean to write for oneself.[13] I will discuss this question further in the last section of this chapter. At the very least, one can say that the *Reveries*, like the *Confessions* and the *Dialogues*, harbor the desire to correct public opinion in view of the fact that what Rousseau attempts in his autobiographies is a *truthful* self-portrait.

Leaving aside the question of Rousseau's paranoid schizophrenia, one can read in his attempt to correct public opinion through autobiographical writings the alienation and anxiety arising from increased commodification in the cultural realm.[14] The expression of specific fears concerning the production, dissemination, and reception of his writings, which occurs throughout the three texts, documents Rousseau's awareness of the relationship between the reception and interpretation of his writings and the construction of his public persona.[15] I will take as a paradigmatic episode one of the incidents involving unauthorized dissemination and willful misinterpretation of works by Rousseau, recounted in *Rousseau Judge of Jean-Jacques*, to explore several of the implications of the commodification of literature for Rousseau.

In a passage from the first dialogue, the Frenchman (a member of the league of conspirators and an enemy of Jean-Jacques) cites a *maxim* from one of Jean-Jacques's works to justify the entire conspiracy against him:

> Frenchman: On this you don't think like J.J.
> *It is by betrayal that traitors must be punished.*
> Here is one of his maxims; what do you say to that? [*749*]

Rousseau then inquires about the textual origin of this maxim, not remembering ever having read such a line in the works of Jean-Jacques:

> Rousseau: Where, then, did he establish this new precept so contrary to all the others?
> Frenchman: In a line of comedy.
> Rousseau: When did he have this Comedy performed?
> Frenchman: Never.
> Rousseau: Where did he have it published?
> Frenchman: Nowhere.
> Rousseau: My God I don't understand you.
> Frenchman: It's a kind of farce that he once wrote hastily and almost impromptu, in the country, in a moment of gaity, that he didn't even bother correcting, and that our Men stole from him like a lot of other things that they adjust in their way for public edification. [750]

The Frenchman's response indicates that part of the conspiracy against Jean-Jacques involves stealing and falsifying manuscripts in order to publish them under Jean-Jacques's name. In the above-cited case, the conspiracy involves stealing, altering, and publishing a text that was never intended for *public* consumption. The little impromptu comedy, which contains the dreaded maxim, was dashed off in a frivolous moment, never edited, and clearly not intended for the public gaze. Part of the betrayal of Jean-Jacques, which his own *maxim* theoretically justifies, involves publishing his works without his consent. Moreover, the conspirators take the liberty of altering these works to suit their own purposes. As if this were not enough, the Frenchman as part of the conspiracy also exemplifies the type of *reading* Jean-Jacques's texts receive, once they are distributed to the public:

> Rousseau: But how is this line used in the play? Is it he himself who pronounces it?
> Frenchman: No; it's a young woman who, believing herself betrayed by her lover, says it in a moment of spite in order to encourage herself to intercept, open and keep a letter written by this lover to her rival. [750]

Rousseau's tirade, which follows this explanation, indicts the conspirators not only for stealing, altering, and publishing this manuscript, but also for willfully misreading the *maxim*:

> Rousseau: What, sir, is talk said by a young girl in love and vexed in the gay plot of a farce written long ago in haste, and never corrected, nor printed, nor performed, this idle talk which she, in her anger, uses to justify an act which on her part is not even treason; is this talk out of which you choose to make one of J.J.'s maxims the unique authority on which your men have woven a frightful web of treason in which he is enveloped? [751]

Willful misreading of Jean-Jacques's texts, at some level, constitutes the most treasonous act committed by the conspirators.[16] Although other passages mention elaborate pains taken to prevent Jean-Jacques from writing, or to prevent his manuscripts from ever being published and disseminated,[17] it is nevertheless evident that the most serious act of treason involves misreading his works, and thus misreading Jean-Jacques.[18] According to the Frenchman, the conspirators read Jean-Jacques's works in order to extract the venomous poison contained within them. According to Rousseau, a reader who reads Jean-Jacques's works as they were intended to be read, finds no venom in them. According to Rousseau, there is no poison in Jean-Jacques's works, only poisonous interpretations. Rousseau further maintains that if the works were read in their entirety, no one would or could claim that they contained any *poison*:

> Rousseau: As the only response to these sinister interpreters and as their just punishment, I would have them read aloud the entire work that they tear in this way to bits in order to taint it with their own venom; I doubt that having finished this reading there would be a single one of them impudent enough to dare renew his accusation. [695]

Thus, willful misreading of Jean-Jacques—the most treasonous act imaginable—constitutes the remaking of his works. The conspiracy against him involves manipulating public opinion about Jean-Jacques by both controlling his access to the public realm by stealing, altering, publishing, or preventing publication of his works, but also by manipulating public reception of his works through the dissemination of *bad* interpretations of them. These *bad* interpretations, in turn, determine how the public views Jean-Jacques himself. Not only does the public rely upon bad interpretations of his works to misread them, it also relies upon these same bad interpretations to construct a misrepresentation of the author.[19] What this collapsing of work and author demonstrates is the degree to which Rousseau is aware that not only his works circulate in the public sphere as commodities, but that he himself does as well. The interpretation of his works as cultural products is not guaranteed, nor is the interpretation of the author—a *by-product* of the cultural products themselves. In effect, the act of reading involves a reconstitution of both the work read and the author who produced it. Since meanings are no longer secured by a religious-metaphysical worldview (and in fact authors like Rousseau encourage the public to think for themselves), his own works are subject to misreading and misinterpretation.

Perhaps, at one level, this has always been true: writers have always been at the mercy of their readers. But it is clear that in the bourgeois public realm, this effect is exacerbated by the very project of enlightenment. The enlightenment project encourages novel and critical ways of thinking and reading, which in turn threaten to undermine the expressed "intentions" of the works read. For Rousseau, this threat of misreading and misinterpretation is also experienced as the threat of reconstruction of both his works and himself as author of those works. At one level this fear is perfectly justified: Rousseau's works were altered without his consent for a variety of reasons concerning the particular circumstances of the literary market during the period. But at another level, this fear reveals an anxiety about commodification of both literature and authors.

Rousseau is not only afraid that his works are misread, but that he personally is misread and misunderstood, and therefore reconstructed in the public's eye as another person: "Nothing was more different from me than this portrait [*peinture*], I was not better, if you will, but I was other" (*Confessions, 1152*). In other words, Rousseau is aware of the fact that he has become a *public* figure. Thus, Rousseau's paranoia may be read as a symptom of the commodification of both culture and the producers of culture, authors and artists. Rousseau's illness results from the wider social malaise he identifies as the spread of culture in his *Discourse on the Arts and Sciences*, but which he personally experiences as his phantasmagoric life as a fetishized commodity in the public gaze.

In the ninth walk of the *Reveries*, one finds a striking example of Rousseau's awareness of himself as a *public* figure. Occasioned by a discussion of the ephemeral quality of happiness, Rousseau describes an incident in which he meets a young child during a walk in Clignancourt. In his prefatory remarks introducing the episode,

Rousseau goes to great pains to explain why it is that he has difficulty talking to, or even being around, children, and why it is that he
generally tries to avoid being seen by them. In a long and contradictory passage, which includes yet another attempt to justify abandoning his own children to the foundling home, Rousseau maintains that while observing children has taught him some of the most
important lessons in life, and afforded him great pleasure, it also
presents the potential for causing him great pain. Rousseau writes:

> If I have made any progress in the knowledge of the human
> heart, I owe it to the pleasure I took in seeing and observing
> children. . . . But noticing with advancing years that my
> decrepit appearance frightened them, I stopped bothering them,
> preferring to deprive myself of a pleasure rather than disturb
> their happiness; contenting myself thereafter with watching
> games and all their little ways. I found a compensation for my
> sacrifice in the light which these observations shed on the true
> and first impulses of nature, which are a closed book to all our
> men of science. . . . My writings are there to prove that I
> engaged in this study with the attentive care of someone who
> enjoyed his work, and it would surely be the most incredible
> thing if *Julie* and *Emile* were the work of a man who did not
> like children. [*1088*, 140, translation altered]

In the following paragraph, Rousseau continues to answer anticipated criticisms from the *public* about his reluctance to approach
children—and consequently his seeming aversion to them—by citing
his general difficulty speaking when put on the spot. But while this
particular weakness serves in the *Confessions* to excuse inappropriate behavior, among other things, here it signals the pressure of
being a *public* figure:

> I never possessed any presence of mind or ease of speech, but
> since my misfortunes my tongue and my head have become
> increasingly slow and confused. I can find neither the ideas nor
> the words I want, and nothing calls for a clearer head and a
> more careful choice of words than talking to children. *What
> makes things even worse for me is the presence of attentive
> onlookers, the importance they attach and the interpretations
> they give to everything said by someone who has written
> specifically for children and is therefore supposed to utter noth-
> ing but oracles when talking to them.* This extreme awkward-

ness and the awareness of my incompetence embarrasses and disconcerts me, and I should be more at home meeting some Asiatic potentate than getting a little child to chat with me. [*1088*, 140-41, my emphasis]

Rousseau's insistence on the added pressure of being identified as an author who wrote works specifically addressed to children, and consequently of the *attention, interpretation and weight* given to what he says to children, signals his awareness of his status as a *public* figure. His anxiety over talking to children arises precisely because of his public persona, which has been constructed through works such as *The New Heloise* and *Emile*. Jean-Jacques Rousseau has become, in the public eye, an expert on children who should have no difficulty making them coo. Not only is he under pressure to perform minor miracles around children, he also feels pressure to produce *oracles* while around them. In effect, his daily practice has become a matter for public attention and public interpretation. His life has been textualized and is subject to interpretation. For Rousseau, the awareness of the attention paid to his life, and in particular, of the fact that he and his life are subject to interpretation by the public, causes anxiety. This means that he runs the risk of being misread, misinterpreted, and therefore constructed in a way that is not consistent with his "true" self. The public construct "Rousseau" may not coincide with the *real* Jean-Jacques.

An episode recounted in the *Dialogues* concerning the painting and engraving of Rousseau done at the request of David Hume during Rousseau's stay in England, again underscores Rousseau's concern over the remaking of his image within the public sphere.[20] Rousseau claims that Hume deliberately instructed the painter to make him look bad. As "Rousseau" explains in the second dialogue:

David Hume, closely tied in Paris to your Men without forgetting the Ladies [*the conspirators*], becomes, somehow, the patron, the zealous protector, the most excessive benefactor of J.J. and does so much in concert with them that he finally manages, despite all the repugnance of the latter, to lead him to England. There, the first and most important of his cares is to have painted by Ramsay, his personal friend, the portrait of his public friend J.J. He desired this portrait as ardently as a very taken lover desires that of his mistress. By means of importunity he obtains the consent of J.J. J.J. is made to wear a very black hat, very brown clothes, he is placed in a very somber setting, and there, in order to paint him seated, he is made to stand-up, hunched over, supported by one of his hands on a very low table, in a posture such that his muscles, which are extremely strained, alter the traits of his face. The result of these precautions had to be a very unflattering portrait even if it were faithful. You have seen this terrible portrait; you will judge the resemblance if you ever see the original. During the stay in England, this portrait was engraved, published, sold everywhere there without his ever having been able to see this engraving. [779]

Rousseau's obsession with the production and dissemination of this *likeness* of him underscores his concern with having a separate identity in the public sphere over which he has no control. Not only do the clothes, the pose, and the somber setting make him look bad, they actually deform him. That is to say that the bad portrait, the misrepresentation, actually changes his form in the public realm. Moreover, the wide dissemination of this image in the form of the engraving suggests that Rousseau is aware of the fact that he has been commodified. When the Frenchman objects that bad portraits are produced every day, Rousseau counters that this particular portrait is significantly different:

I agree: but these disfigured copies are the work of eager, bad workers, and not the productions of distinguished artists, nor the fruits of zealous friendship. They are not extolled with a lot of noise all over Europe, they are not announced in the public papers, they are not displayed in residences, adorned with glass and frames; they are allowed to rot on the quays or decorate the rooms of cabarets and barbers' shops. [780]

The difference lies in the fact that this portrait clearly inhabits the public sphere. Its prominence within the public sphere torments the *real* Rousseau precisely because it does not represent the *real* Rousseau. This portrait is a crude misrepresentation, a disfiguring copy that poses a serious threat.

The question becomes why does a misrepresentation pose a threat to the *real* Rousseau? If the real Rousseau is the original, upon which the copies are based, how do the copies threaten to undermine or deform the original? The very existence of the perceived threat and of Rousseau's obsessive anxiety suggest the answer. There is no *real* Rousseau, only opposing representations. In the bourgeois public sphere, which requires the interpretation of representations, no single interpretation is guaranteed. Rousseau and his works are subject to the critical gaze of the public, and thus subject to reinterpretation and re-representation. Interestingly, Rousseau's autobiographical writings both affirm and deny this proposition. He takes up his quill to correct the misrepresentations through autobiography, only to offer yet another representation in their stead.[21] While Rousseau asserts the originality and uniqueness of his *true* self in autobiography, the autobiographical project denies the possibility of inscribing the *true, private* self.[22]

The Subject/Object Problem Revisited: The Impossibility of Autobiography

So far in my discussion, I have implicitly established the binary opposition between public and private, and have associated the public with representation and the private with the origin, the real or the true self. Rousseau's anxiety about the way in which he is represented in the public realm implies that there exists a parallel private realm in which the *true* self dwells. The second dialogue of *Rousseau Judge of Jean-Jacques* at one level confirms this equation of public sphere with *false* representation and private sphere with *true* self. Rousseau's visit to meet the *real* Jean-Jacques is aimed at discovering the *true* nature of the author:

> My initial research having thrown me into *the details of his domestic life*, there I particularly applied myself, persuaded that I would pull from it information on my object of study more certain than all he might have said or done *in public*, and besides which I had not seen for myself. It is in the familiarity of intimate contact [*commerce*], *in the continuity of private life that a man in the end allows himself to be seen as he really is; when the incentive for self-awareness is allowed to relax [quand le ressort de l'attention sur soi se relâche], and forgetting the rest of the world, one frees oneself to the impulse of the moment.* [794, my emphasis]

On the one hand, private life, out of the public gaze, is privileged as site of the *true* self. Without the threat of continual observation, one can *be oneself*, act spontaneously, let down the mask, forget about the other's gaze. This would seem to confirm the correlation between, on the one hand, *false* representation and the public sphere and, on the other, *truth* and the private sphere. However, it is also true that through the course of the *Dialogues* the Frenchman too comes to know the *true* Jean-Jacques. The Frenchman does not, however, come to *know* Jean-Jacques through personal contact, but through reading his works. The *conversion* of the Frenchman through the reading of Jean-Jacques's texts is in fact one of the key objectives of the *Dialogues*. This objective is not only consistent with, but is also emblematic of, the process of enlightenment. Clearly the *philosophes* do not intend to personally enlighten the masses through actual contact. Publication and dissemination of their works provide the means of access to the public and as such constitute the vehicle for enlightenment.

However, the conversion of the Frenchman through the reading of Jean-Jacques's texts seemingly poses a problem for the dichotomy established between public-representation and private-true self. The Frenchman is able to *know* the true Jean-Jacques through his works, because reading Jean-Jacques's texts has fundamentally altered his reading practice. The Frenchman has been taught how to critically read and evaluate texts. This, in effect, is the principal goal of enlightenment: to inculcate a critical reading practice in the general public. But the conversion of the Frenchman not only implies that Jean-Jacques's texts have enlightened him in a general sense, but that they have also provided specific and accurate knowledge about the writer of the texts. The Frenchman has been enlightened about the true nature of Jean-Jacques by reading his works. Thus, the conversion of the Frenchman implies that the *true* Jean-Jacques is inscribed within his texts; that if one reads properly—that is to say, in accordance with the constraints established by the author—one will gain *true* knowledge of the author's self.

To say that Jean-Jacques is inscribed within his texts seemingly contradicts the earlier claim that the *true* Jean-Jacques is the private Jean-Jacques, the one not subjected to the gaze of others. Clearly, the act of publication, the making public of texts, renders highly problematic any claim to knowledge of the *private* self. How can the private self be inscribed within texts destined for the public eye? Is not the writing of texts inherently a *public* act? Are not Rousseau's claims to write autobiography for himself highly suspect, most of all because they seemingly help maintain the strict oppositions between public and private, representation and original, appearance and essence, false and true?[23]

Thus, the project of autobiography, the writing of the self, poses many interesting problems and paradoxes. If, on the one hand, the autobiographical texts are aimed at correcting public opinion, as I have previously maintained, then they tacitly acknowledge that there is no such thing as a *true* self. Rousseau's awareness of his existence as a public figure, a socially constructed representation, implies that any attempt by him to refashion this representation amounts to nothing more than offering a counter-representation. He can claim no privilege for his own self-representations over other representations circulating in the public sphere. His portrait of himself is only another *public* image circulating in the public sphere and subject to the public gaze. If, on the other hand, we read the autobiographical texts not as corrective measures taken to reform Rousseau's public image, but as *private* writings in which Rousseau writes his *self* to himself, then we are faced with even more paradoxes.

Using elements of Adorno's theoretical framework from *Negative Dialectics*, I will attempt to bring to light the philosophical paradoxes that Rousseau's autobiographical writings present.[24] At the most fundamental level, the task of writing the self or the subject is not only an inexhaustible task, but one that will *necessarily* never be completed. To exhaust the subject, to contain and inscribe it within writing, implies objectifying the subject. This necessarily results in a paradox: any subject that has been objectified is no longer a subject but an object.[25] In Adorno's language, this proposition is the very foundation of dialectics. In terms of the project of autobiography, Adorno's dialectical critique proclaims the necessary inadequacy of any *portrait* of the subject. Any autobiographical portrait leaves behind a remainder, which bears witness to the *untruth* of the portrait. According to Adorno, all identitarian thinking that establishes equations between like things as a foundation for knowledge, denies the fundamental dissimilarity between those things.

The desire for this type of adequation is, at least in part, motivated by the forces of a market economy and the exigencies of science combining in the early modern period to serve rational domination. The error lies in maintaining that the universal or concept could ever be adequate to the particular or object. As an example of identitarian thinking, autobiography posits the adequacy of the portrait—in this case an example of the *universal* or *concept*—to the particular or subject *represented*.

Inevitably, however, the excess or remainder must confront the subject who has attempted to contain the object within thought. Adorno writes:

Whichever part of the object exceeds the definitions imposed on it by thinking will face the subject, first of all, as immediacy; and again, where the subject feels altogether sure of itself—in primary experience—it will be least subjective. The most subjective, the immediate datum, eludes the subject's intervention. Yet such immediate consciousness is neither continuously maintainable nor downright positive; for consciousness is at the same time the universal medium and cannot jump across its shadow even in its own *données immédiates*. They are not the truth. [39-40]

In the case of autobiography, the subject is necessarily confronted with the inadequacy of its own *representation* of itself in the form described by Adorno of immediacy. The subject, through an act of mediation (writing), has produced an objectified version of itself. But this *concept* or representation, which the subject has produced, is never fully adequate to the *object* it seeks to contain—in this case, the subject itself. The remainder or excess, not contained within the representation, confronts the subject as pure immediacy. In this case, the subject's immediate awareness of itself as a subject confronts it as that which cannot be inscribed within the representation. Thus, the act of writing constitutes a mediation that can never testify to the subject's immediate knowledge of itself. Instead, Rousseau's attempt to discover the private *self* in writing only emphasizes the paradoxical nature of the subject's *immediate* or private knowledge of itself. The represented or objectified self fails to be adequate to the immediate self, precisely in the realm of immediacy.

According to Adorno, this problem arises precisely because of the nondialectical character of the relation between subject and object in identitarian thinking. Rather than conceive their relation dynamically, both subject and object become reified in this type of thinking:[26]

> The reduction of the object to pure material, which precedes all subjective synthesis as its necessary condition, sucks the object's own dynamics out of it: it is disqualified, immobilized, and robbed of whatever would allow motion to be predicated at all. [91]

In the case of Rousseau, the autobiographical project oddly reifies both subject and object, precisely because of their coincidence. Writing the self in effect objectifies the subject. The autobiographical project, at its core, denies the dynamic relation between subject and object in its attempt to adequately represent the subject. A dynamic relation between subject and object—one that would enable the subject to know itself—would stress the *process* as opposed to the *product*. In other words, the subject would know itself either in the constitutive *act* of writing or in the act of interpretation. This emphasis upon process and activity would avoid the trap of reifying either of the poles.[27] Instead the relation between subject and object conceived as dynamic process would also highlight the fundamental inadequacy of the representation to the subject represented, while at the same time preserving the dynamic character of the representation itself.

In his discussion of freedom and determinism, Adorno further elucidates the problem of the reification of the subject.[28] The immediacy and spontaneity of the *private* self—its freedom as a subject that Rousseau seeks to *represent* in his autobiographies—is precisely that which defies representation. To write the self is to determine and mediate the self, thus vitiating any claim to either freedom or immediacy. Ultimately, we are faced with the inherently public nature of writing.

Adorno's claim that any knowledge of the self is necessarily mediated not only denies the possibility of knowing the *private* self in any way other than through an act of mediation, but it also implies that the *private* self is necessarily mediated by the *public* self. Because of their dialectical interdependence the *private* and *public* selves are, finally, inseparable.

A striking episode from the seventh walk of the *Reveries* illustrates metaphorically the penetration of the public self into the realm of the private. I will cite the entire passage:

> I shall remember all my life a botanical expedition I once made on the slopes of the Robeila, a mountain belonging to Justice Clerc. I was alone, I made my way far into the crevices of the rocks, and going from thicket to thicket and rock to rock I finally reached a corner so deeply hidden away that I do not think I have ever seen a wilder spot. Black fir trees were mingled and intertwined with gigantic beeches, several of which had fallen with age, and they formed an impenetrable barrier round this secret refuge; through the few gaps in this dark wall one could see nothing but sheer rock faces and fearful precipices which I dared only look at lying flat on my face.

From the mountain gorges came the cry of the horned owl and the eagle, while from time to time some more familiar birds lightened the horror of this solitary place. . . . Gradually succombing to the powerful impressions of my surroundings, I forgot about botany and plants, sat down on pillows of *lycopodium* and mosses, and began dreaming to my heart's content, imagining that I was in a sanctuary unknown to the whole universe, a place where my persecutors would never find me out. Soon this reverie became tinged with a feeling of pride. I compared myself to those great explorers who discover a desert island, and said complacently to myself: "Doubtless I am the first mortal to set foot in this place." I considered myself well-nigh a second Columbus. While I was preening myself on this notion, I heard not far off a certain clicking noise which sounded familiar. I listened: the same noise came again, then it was repeated many times over. Surprised and intrigued, I got up, pushed through a thicket of undergrowth in the direction of the noise, and in a hollow twenty yards from the very place where I thought to be the first person to tread, I saw a stocking mill. [*1070-71*, 117-18]

Without going into too much detail in reading this passage, I would suggest that Rousseau's solitary walk into the Alpine wilderness represents his voyage of self-discovery in the *Reveries*. As he travels deeper and deeper into this wilderness, he discovers a hidden retreat surrounded by a barrier formed of immense fallen trees and sharp precipices. This hidden retreat, actually the deepest recesses of his consciousness, has a *savage* look, which is somewhat tempered by other familiar objects. Indeed the deepest recesses of the self, as Freud was to discover later, have a frightening aspect. The familiar objects perhaps represent pleasant memories or thoughts that occur often to Rousseau. Like Columbus discovering the new world, or Freud discovering the unconscious, Rousseau is an explorer on a voyage of self-discovery. He is not only the first, but the only mortal ever *to penetrate this far*. But precisely in this moment of self-recognition and discovery, Rousseau hears the familiar and repeated noise that pierces his consciousness. At the moment of penetration to the private, immediate self, Rousseau discovers that even this isolated space is marked by the presence of the public sphere. The stocking factory signals the penetration of wilderness by civilization and technology, but also suggests metaphorically the penetration of the private by the public.

Consistent with Adorno's insight into the dialectical character of subject/object relations, I would suggest that the above cited passage illustrates the sense in which Rousseau's notion of the private self denies two dialectical relations. On the one hand Rousseau's conception fails to recognize the dialectical relation between subject and object in his belief in the adequacy of the portrait (or the concept) to the object (in this case the subject). On the other hand his autobiographical writings deny the dialectical relationship between public and private by failing to recognize the mediated character of knowledge of the self. The above passage from the *Reveries* signals the intrusion of the public into the private with the presence of the stocking factory in the wilderness. As my reading of the passage suggests, the wilderness of Rousseau's *private*, immediate self is marked by the presence of the *public* stocking factory. Even in moments when he believes he has penetrated to a space untouched by other mortals—his own *private* consciousness—he is confronted with the *reality* of his mediated and, therefore, public knowledge of himself.

Thus, Adorno's insights from *Negative Dialectics* have suggested the impossibility of autobiography conceived as *private* writing. If *private writing* amounts to writing the *private self*, then I have demonstrated the sense in which this constitutes paradox. Instead, Rousseau's autobiographical projects will always end in the frustration of further and further alienation from the *private* and true self.

One final example from the *Reveries* illustrates the impossibility of the task of autobiography due to the coincidence of the two contradictory goals of Rousseau's autobiographical writings: correcting public opinion and writing (for) the *private* self. This example also clearly demonstrates the sense in which the self is endlessly refracted through the process of writing, thereby rendering both goals unattainable. In his discussion of lying in the fourth walk, Rousseau again raises the question of *truthful* self-representation in the *Confessions* and by extension in autobiography generally. Rousseau writes:

> I have never felt my natural aversion for falsehood so clearly as when I was writing my *Confessions*, for this is where temptations would have been frequent and strong had I been so inclined. But far from having concealed or disguised anything which was to my disadvantage, by some strange quirk which I can hardly understand and which is perhaps due to my distaste

for all forms of imitation, I felt more inclined to err in the other direction, condemning myself too severely rather than excusing myself too indulgently. [*1035*, 76, translation altered]

After proclaiming that he always told the whole truth in his *Confessions* ("in this work I carried good faith, truthfulness and frankness as far, further even, or so I believe, than any other mortal" [ibid.]), he claims that although he always told everything, he admits that at times he deliberately made himself look worse than he really was, and at other times he left out important episodes:

> I never said less than the truth; sometimes I went beyond it, not in the facts but in the circumstances surrounding them, and this *kind of lie* [*espèce de mensonge*] was more the effect of a delirious imagination rather than an act of will. [*1035*, 76, translation altered, my emphasis]

Although in the next sentence he maintains that this is not lying per se, and in the following lines blames his faulty memory and his old age, the admission of this *espèce de mensonge* reveals his awareness of the constructed, and therefore *artificial*, character of the portrait offered in the *Confessions*. In the following paragraph, he offers an overall justification for the *lying* in the *Confessions*, which amounts to a quid pro quo: lies that enhance his good qualities are offset by the lies that accentuate the bad. Rousseau explains:

> If sometimes without thinking about it I involuntarily concealed the deformed side by presenting myself in profile, these omissions [*réticences*] were more than made up for by my other stranger omissions, for I was often more careful to conceal my good points than my shortcomings. . . . I often presented what was bad in all its baseness, but I rarely presented what was good in the most attractive light, and often I left it out altogether because it did me too much honour, and I would have seemed to be singing my own praises by writing my confessions. [*1036*, 77, translation altered]

Rousseau then supplies two additional episodes to his childhood memories that he more or less deliberately left out of the *Confessions* because they made him look too good. These two episodes, as supplements to the *Confessions*, signal the endless refraction of "Rousseau" which takes place in the autobiographical writings. Not only does Rousseau the author tacitly acknowledge that he is different from the young Rousseau who was the subject of this life experience (the faulty memory signals this *difference*), but he also acknowledges that there is a slippage between the young Rousseau who had the experiences and the "Rousseau" depicted in the *Confessions*. The episodes of the *Reveries*, read as supplement to the *Confessions*, further indicate that there is slippage between differing *representations* of Rousseau. Read in the Derridean sense, all these supplements undermine the primacy of any original source or, in this case, the real, true, original, or private Rousseau.[29]

The multiplication of "Rousseau" through the refracted mirror of writing inhibits access to the private self. Consistent with Adorno's reading of the remainder or excess, which always eludes adequation by the concept, the autobiographical portraits remain inadequate in relation to the *real* Rousseau. The various portraits of the *Confessions*, *Dialogues*, and *Reveries* in fact assert that no single representation would ever be adequate to the task. As part of the public realm they affirm the *public* nature of representation. As Habermas points out, "representation can only occur in public." But these portraits belong specifically to the bourgeois public sphere. Their very multiplicity signals the problems of interpretation and reception that attend the bourgeois public realm.

My reading of the autobiographical materials as corrective measures taken against misrepresentations in the public sphere has demonstrated the sense in which the *private* is mediated by the *public*. Because of the rise of the bourgeois public sphere and the concomitant commodification of both cultural products and their producers, one finds in the texts of Rousseau in particular an ideological emphasis upon the *private* as a haven from the alienating *public* realm that parallels his bias in the *Second Discourse*.[30] His retreat from the public sphere in these texts in order to avoid its alienating effects, and his consequent overemphasis on the distinction between public and private, only returns to haunt him as the spheres become impossible to separate.

On the one hand, I have read Rousseau's autobiographies as an attempt to correct his public image. But if they are read in this manner, they tacitly acknowledge and participate in the commodification of Rousseau by repeating the gesture of the public realm: Rousseau merely attempts to replace a bad representation with a good one. I have also attempted to read the autobiographical texts as *private writing*, and in so doing have demonstrated the problems and paradoxes that attend such a conception. These problems are perhaps less a result of the historical context that gave rise to them than to the conception of the subject that operates in Rousseau's works. Nevertheless, this conception of the subject—philosophically indebted to both rationalism and empiricism—may be linked to historical developments of the seventeenth and eighteenth centuries. Specifically, the rise of capitalism and its bourgeois possessive individual intent upon protecting *private property* motivate both the creation of the public sphere and the private self.[31] As Habermas deftly summarizes the nature of the public realm, it is "the sphere of *private people* come together as a public" (27, my emphasis).

Although the public sphere relies in part for its constitution on the distinction between itself and the private sphere, their dialectical relation continually subjects that distinction to close scrutiny. As we have seen with Rousseau's autobiographies, every attempt to represent the private sphere amounts to a publication of it. Our only knowledge of the private is mediated by the public—a fact that becomes apparent only in the historical moment of their coappearance. Moreover, the rationality characteristic of the public sphere works to critically analyze and dismantle the private sphere upon which it depends.

Ultimately, I read Rousseau's classically bourgeois invocation of a private self in his autobiographical texts as an attempt to fight the alienation and commodification that attend the rise of the bourgeois public sphere. As I noted, the increased rationalization of the public sphere, which serves a positive function in carving out a space for critical debate, at the same time creates the possibility for consumer markets. Subject to the means-ends rationality of capitalism, these markets are in turn easily exploited for financial gain. As the examples from Rousseau's autobiographies analyzed here demonstrate, he was keenly aware of the circulation of both his texts— and by extension himself—in these markets. The fact that many of his texts were banned in France clearly only exacerbated his perception that he had lost control of his work, and therefore of his public persona. As pirated editions of his works circulated, he perceived that even his *private* life was a reified commodity within a consumer market. For someone subject to paranoid delusions, it is not a huge step in logic to further imagine the conscious manipulation of consumer opinion through the manipulation of the market. In Rousseau's defense, it seems appropriate to remember that writers were subject to real prosecution and persecution during this period, and that the court was also capable of using the public sphere for its own political ends. Rousseau's paranoid emphasis on the willfull manipulation of his texts—by theft, alteration, and publication of them without his knowledge—as well as his concerns over their reception and interpretation anticipate the processes of the culture industry and the careful creation and control of mass markets in the pursuit of profit.

The *coincidence* of paranoia in a public figure with the historical rise of the bourgeois public sphere suggests that manipulatable mass markets could be foreseen, given the rationalization that underpins both the public sphere and capitalism. Cultural products severed from the institutionally generated and maintained interpretations of the court and church were free to circulate subject to a new critical gaze. They were also available for exploitation for financial gain. As cultural commodities, Rousseau's writings testify to the growing awareness of the potential for mass markets opened by the project of Enlightenment.

Transitional Interlude

Before turning to Diderot and his recasting of the philosophical problems already discussed, it seems appropriate to reflect upon and synthesize the themes generated in the preceding analyses of Rousseau. The specifics of textual interpretation tend to detract from the overall similarities linking the problematics raised. I would like to reiterate the themes of the introduction here while at the same time suggesting ways in which my readings of Rousseau contribute to the general argument of this book concerning mass enlightenment.

I have opened with Rousseau's social and political theory to demonstrate the ways in which his concerns testify to his awareness of the potential problems attending the project of enlightenment. Specifically, I have concentrated on his diagnosis of certain features of the dialectic of enlightenment as understood by Horkheimer and Adorno. His attempts to avoid reason as a form of domination in the *Second Discourse* are evidenced in his preference for small family groups working for their own subsistence. Rousseau identifies the invention of property—with its attendant division of labor and expansion of needs—as the *original* source of inequality that leads to exploitation. Thus, on Rousseau's reading, reason conceived as domination may be avoided by sidestepping the development of technological societies. Small, independent family units escape the exploitation and inequality of means-ends rationality as they pursue their limited interests in a protected private sphere.

This preference for isolation as a hedge against technological domination reappears in Rousseau's advice for Corsica and, to a lesser extent, Poland. For Corsica, he advocates maintaining national independence at the expense of commercial growth and development. The imposed agrarian economy in Corsica serves to protect this nation from outside domination, while at the same time providing a national identity for its citizens. In the case of Poland, national independence is preserved through carefully orchestrated indoctrination to patriotism in a system of public education for the citizenry. The advice to both Poland and Corsica exhibits the same wariness with regard to potential exploitation from without—bad treaties with or outright domination by other countries—that is evident in the *Discourse on Inequality*. Rousseau's practical political advice to these nations again testifies to his concerns about technological progress spurred by instrumental reason.

The effort to avoid the advance of technological domination in Rousseau's social and political philosophy stems from a diagnosis of alienation. In the *Second Discourse*, alienation appears first as alienated labor. The division of labor forces humans into a kind of slavery in which they perform tasks that do not directly provide the means of subsistence. In addition, the expansion of needs that attends the division of labor alienates humans from their true needs, by creating dependency on certain material goods. Rousseau, here, identifies possessive individuals of capitalism as ready slaves to rational domination. They either dominate themselves or are dominated by one another. In either case, rationality only leads to dependence and alienation with respect to material survival.

The concern over alienation is recast in Rousseau's advice to Corsica and Poland. Rather than expressing a concern over the possessive individuals' alienation from their material needs and the means to satisfy them, these texts attempt to guard against the individuals' alienation from the community. Specifically in the *Considerations on Poland*, Rousseau includes a lengthy discussion of public education aimed at instilling a sense of civic pride and national identity in each one of the citizens. The state serves a parental function with respect to the citizens, whose arrested psychic development enables them to substitute the state for their ego-ideal. The end result—a mass society with a coherent national identity— prohibits alienation from developing, because all citizens identify strongly with the state.

Despite the seeming divergence, the concern over alienation in the texts on Poland and Corsica is not very different from its articulation in the *Second Discourse*. Although in the latter Rousseau seems more concerned with individuals' alienation from their own needs and means for survival than with their sense of belonging to a community, there is nonetheless a theoretical link between the two. For Rousseau, the *advance* of enlightenment in the form of technological development is ultimately responsible for both forms of alienation. It is due to the increase in private interest that creates commercial ties and, therefore, relationships of dependence between persons and nations, that alienation from the community

occurs in the first place. Rationality—which in the service of capitalism seeks to maximize profit through any and all means available—subordinates communal ties to private interests. Thus, possessive individuals become alienated from themselves and their
community in the interest of financial gain.

By establishing a form of individual identity dependent on the
state and, therefore, the interests of the community, Rousseau seeks
to preclude the development of particular interests that override
general, communal ones. Thus, both forms of alienation are tied to a
concern over rational domination in the service of private interest
characteristic of capitalism.

For Rousseau, the alienating effects of reason are felt in their
potential to transform private interests into a motivation for domination and exploitation of others. These effects are evident in economic, political, and social relations between members of a community. Rousseau's social and political theory attempts to minimize
the alienation of the public sphere by either limiting contact
between citizens (*Discourse on Inequality, Social Contract*) or by
having the state mediate relations between citizens (*Corsica,
Poland*). In either case, his theory signals his awareness of the tendency toward alienated social relations brought about through the
growth of rationalization.

Thus, the public sphere emerges as a problematic realm in
Rousseau's theory. On the one hand, a zealous defender of Republicanism, Rousseau cannot recommend public celebrations and festivals enough. On the other hand, a fierce protector of the rights of the
individual, he shields his farmer-citizens from too much involve-
ment in the business of government. To make matters worse, as we
have seen, his autobiographies reenact this ambivalence toward the
public sphere. Clearly destined for some public, they tacitly
acknowledge Rousseau's concern with public opinion. Yet steadfastly *private*—at least in some sense—they attempt to reserve a
space for the private self.

Rousseau's alternative engagement with and retreat from the
public sphere, in his autobiographies in particular, is consistent with
his nuanced appreciation of historical change. As I have tried to suggest, using Habermas's conception of the public sphere, the political
benefits to liberal democracy are inseparable historically from the
negative effects of a market economy. That is to say, critical public
debate appears contemporaneously with the rise of capitalism,
including alienated labor and commodification.[1] For, as Habermas
argues, the appearance of the bourgeois public sphere coincides with

the *expansion and liberation of the sphere of the market* (74). The same bourgeois individuals who, freed from the state's authority with respect to social reproduction under capitalism pursued their own economic interests with relative autonomy, also engaged in critical debate in the newly created social space of the public sphere. A *free* capitalist market aided the establishment of the bourgeois public sphere, but also conditioned the nature of relations within that sphere. As Habermas notes, "in proportion to the increasing prevalence of the capitalist mode of production, social relationships assumed the form of exchange relationships" (ibid.).[2] In this respect, the appearance of a bourgeois sensibility, which extends beyond the class directly involved with market pursuits, is nonetheless shaped and determined by market forces. Social relations and even social values (inheritance plans, notions of marriage and family) are conditioned by the appearance of a market in spite of the fact that these values and the individuals who hold them seem at first glance not to be in any way tied to the market. Thus, Habermas's insistence on the public sphere as a *category of bourgeois society*.

Rousseau's characterization of the public sphere in his autobiographies identifies its double nature. On the one hand, his faith in his readers, expressed in his ill-fated attempts to publish the works, speaks to his continued confidence in public opinion. He believes that he will ultimately be vindicated in the republic of letters. On the other hand, his paranoia concerning his reputation and the ease with which the conspirators, he believed, had successfully duped the multitudes, suggests a prescient fear of the manipulability of mass markets.

Although Rousseau never directly cites profit as a motive behind the "conspiracy," publishing conditions in eighteenth-century France lend credence to many of his charges in the *Dialogues*. In particular, his claim that editions of "his works" circulated, which were nothing but the works of others with a few of his most famous sentences sprinkled in, are plausible in the context of the clandestine book trade. Pirated editions of both legal and banned books circulated, as well as pamphlets that often "cited" Rousseau. Rousseau's popularity among the hack writers no doubt ironically contributed to his feelings of being manipulated and used for others' ends.[3] Rousseau was *commodified* as a writer to the extent that his recognizable name nearly guaranteed a profitable printing enterprise to printers and booksellers. Compared to the booktrade in England in the mid-eighteenth century—which also had its share of debates concerning literary property, copyright law, plagiarism, and the like—the book trade in France is far more complicated due to the added pressures of censorship and the black market in books.[4] Authors sold their rights to manuscripts directly to printers who then legally controlled the works. Pirated editions of works were often printed from stolen manuscripts (hence Rousseau's fear of having his works stolen), and may or may not have been faithful to the authors' texts. Added to this market were books from printers across the border who smuggled either explicitly banned works or texts that had never been submitted to the censor.

Thus, our understanding of the book in eighteenth-century France cannot be separated from an understanding of the processes of its production and distribution. The fact that there was a significant clandestine book trade underscores the profit motive in producing literature. The public sphere of the republic of letters, though clearly an essential feature of early liberal democracy, is nonetheless thoroughly marked by its market structure. This is not to suggest that the public sphere was not a site for critical debate, for indeed these works sparked ideas that circulated broadly enough to inspire a revolution. What I would like to suggest is that the way in which ideas circulated was in the form of commodities. Books were rented by the hour in subscription libraries or purchased by individual readers.[5] They were also reviewed in gazettes with increasing frequency throughout the century. They were no doubt discussed, analyzed, and fought over in coffeehouses and salons. They were, nevertheless, the means of subsistence in some instances for their authors and certainly for printers and booksellers in France and over the border.

Thus, Rousseau's ambivalent attitude about the public sphere, and his own circulation within it, is in part a reaction to his own commodification through the book market. His name, his works, and to a certain extent Rousseau himself as a public figure are being marketed for profit. Consistent with his aversion to alienated labor and the expansion of needs due to technological development expressed in the *First* and *Second Discourse* as well as in the *Project for Corsica* and *Considerations on Poland*, his paranoia about his public image stems from the same market forces that influence him directly as a writer of commodified texts. In this sense, the autobiographies express many of the same concerns about the development of markets and technology that are more directly articulated in his social and political philosophy.

Rousseau's perception of the public sphere in eighteenth-century France—though no doubt distorted to a certain extent by his particular psychoses—nonetheless anticipates the appearance of a culture industry. As I have argued in the introduction, the move toward mass culture is less a question of quantity than it is an issue of quality. To perceive the reading public as a mass of individuals requires a shift in thinking rather than an exponential leap in production and distribution. Authors and, to an even greater extent, printers and booksellers merely have to see the possibility of a bestseller—one they clearly saw with *La Nouvelle Héloïse*.[6] The appearance of the phenomenon does not necessarily require marketing strategies. But once a bestseller appears, the market event can be reproduced using marketing strategies that were already employed in the eighteenth century. These strategies included reducing the format in order to make volumes more affordable, printing texts anonymously and then revealing attributions, making texts available as they were being written (almost in the form of serials), classifying works as *oeuvres philosophiques* to pique interest, having books reviewed in gazettes, and so on. Thus, the sale of books could be increased through strategic manipulation of the market.

In a sense, the very project of enlightenment calls for *marketing strategies*. Given the historical co-genesis of the public sphere and capitalism, it seems in retrospect fairly apparent that the Enlightenment was deeply marked by the mechanisms of capitalism. What I have hoped to demonstrate in the foregoing analyses of Rousseau, is that even in the eighteenth century many of these negative effects of enlightenment were evident. Rousseau was particularly sensitive to issues concerning alienation, commodification, and ultimately domination. His social and political philosophy as well as his autobiographies testify to his concerns about rationality in the service of technological development and its potential to overrun the public sphere. Keenly aware of the problem of private interest, he forecasts the growth of mass markets.

Turning from Rousseau to Diderot changes the character of the problems under analysis. As I have already indicated in the introduction, to a great extent Rousseau is a dialectical thinker who never seems to harness dialectics to his advantage. He thinks dialectically in spite of himself, often pointing out the dangers of certain aspects of bourgeois ideology, only to fall into the trap of their negation. Diderot by contrast qualifies as a dialectical thinker who harnesses paradox and works it to his advantage. Thus, the second half of the book engages Diderot in direct dialogue with his philosophical *progeny*: Hegel, Marx, and Adorno.

Consistent with the shift to properly dialectical philosophy, the second half of *Mass Enlightenment* leaves social and political philosophy behind to engage in questions concerning epistemology, ethics, and aesthetics. These topics will be explored in relation to the same theoretical issues that inform the first half of the book— namely, the negative effects of enlightenment rationality in the service of capitalism as they influence cultural production. In the case of Diderot, the issues are merely broadened to include more far-reaching philosophical consequences. In keeping with Diderot's supple and subtle dialectical style, the construction of my own arguments and analyses attempts to follow his lead. Thus, the division between the two halves of the book is marked not only by a shift in author and emphasis, but also in a change in style of argumentation.

It is also important to note in this moment of transition between the two halves of the book that Diderot's relation to the *business* side of literature appears less naive than Rousseau's. As director of the *Encyclopédie* project, Diderot has a more nuanced understanding of the market mechanisms that impinge on literary production. While at times he bemoans the commodification of culture, sounding a lot like Rousseau (see chapter 6), at others he seems more accepting of the effects of the market, and even engages in playful cynicism (see chapter 5). Overall, his dialectical perspective enables him to appreciate the interrelation of philosophical questions in a way that anticipates later critical theorists. But like Rousseau, Diderot recognizes the determining effects of the market on culture during his own time and anticipates the appearance of mass markets in the late nineteenth century. In this respect he shares with Rousseau an anticipatory vision of cultural modernity.

4 Materialist Hermeneutics: Diderot's *Rêve de d'Alembert*

> The philosophers have only *interpreted* the world, in various ways; the point, however, is to *change* it.
> —Karl Marx, *Theses on Feuerbach*

French materialism of the eighteenth century shares with its philosophical precursors—Continental rationalism and British empiricism—an emphasis on the primacy of the subject and of the senses as the point of origin of all knowledge.[1] Although French materialism informs a worldview that is not static, it nonetheless tends to offer mechanistic, causal explanations of events. Thus, the French materialist episteme differs only slightly from the earlier classical episteme—described in Foucault's analyses of the Port Royal grammar and logic—in its incorporation of a mechanistic conception of change.[2] Diderot, however, stands out among the French materialists for his development of a dynamic, organic form of materialism. Anticipating discoveries in biology and physics, Diderot's materialism allows for theorizing more radical forms of change over time. His use of theories of evolution and of particles in motion undergirds a theory that is qualitatively different from the materialisms of his contemporaries.[3]

The following analysis proposes a reading of Diderot's organic materialism as a direct precursor of Hegel's historical dialectics and Marx's dialectical materialism.[4] I will argue that it is Diderot's emphasis upon *process* that sets the stage for later dialectical materialists. In particular, his development of a materialist epistemology and hermeneutics represents a dramatic break with the static, classical episteme, one that enables theorizing significant change over time. In the historical context of the late eighteenth century, Diderot's materialist epistemology and hermeneutics signal important social and cultural changes that necessitated theories both dynamic and critical. Thus, my reading of *Le Rêve de d'Alembert* analyzes Diderot's materialist epistemology and hermeneutics in view of the social and cultural changes of the late eighteenth century. I maintain that Diderot's critical, dialectical epistemology and hermeneutics lay important groundwork for nineteenth-century philosophers and theorists.[5]

In the opening of *The Grundrisse*, Marx explains the dialectical nature of the relation between production and consumption. According to his analysis, the act of production is only completed in consumption. Likewise, consumption must be understood as an act of production. Marx writes:

> It is clear that in nutrition, for example, which is but one form of consumption, man produces his own body; but it is equally true of every kind of consumption which goes to produce the human being in one way or another. It is consumptive production. . . . *Production is thus at the same time consumption, and consumption is at the same time production. Each is directly its own counterpart. But at the same time an intermediary movement goes on between the two. Production furthers consumption by creating materials for the latter which otherwise would lack its object. But consumption in its turn furthers production, by providing for the products the individual for whom they are products. The product receives its last finishing touches in consumption.* [24, emphasis added]

Marx's analysis presents a classic example of dialectical materialism: first, production and consumption—normally conceived as opposites—are shown to be linked and in fact dependent upon each other. The opposites constantly further each other's ends in a dialectical dynamic. Second, although Marx's reading applies to economic processes, he nevertheless uses the example of the body to illustrate his point. The destructive process of consuming food may also be understood as productive of the body. Conversely, the production of the body necessitates the destruction or consumption of food. Thus, dialectical forces are shown to determine even the most elementary processes.

Marx's reading of production and consumption in *The Grundrisse* coincides perfectly with Diderot's fantastical defense of materialism in *D'Alembert's Dream*. Arguing against spirit-matter dualism, Diderot maintains that all matter is sentient. He distinguishes between matter possessing active sensibility and matter possessing only inert sensibility. Consistent with his materialism, he holds that any object of inert sensibility may be rendered active, and vice versa: all matter in the universe forms a dynamic continuum. In the opening "Entretien" with d'Alembert, Diderot proposes the process of alimentary consumption to illustrate:

> For what do you do when you eat? You remove the obstacles which were resisting the active sensitivity of the food [*sensibilité active*]. You assimilate the food with yourself, you turn it into flesh, you animalize it, make it capable of feeling. What you do to that food I will do to marble, and whenever I like. [93, 151]

D'Alembert challenges Diderot's thesis, doubting the edibility of an inert statue, and hence the possibility of bringing it to life:

> D'Alembert: Make marble eatable . . . doesn't sound very easy to me.
> Diderot: It's my business to show you how it is done. I take this statue you can see, put it into a mortar, and with some hard bangs with a pestle. . . .
> Diderot: When the marble block is reduced to the finest powder I mix this powder with humus or compost, work them well together, water the mixture, let it rot for a year, two years, a century, for I am not concerned with time. When the whole has turned into a more or less homogeneous substance—into humus—do you know what I do? . . . I sow peas, beans, cabbages and other leguminous plants. The plants feed on the earth and I feed on the plants. [94-95, 151-52]

Consistent with Marx's thesis, Diderot's example illustrates what Marx calls *the intermediary movement* between production and consumption. Again citing the passage from Marx above: "Production furthers consumption by creating materials for the latter which otherwise would lack its object. But consumption in its turn furthers production, by providing for the products the individual for whom they are products." In Diderot's example, pulverizing the statue and producing humus furthers consumption by ultimately issuing in vegetables destined to be eaten. In turn, eating the vegetables helps to sustain the individual—here Diderot—for whom they are products. Thus, for both Marx and Diderot, dialectical materialism implies a fundamental interdependence between the processes of production and consumption. Moreover, for both thinkers, the materialist world-view entails analyzing processes such as these in a broad historical context, which is able to recognize change over time.

Diderot's Materialism

In *D'Alembert's Dream,* Diderot maintains that the entire universe is composed of indivisible units that combine and recombine to form various types of matter (*107,* 160).[6] He further suggests that all matter—organic and inorganic—must be understood as part of a larger whole. Thus, he defends a *metaphysics* of perpetual flux:

> All creatures are involved in the life of all others [*tous les êtres circulent les uns dans les autres*], consequently every species . . . all nature is in a perpetual state of flux. Every animal is more or less a human being, every mineral more or less a plant, every plant more or less an animal. . . . There is nothing clearly defined in nature. . . . Is there in nature any one atom exactly similar to another ? No. . . . Don't you agree that in nature everything is bound up with everything else, and that there cannot be a gap in the chain? *Then what are you talking about with your individuals? There is no such thing; no, no such thing. There is but one great individual, and that is the whole.* [138-39, 181, emphasis added]

As a result of the thesis of perpetual flux, Diderot maintains that there are no types and essences: "so nothing is of the essence of a particular being [*rien n'est de l'essence d'un être particulier*]" (138, 181). Since all matter is part of the larger whole that is subject to perpetual metamorphosis, there are no essences, only temporary tendencies.

The thesis of perpetual flux and its corollary concerning the impossibility of identifying *individuals* (types or essences) pose serious difficulties for any theory of knowledge, because they ultimately frustrate attempts to assign identity.[7] For example, in contrast to Descartes's certainty regarding the continuity between the melted and hardened wax, Diderot's flux thesis cannot ground such certainty. Although he would maintain that there are units that recombine to form new material, these *atoms* hardly ensure that our knowledge of the continuity of the *wax* is correct. On the contrary, in order to be consistent with the thesis of perpetual flux, one would have to maintain that both the melted and hardened states of wax are only temporary and ephemeral forms. Rather than insist on the continuity of identity through change like Descartes, Diderot finds the mere fact of change significant. Recognizing the continuity of matter through a succession of forms is less important for Diderot than recognizing that there is a succession of forms.[8]

Moreover, many of Diderot's examples call into question the very idea of continuity by blurring the distinction between continuity and contiguity. Or, put another way, Diderot undermines the possibility of establishing identity by challenging our ability to distinguish between contiguous and continuous objects. In one of his most colorful examples, Diderot proposes a swarm of bees acting in concert that are metamorphosed into a single creature:

> Have you ever seen a swarm of bees leaving their hive? . . .
> The world, or the general mass of matter, is the great hive. . . .
> Have you seen them fly away and form at the tip of a branch a
> long cluster of little winged creatures, all clinging to each other
> by their feet? This cluster is a being, an individual, a kind of liv-
> ing creature. . . . But these clusters should be all alike. . . . Yes,
> if he admitted the existence of only one homogeneous sub-
> stance. [*120, 168*]

As the doctor explains to Mademoiselle de l'Espinasse, if the bees were of a homogeneous material, then they would form one continuous animal. If each bee is considered to be heterogeneous, then they form a mass composed of contiguous organisms. Maintaining the distinction between continuous and contiguous bees—although difficult in the dream state—ought to be easy enough in the waking state. However, as the subsequent examples demonstrate, it is not always easy to distinguish between continuous and contiguous organisms.

Representing a human analogy to the swarm of bees, Doctor Bordeu suggests the problem of Siamese twins. Although Siamese twins are seemingly two contiguous organisms joined together through some sort of biological accident, from another perspective they are continuous—at least in body. Regardless of the scientific merit of the example, the Siamese twins demonstrate the epistemological problem of maintaining a hard and fast distinction between continuous and contiguous organisms. These human polyps, as Diderot calls them, raise serious questions concerning epistemological certainty in a world subject to change. If I cannot know with absolute certainty whether Siamese twins are contiguous though joined or really continuous, how then do I classify them? How do I know if they are one being or two? Or something in between? How do I establish its/their identity? How then can I be certain about the nature of matter in the universe? Without Cartesian certainty, what type of knowledge is possible? In other words, the thesis of perpetual flux, as Diderot articulates it, makes it extremely difficult, if not well nigh impossible, to get a *fix* on reality. As matter changes forms—combines and recombines—it is at once separate and distinct units, and merely part of a larger whole. The distinction between contiguous and continuous organisms is blurred, because all matter is simultaneously both continuous and contiguous with all other matter according to the thesis of perpetual flux. In other words, establishing and maintaining identity even through a succession of forms is highly problematic, given Diderot's version of materialism.[9]

The problem of knowledge is further complicated in *D'Alembert's Dream* by Diderot's undermining of the Cartesian cogito. Whereas direct and indubitable knowledge of self and God ground knowledge in Descartes, direct and indubitable knowledge of anything would seem all but impossible for Diderot. In the opening "Entretien," Diderot and d'Alembert presumably agree that memory plays the key role with respect to both the formation of subjective identity and coherent knowledge of the world:

> Diderot: Could you tell me what the existence of a sentient being means to that being himself?
> D'Alembert: Consciousness of having been himself from the first instant he reflected until the present moment.
> Diderot: But what is this consciousness founded on?
> D'Alembert: The memory of his own actions.
> Diderot: And without that memory?
> D'Alembert: Without that memory there would be no "he," because, if he only felt his existence at the moment of receiving an impression, he would have no connected story of his life. His life would be a broken sequence of isolated sensations. [99-100, 155]

According to this passage, and consistent with other empiricists, Diderot asserts the primacy of memory in both shaping identity and ensuring that the subject formed as a result of that memory has a coherent experience of the world. Without memory, life would be nothing but a chaotic series of disparate sense experiences.

Despite Diderot and d'Alembert's agreement in the "Entretien," the representation of dream experience in the succeeding "Rêve" undermines the force of the argument. In particular, Diderot suggests in the second dialogue that even normally functioning memory is subject to lapses. When d'Alembert awakens from the dream state, he asks the doctor to explain the *continuity* of identity over time:

> D'Alembert: Doctor, just one more word and I'll let you go to your patient. Taking into account all the changes I have undergone in the course of my life, and in view of the fact that at present I probably haven't a single one of the molecules I brought with me when I was born, how have I kept my personality for myself as well as for others?
> Bordeu: You told me how during your dream.
> D'Alembert: Have I been dreaming [*est-ce que j'ai rêvé*]? [163, 201]

The doctor goes on to assert the importance of memory for the formation of identity—the idea expressed by the sleeping d'Alembert—but d'Alembert's failure to remember his own dream undermines the persuasive force of the answer. His lack of awareness of having dreamt, much less of the content of the dream, demonstrates a fundamental lack of continuity between waking and dreaming states. Consequently, the assertion that memory provides the continuity necessary for identity, and therefore knowledge, is contradicted by d'Alembert's own experience. At best, memory is selective or faulty, and as such cannot provide a certain ground for either subjective identity or knowledge. Diderot's undercutting of Cartesianism seemingly leaves him without *stable* epistemological ground. Instead, knowledge seems mired in a quicksand of perpetual flux.

Surprisingly, Diderot's dialogue does not issue in radical philosophical relativism. Despite his assertion that matter is subject to constant change, Diderot does not preclude the possibility of knowledge. Rather, he invokes a dynamic conception of knowledge that will be adequate to his dynamic, materialist (meta)physics. The dialogue as a whole illustrates the form of knowledge Diderot proposes.[10] In fact, the dialogic form enables Diderot to represent the passage of knowledge from one person to another, and therewith its continual change and mutation. In other words, the dialogue enacts the perpetual flux of knowledge that coincides with the perpetual flux of matter. The ideas from the "Entretien" are transformed in the "Rêve," first by the sleeping d'Alembert, and then by the interpretations of Mademoiselle de l'Espinasse and Bordeu. In turn, the moral consequences of these ideas are developed in the concluding "Suite." The dialogue as a whole traces the changes undergone by the ideas as they pass from one person to another. Thus, the text suggests that knowledge, like reality, is subject to change, because it is subject to constant revision.

Returning to my earlier discussion of production and consumption, I would argue that, for Diderot, knowledge like any other *material* participates in this dialectical process. Knowledge is produced as it is consumed and consumed as it is produced. Put another way, to think is to interpret, and to interpret is to think. The waking d'Alembert listens to Diderot's ideas—consumes them—only to *re*produce them in the form of new ideas in his dream. Likewise, Mademoiselle de l'Espinasse and Bordeu consume the ideas of the dream in order to produce their own ideas. Without consumption— that is to say, interpretation—the production of ideas is incomplete. And without production there is no interpretation. New ideas are produced and consumed in a never-ending dialectical process that coincides with the dynamics of perpetual flux. For Diderot, reality is not static, and neither is knowledge.[11]

Materialist Epistemology: Fallibilistic Hermeneutic Holism

Diderot's thesis of perpetual flux and his corollary conception of knowledge in perpetual flux represents a significant break with other eighteenth-century versions of materialism. In particular, his thesis of perpetual flux, which incorporates theories of evolution and of perpetual motion in the universe, challenges the mechanistic, cause and effect materialism of the day. Moreover, his development of an epistemological position, which coincides with his *metaphysics*, heralds the coming of history and anthropology as new *disciplines* in the nineteenth century.[12] But Diderot's organic materialism represents more than a revision of earlier materialism. Its epistemological implications offer the possibility for critical insight into perceived changes in social and historical reality. It is precisely the critical component of Diderot's materialism which sets it apart from other eighteenth-century theories.[13]

Diderot's theory of the production and consumption of ideas through the dynamics of interpretation escapes the stasis of identitarian thinking and envisions a truly dialectical materialism. Anticipating Marx and Adorno, Diderot's text offers an example of negative dialectics. In order to better examine the implications of Diderot's materialist epistemology, and in particular its nonidentitarian, negative dialectical character, it will be useful to contrast it with a counterexample. Toward this end, I will use Freud's theory of primary narcissism as an example of a nondialectical theory of consumption.

According to Freud's well-known narrative of infantile development, the child passes through the succession of oral, anal, and genital phases. In the oral phase, the ego is in the process of differentiating itself from the id, and consequently the child does not yet possess a fully independent conception of self. It is during this phase that the child derives pleasure by incorporating objects into its mouth. At this stage the id forms object-cathexes, which are not yet distinguishable from identifications.[14] The child identifies with/cathects onto external objects and then makes them part of the self through incorporation. Thus, the pleasure of incorporation and consumption in part derives from the expansive id's identification with surrounding objects.[15]

According to Freud, despite the pleasure of incorporation, primary narcissism originates in self-preservation.[16] The child perceives a threat and uses incorporation and consumption as a strategy of containment. In a denial of difference, eating the *object* nullifies the threat posed by the foreign body by making it part of the self. Freud's theory of primary narcissism is thus inherently undialectical. The eat or be eaten mentality of self-preservation contains no internal dynamic. Rather, the annihilation of the foreign body motivates consumption.

By contrast, a dialectical theory of consumptive production or productive consumption requires recognition of the external object as object apart from the subject.[17] Marx writes in *The Grundrisse*:

> Consumption produces production in two ways. In the first place that the product first becomes a real product in consumption; . . . consequently, a product, as distinguished from a mere natural object, proves to be such, first *becomes* a product, in consumption. Consumption gives the product the finishing touch by annihilating it, since the result of production is a product, not as a material embodiment of activity but only as an object for the active subject.

> In the second place, consumption produces production by creating the necessity for new production. . . . It is clear that while production furnishes the material object of consumption, consumption provides the ideal object of production, as its image, its want, its impulse and its purpose. [24-25]

Although Marx stresses the annihilation of the product in the act of consumption, he emphasizes that it is necessary that the object be recognized as such by an active subject. In other words, consumption dialectically completes production because it entails a specific type of subject-object relation. In Freud's primary narcissism, there is only the child-subject—no external world and no other objects.[18] The act of incorporation seeks to perpetuate the infantile denial of the threat of the external world. It does not recognize the object as object.

Marx's second point is also denied in infantile primary narcissism: the act of incorporation does not promote production. Although, strictly speaking, eating does help to produce the child, this is not the child's aim in primary narcissism. On the contrary, the child does not wish to encounter other threats from the external world. Even though the act of incorporation offers a pleasure that could stimulate a desire for more consumption—the child might seek other objects to put in its mouth—Freud always couples the desire for incorporation with the perceived threat of the foreign body. Thus, primary narcissism, because it seeks to deny the relation between subject and object, also denies a dialectical relation between them.

Ultimately, the difference between Freud's primary narcissism and Marx's productive consumption lies in the focus of their analyses: whereas Freud emphasizes the subject who makes the object or product part of the self, Marx highlights the *process*. Marx's analysis of labor thus focuses on the activity of production, not on the static objects produced. Likewise, Diderot's epistemology stresses the activity productive of thought, and not the ideas themselves. In fact, Diderot's metaphysics and epistemology are coincident on this point: both stress the process of continual change as opposed to a mapping of knowlege onto reality.

In an example of materialist epistemology from the "Entretien," Diderot compares the process of thinking to the vibrating strings of a clavichord. He imagines the human mind as a set of feeling strings that interact to produce different *harmonics* or associations of ideas. Diderot explains:

A sensitive vibrating string goes on vibrating and sounding a note long after it has been plucked. It is this oscillation, a kind of necessary resonance, which keeps the object present while the understanding is free to consider whichever of the object's qualities it wishes. But vibrating strings have yet another property, that of making others vibrate, and it is in this way that one idea calls up a second, and the two together a third, and all three a fourth, and so on; you can't set a limit to the ideas called up and linked together by a philosopher meditating or communing with himself in silence and darkness. This instrument can make astonishing leaps, and one idea called up will sometimes start an harmonic at an incomprehensible interval. If this phenomenon can be observed between resonant strings which are inert and separate, why should it not take place between living and connected points, continuous and sensitive fibres? [*101-2*, 156]

According to Diderot's model, thinking itself entails a material process of production, which involves both stimulation from external objects and physical activity within the mind. His vibrating chords produce harmonics or associations between ideas, which are at times unexpected.[19] Most importantly, thought requires material production and consumption conceived according to a musical model: the human instrument consumes the world in order to produce its music. That is to say, that objects touch off series of harmonics within the mind. The mind then produces new music (thoughts and ideas), which in turn stimulates new chords. Every act of consumption—the vibrating of the strings of the mind—entails production of some sort. No matter how simple the sense impression, there is always the possibility of producing a creative harmonic series, or a radically new way of thinking. Thus, Diderot's materialist conception of the workings of the mind stresses the activity of thought as opposed to passive receptivity. It also entails a dynamic relation between the subject and the objective world.

Ultimately, Diderot's epistemology allows for a dynamic conception of knowledge because it amounts to a fallibilistic form of hermeneutic holism.[20] In other words, knowledge is subject to constant revision because it entails a continuous process of interpretation.

Diderot's opinion on a well-known debate among eighteenth-century philosophers clearly illustrates his position. Voltaire, Locke, and Condillac, among others, were engaged in a debate concerning the ability of a person whose cataracts had been removed to visually identify a sphere and a cube. Whereas Condillac held that the formerly blind person would be able to distinguish the two shapes, without the aid of the sense of touch, Locke and Mollineux maintained that tactile verification would be necessary. Diderot's position on the question lends insight into his hermeneutic holist theory of knowledge. In the *Lettre sur les aveugles*, he contends that the formerly blind person would not be able to distinguish between the two objects immediately. Only after reflection and comparison would the person be able to distinguish between the sphere and the cube by sight.[21] However, he does not hold that touching the objects would be required for verification. Using the extreme example of a disembodied eye as a limit case, Diderot maintains that eventually even an eye would learn to read what it sees, without the aid of the other senses:

> A living and animate eye would no doubt have some difficulty in assuring itself that exterior objects were not part of itself; that it is sometimes next to them, sometimes far away; that they are represented, that some are larger than others, that they have depth, etc. . . . but I have no doubt that it would see them in time, and that it would see them distinctly enough to discern at least the gross limits of them [*mais je ne doute nullement qu'il ne les vît à la longue, et qu'il ne les vît assez distinctement pour en discerner au moins les limites grossières*]. [63]

Likewise, the blind person, upon seeing for the first time, would learn to judge the visual impressions without the input of the other senses. More importantly for our purposes, Diderot implies that sight—and all the other senses—are languages that require interpretation. Raw sense data, like a foreign language, remains meaningless without the proper decoding.

Thus, Diderot's position in the *Letter on the Blind* goes beyond traditional empiricism.[22] Rather than merely replace the notion of innate ideas with the notion of ideas derived from sense data, he incorporates a hermeneutic thesis. Sense impressions alone are insufficient for knowledge: the thinking subject must actively judge sense data in order to produce knowledge. Anticipating Kant, Diderot's position implies an act of synthesis on the part of the formerly blind person who correctly identifies the sphere and cube.

Moreover, this knowledge is not static. According to the *Dream*, knowledge—like all other matter—is subject to change. As the clavichord model illustrates, thought is inherently active and changing as the strings of the mind continually produce new harmonic series. Thus, Diderot's epistemology is not a static correspondence theory, but rather an extension of his organic materialism into the realm of thought. His materialist epistemology represents a form of fallibilistic hermeneutic holism, in the sense that all knowledge requires interpretation and revision.

Diderot's position, as I have analyzed it so far, entails a dialectic at two levels: at the first level, knowledge or interpretation entails the dialectical hermeneutic relation between part and whole. No single piece of information can be said to be meaningful without the projected backdrop of the whole. Similarly, each new interpretation of a part requires the revision of the conception of the whole. At the second level, Diderot's materialist hermeneutics implies that subjective identity itself is revised in the process of interpretation. Representing an ontological aspect of his hermeneutics, this level of the dialectic implicates the subject in every act of interpretation. The subject itself undergoes a process of revision as it continually revises its conception of the world.

Finally, it must be noted that Diderot's hermeneutics extends beyond mere textual interpretation.[23] For Diderot, all knowledge implies these two simultaneous dialectics—the hermeneutical dialectic between part and whole and the ontological dialectic. Thus, Diderot's fallibilistic hermeneunics emphasizes *process* over *product*. Knowledge implies a continuous process of production.

Negative Dialectics

So far I have demonstrated that Diderot's materialist epistemology amounts to a form of fallibilistic hermeneutic holism, but I have not yet addressed the question of a negative dialectic. As we have seen, the fallibilistic aspect of his epistemology implies a dynamic element—one that subverts the possibility of a Hegelian type of *telos*. Moreover, Diderot's emphasis upon interpretation implies both the part/whole and ontological hermeneutical dialectics. But neither fallibilism nor hermeneutics necessarily imply a negative dialectic. The negative dialectical component in Diderot's materialist epistemology lies in its nonidentitarian character. In order to explore the subtleties of nonidentitarian thinking, and specifically the negative dialectical aspect of Diderot's work, it will be necessary to return to Adorno's critique of identitarian thinking in *Negative Dialectics*.

Adorno's critique of Hegel, and of idealism in general, depends upon revealing the nonidentity concealed within identity.[24] In other words, Adorno is interested in the epistemological problem of the adequacy between thought or concept and thing.[25] His method relies upon discovering the contradiction inherent in predicative relations. He maintains that all relations of identity (between thing and concept) imply a nonidentity. In traditional identitarian thinking, the predicative relation asserts the adequacy of the relation between concept and thing. Adorno writes:

> In idealism, the highly formal identity principle had, due to its formalization, an affirmative substance. This is innocently brought to light by terminology, when simple predicative sentences are called "affirmative." The copula says: It is so, not otherwise. The act of synthesis, for which the copula stands, indicates that it shall not be otherwise—else the act would not be performed. The will to identity works in each synthesis. As an a priori task of thought, a task immanent in thought, identity seems positive and desirable: the substrate of the synthesis is thus held to be reconciled with the I, and therefore to be good. [147-48]

In other words, the identitarian thought process requires synthesis or a relation of adequation between a thing and a concept. For example, a simple proposition asserts that $2+3=5$. The affirmative character of the predicate $(=)$ denies any difference between the things being equated.

The problem arises for Adorno when we recognize that identity depends, in fact, on nonidentity. To assert that $5=5$ is a tautology. However, to assert that $2+3=5$ requires effacing the fundamental nonidentity that makes this an interesting, albeit simple, proposition. The assertion $2+3=5$ denies that $2+3$ is at some level different from 5, as is $3+2$ or $1+4$. In other words, predicative relations and other forms of definition entail the masking of nonidentity. However, Adorno asserts:

> Definition also approaches that which the object itself is as nonidentical: in placing its mark on the object, definition seeks to be marked by the object. Nonidentity is the secret *telos* of identification. It is the part that can be salvaged; the mistake in traditional thinking is that identity is taken for the goal. The force that shatters the appearance of identity is the force of

thinking: the use of "it is" undermines the form of that appearance, which remains inalienable just the same. *Dialectically, cognition of nonidentity lies also in the fact that this very cognition identifies—that it identifies to a greater extent, and in other ways, than identitarian thinking. This cognition seeks to say what something is, while identitarian thinking says what something comes under, what it exemplifies or represents, and what, accordingly, it is not itself.* [149, emphasis added]

Identitarian thinking effaces the very particularity of the particular by making it an example of the rule or universal. Thus, epistemological systems that rely upon categorization deny the dynamic relation between particular and universal, because they assert the identity between particular and universal.[26] For example, botany requires that flowers be identified according to a complex classificatory schema. As an epistemological system, this classificatory schema maintains the correspondence between particular (a flower) and universal (Latin name, ideal type). While botany as a science recognizes differences between species, it cannot recognize differences between two flowers of the same species. Nor can it account for any tension between the particular and the universal—for example, that this particular flower has flaws and thus does not embody the ideal type.[27]

In Diderot's text, it is clear that identitarian thinking is inadequate to a world subject to perpetual flux. As we have already seen, Diderot clearly maintains that types and essences are vain philosophical concepts that deny the ephemeral character of any particular form that matter might take. Instead, the thesis of perpetual flux necessitates a new epistemology that does not deny the inherently changing nature of matter.

Adorno proposes nonidentitarian thinking as an alternative epistemology to identity:

To define identity as the correspondence of the thing-in-itself to its concept is *hubris*; but the ideal of identity must not simply be discarded. Living in the rebuke that the thing is not identical with the concept is the concept's longing to become identical with the thing. *This is how the sense of nonidentity contains identity.* The supposition of identity is indeed the ideological element of pure thought, all the way down to formal logic; but hidden in it is also the truth moment of ideology, the pledge that there should be no contradiction, no antagonism. [149]

As Adorno describes it, nonidentitarian thinking does not eliminate identity altogether. However, it recognizes the contradiction inherent in the claim of identity. Rather than deny the tension between particular and universal, nonidentitarian thinking uses this tension in order to create a dynamic form of knowledge. Negative dialectics, thus, evades the trap of synthesis (idealism) by perpetuating the dynamic tension between subject and object. Knowledge represents a continual striving to abolish the nonidentity—a continual attempt for concept to be adequate to thing—but one that necessarily perpetuates itself. Here the difference between the Hegelian conception of the dialectic, which stresses the *Aufhebung*, and Adorno's negative dialectics is clear. Whereas Hegel's idealism highlights the moment of synthesis, Adorno's materialism perpetually staves off synthesis, because there is always a remainder that resists sublation. In other words, there can never be final synthesis for Adorno because matter (object, thing-in-itself) always resists adequation to its concept. The concept for Adorno, unlike for Hegel, will always be inadequate to the particular:

> In [identitarian] epistemology the inevitable result is the false conclusion that the object is the subject. Traditional philosophy believes that it knows the unlike by likening it to itself, while in so doing it really knows itself only. *The idea of a changed philosophy would be to become aware of likeness by defining it as that which is unlike itself.* [150]

Adorno's description of dialectical epistemology very nearly approaches Diderot's materialist epistemology in *D'Alembert's Dream*. Like Diderot, Adorno asserts the importance of recognizing difference. The source of this difference for both Diderot and Adorno lies in the tension between particular and universal, thing and concept.[28] Preserving this difference allows for theorizing change. For Adorno, a static epistemology is nothing less than ideological, because it necessarily denies difference, and therefore change, in favor of synthesis and stability. Traditional epistemology—most obviously Hegel—tends to efface the difference between subject and object in favor of the subject. Adorno proposes an alternate negative dialectical epistemology that will be able to recognize and theorize change:

> On its subjective side, *dialectics amounts to thinking so that the thought form will no longer turn its objects into*

immutable ones, into objects that remain the same. Experience shows that they do not remain the same. The unstable character of traditional philosophy's solid identity can be learned from its guarantor, the individual human consciousness. To Kant, this is the generally predesigned unity underlying every identity. In fact, if an older person looking back has started early on a more or less conscious existence, he will distinctly remember his own distant past. It creates a unity, no matter how unreal the elusive picture of his childhood may seem. Yet the "I" which he remembers in this unreality, the I which he was at one time and potentially becomes again—this I turns simultaneously into another, into a stranger to be detachedly observed. [154, emphasis added]

Adorno, again like Diderot, signals the importance of revising identity in both senses of the word: not only must we revise our thinking about objects in the world, we must also reconsider the unity and stability of our own subjective identities.[29] The two are in fact predicated on one another. In traditional philosophy, the unity of the subject provides the stable ground for knowledge of the world. Uncharitably citing Kant as a prime example, Adorno explains that the stability of knowledge in the traditional sense rests on the double denial of nonidentity: traditional epistemology denies both change in the world and change in the subject. Dialectical epistemology proposes recognizing the nonidentity at the heart of identity. In other words, it allows us to account in some way for that which resists definition—both in things in the world and in our own identities.

As we have already seen, Diderot's text addresses this problem head-on. D'Alembert's failure to remember the content of his dream—a content that asserts the primacy of memory for the unity of subjective identity—signals a fundamental lack of continuity between waking and dreaming states. While Diderot asserts the traditional position that memory provides the stable ground for subjectivity and knowledge, he simultaneously recognizes that neither the subject nor the world are stable. In his critique of Cartesianism, Diderot unearths what Adorno calls the nonidentity of identity. Moreover, his use of metaphor and concrete examples testifies to his commitment to a truly materialist epistemology.[30] Each succeeding example creates new possibilities without ever exhausting the previous metaphor. In other words, Diderot's text enacts a nonidentitarian epistemology in its use of literary tropes to address philosophical problems.[31]

An example of a series of related metaphors illustrates Diderot's avoidance of synthesis and sublation in favor of a negative dialectical approach to epistemology. Beginning in the "Entretien," Diderot uses the example of the clavichord, as we have already seen, to illustrate his conception of the workings of the mind. In the "Rêve," d'Alembert introduces the example of bees to problematize the relations of continuity and contiguity. Although at first glance it does not seem that the bee metaphor is related to the clavichord metaphor, in fact both metaphors address the problem of continuity and contiguity with respect to the parts of the human body and their relation to a central consciousness.

Julie de l'Espinasse next introduces the metaphor of the spider in its web to help elucidate the epistemological problems at hand:

> Doctor, come nearer. Imagine a spider at the centre of its web. Disturb a thread and you will see the creature rush up on the alert. Now suppose that those threads that the insect draws from its own body and draws in again at will were a sensitive part of itself. [140, 182]

The relation between the spider in its web and the clavichord is apparent: both metaphors incorporate vibrating strings to illustrate the transmission of information as sense data are received. However, the spider metaphor distinguishes between the material aspect of the body (web) and the central consciousness or mind (spider), whereas the clavichord metaphor did not. The further elaboration of the spider metaphor demonstrates its relation to the metaphor of the bees, and by extension, the link between the clavichord and bee metaphors:

> Mademoiselle de l'Espinasse: But if the smallest speck of matter makes one thread of the web vibrate, the spider is alerted, excited and darts here or there. At the centre she is conscious of what is going on at any point in the huge mansion she has woven. Why don't I know what is going on in my own system or in the world at large, since I am a bundle of sensitive particles and everything is touching me and I am touching everything else? [141, 183-84]

Mademoiselle de l'Espinasse's question concerning her own inability to receive sense impressions from parts of her body or, more generally, objects in the world, links the spider and clavichord metaphors to the bees. The question poses the problem of contiguity and continuity in relation to sense impressions and their reception. Put another way, Julie would like to know why the strings of her web (or her clavichord) do not start vibrating when something happens in the next room. This question closely resembles the one raised by the bees—namely, what distinguishes contiguous from continuous organisms?

Although none of these metaphors offers any ultimate solution to the epistemological/metaphysical questions raised, Diderot's use of metaphor goes a long way in illustrating an epistemology that uses nonidentitarian thinking. The succession of metaphors resists synthesis or sublation, and instead offers "answers" that require interpretation and revision. In fact, each successive metaphor may be read as both an interpretation and revision of the preceding metaphors. These *metaphoric interpretations* do not, however, offer any kind of final solution. On the contrary, they invite more revision and interpretation.[32] Thus, Diderot's use of metaphor illustrates his fallibilistic hermeneutic holism, while at the same time clearly indicates a negative dialectical component of his thought. The metaphors fuel an endless process of interpretation precisely because they contain a *material* residue that resists synthesis.[33]

This *material residue* or literary/artistic aspect of the metaphors, which resists a final interpretation, signals a critical element in Diderot's epistemology. Diderot's text requires an active reading practice (as does Adorno's). The reader will be called upon to interpret the text, and will not be allowed to passively receive it. The act of reading, thus, entails an act of production. Consuming the text requires producing the text. In a dialectical hermeneutic, Diderot ensures the critical engagement of his reader with the text. Returning to my epigraph from Marx's *Theses on Feuerbach*, it is clear that for Diderot, not only interpreting the text, but also interpreting the world necessarily entails changing it. All acts of judgment require critical-practical engagement with the world.

As we have already seen in the previous chapter, Jürgen Habermas argues that the rise of a critical reading public must be situated historically within the eighteenth century. The Enlightenment project encourages the active participation of readers who ideally will engage with the texts they are *consuming*. Diderot's materialist epistemology goes perhaps a step further than the Enlightenment goal of educating a public. His fallibilistic form of hermeneutic holism implies that the goal of enlightenment will never be attained. In fact, the text as material is merely part of the dialectic of knowledge as it passes through a succession of forms. The reader's active participation in *producing* the text implies that Diderot claims no privileged access to the "truth" or "knowledge" for himself. Rather, knowledge only appears momentarily in the interstices between reader and text.

In the context of the rapid social and cultural changes occurring in French society in the second half of the eighteenth century, Diderot's materialist hermeneutics represents an important contribution to philosophical work, which enables theorizing such change. The spread of a consumer market and the dawning of mass culture clearly contribute in significant ways to Diderot's ability to theorize change according to a dialectical model that incorporates a sophisticated understanding of the relation between the processes of production and consumption. As director of the *Encyclopédie*, Diderot had privileged access to information concerning changes in the reading public. The *Encyclopédie* itself signals and also clearly perpetuates many of these changes. For example, readers wrote back to Diderot to correct errors in description or explanation in fields in which they were *experts*.

The correspondence between the reading public and the editor of the *Encyclopédie* is characteristic of the type of dialogical and dialectical form of knowledge that Diderot's materialism implies. As I have analyzed it here, Diderot's materialist epistemology takes a great step toward understanding the dynamic of *knowledge* in a world subject to constant and often times radical forms of change. It also clearly acknowledges the important contribution of the public. Without the public to *consume* the texts, the texts themselves would never and could never be *produced*.

5 Diderot and Hegel: Alienation and the Problem of Ethical Life in *Le Neveu de Rameau*

In the preceding chapter I examined Diderot's epistemology as elaborated in *D'Alembert's Dream* in view of establishing lines of correspondence between what I called his materialist hermeneutics and Adorno's negative dialectics. Drawing such a parallel places Diderot at the beginning of a philosophical tradition that leads via Kant, Hegel, and Marx to the thinkers of the Frankfurt School. As I have already shown, Diderot's materialist epistemology and hermeneutics anticipate many of the dialectical positions of these later philosophers.

In this chapter, I will analyze in detail Hegel's reading of *Le Neveu de Rameau* from the *Phenomenology of Spirit* in order to further elaborate the relationship between Diderot's dialectical philosophy and the fully developed dialectical philosophies of Hegel, Marx, and Adorno. In particular, the problem of alienation as articulated by Diderot bears a strong resemblance to invocations of the concept by these later thinkers. The appearance of the problem of alienation in Diderot's work—and to a certain extent in Rousseau's, as we have already seen—indicates that historical developments in the second half of the eighteenth century foreshadow problems for later bourgeois society.

Hegel's four citations of *Rameau's Nephew* in the *Phenomenology* do not constitute a detailed reading of Diderot's text however.[1] Rather, the strategic citation of Diderot by Hegel merely suggests the outlines of a reading of *Rameau's Nephew*. In effect, Hegel positions Diderot within a particular historical and cultural context by illustrating his points with "quotations." In order to flesh out a reading of *Rameau's Nephew* from the *Phenomenology* it will be necessary to amplify Hegel's discussion of the Enlightenment and the period preceding it. I will augment Hegel's discussion with insights from later dialectical theorists (Marx, Adorno, and Horkheimer) in view of establishing Diderot's position with respect to this tradition.

Hegel and Diderot on Alienation

Hegel's account of the Enlightenment in the *Phenomenology* is preceded by his analysis of the breakdown of feudal society and the emergence of a secular culture. Hegel highlights the rise of a centralized monarchy, and thus of a nation-state. He also takes note of the importance of wealth and patronage in the period preceding the Enlightenment. It is in this section of the *Phenomenology* that Hegel cites Diderot's *Rameau's Nephew* three times and offers the clearest indication of his reading of the text. In order to fill in Hegel's reading of Diderot, it will be necessary to review Hegel's account of Spirit as it moves beyond feudalism and into bourgeois culture.[2]

This section of the *Phenomenology* traces what Hegel terms the self-alienation of Spirit or culture. By this he means that a self-conscious form of secular culture develops for the first time. Or put another way, "Spirit constructs for itself not merely a world, but a world that is double, divided and self-opposed" (295). Hegel maintains that this doubling is necessary for the development of self-consciousness. In particular, Hegel is interested here in the dialectic between individual and universal that develops out of the feudal world.[3] Thus, his analysis focuses primarily on the individual in relation to the emerging state. His first citation of Diderot in fact occurs in his discussion of the appearance of the individual.

Hegel maintains that it is by and "through culture that the individual acquires standing and actuality" (298). But Hegel goes on to suggest that any notion of the *natural* self must be set aside as erroneous. Because the self necessarily comes to know itself by and through culture, the notion of the *natural* self is false.[4] Ironically, what appears as the *individual* actualized or realized through culture, is actually the universal:

> If, therefore, individuality is erroneously supposed to be rooted in the *particularity* of nature and character, then in the actual world there are no individualities and no characters, but everyone is like everyone else; but this presumed individuality really only exists in someone's mind, an *imaginary* existence which

has no abiding place in this world, where only that which exter-
nalizes itself, and, therefore, only the universal, obtains an
actual existence. That is why such an imagined existence is
esteemed for what it is, for a *kind* of being. [298]

Reminiscent of some of Diderot's pronouncements concerning types and essences in *D'Alembert's Dream*, Hegel here insists on
the dialectical relation between the individual and universal. The
individual can only exist in relation to a universal that ultimately
defines it.[5] Hegel is quick to point out, however, that by *kind* he
does not mean the derogatory term, *espèce*. Citing *Rameau's
Nephew*, he writes:

> "Kind" is not quite the same as *espèce*, "the most horrid of all
> nicknames; for it denotes mediocrity and expresses the highest
> degree of contempt." "Kind" and "good of its kind" are, how-
> ever, German expressions which add an air of honesty to this
> meaning, as if it were not really meant so badly; or, again, con-
> sciousness is, in fact, not yet aware what "kind," and what
> "culture" and "reality" are. [298][6]

In this first citation of Diderot, Hegel distinguishes between what he
means when he proclaims that the individual is necessarily mediated
by the universal—in this case culture—and the nephew's negative
assessment of an *espèce*. Whereas the nephew deplores the term
because of the lack of originality associated with it, Hegel cautions
that "kind" [*Art*] indicates something different. Hegel associates
"kind" with the actualization of the individual through culture,
which entails the mediation by a universal—but one that does not
preclude originality or even genius.

In the historical context that Hegel describes, the rise of the
individual is necessarily mediated by a universal culture. For Diderot
also, as we have seen in *D'Alembert's Dream* and now here in
Rameau's Nephew, the concern over originality and genius arises
at precisely the same historical moment when the bourgeois individual comes into being. It is only in the context of a universal culture that mediates and actualizes the individual that a concern with
individuality can arise.[7] In other words, a dialectical analysis of the
relation between individual and universal insists that without a universal culture there can be no individual. Likewise, without an individual to stand against it, there can be no recognition of the universal. Thus, in both Hegel and Diderot there is a concern with defining

individuality in the face of the homogenizing tendencies of a dominant culture that occurs at the precise historical moment marked by
the appearance of the bourgeois individual.

As Hegel describes the appearance and development of state
power and wealth, and the individual's relation to both, his dialectical history moves toward the eighteenth century. He distinguishes
between what he terms the noble and ignoble forms of consciousness, which describe the individual's relation to state power and
wealth. While the noble consciousness identifies with both state
power and wealth as forms of culture that actualize its own being,
the ignoble consciousness dwells on the *disparity* between itself and
both the sovereign and wealth. The noble consciousness experiences
the state power as a further expression of itself and according to
Hegel, "in the service of that authority its attitude towards it is one
of actual obedience and respect" (305).

By contrast, the ignoble consciousness experiences both state
power and wealth as *fetters*. It "sees in the sovereign power a fetter
and a suppression of its own *being-for-self*, and therefore hates the
ruler, obeys only with a secret malice, and is always on the point of
revolt" (305). Likewise, the ignoble consciousness, although it
obtains some degree of self-satisfaction through wealth, ultimately
experiences this satisfaction and self-realization as transitory "since
through wealth it becomes conscious of itself merely as an isolated
individual, conscious only of a transitory enjoyment, loving yet hat-
ing wealth, and with the passing of enjoyment, of something that is
essentially evanescent, it regards its relation to the rich as also having vanished" (305).

At the historical moment that sees the appearance of the noble
and ignoble forms of consciousness, state power has not yet been
consolidated and has not yet, therefore, achieved self-consciousness.
According to Hegel, state power attains self-consciousness or obtains
a will through the unified identity of the monarch (309). More specifically, it is by and through language—the "I" of the monarch—that
state power becomes self-conscious.

In this section of the *Phenomenology*, Hegel highlights the role
of language in the realization of self-consciousness, specifically the
language of flattery, which the noble consciousness addresses to the
monarch (310). Moreover, because the monarch depends upon the
language of flattery for his own self-consciousness, he finds himself
dependent upon the noble consciousness (312). The monarch or state
power, dependent upon the noble consciousness for its own identity, bestows wealth in exchange for flattery. Thus, Hegel describes

the dialectic between noble and king in the patronage system of the old regime. The noble is grateful to his benefactor, the king, who in turn depends upon his nobles.

The dialectical relation between noble and king is altered, however, by a change in the status of wealth and a concomitant change in the noble consciousness. Whereas wealth previously contained "no intrinsic being of its own" (313), the exchange between wealth and flattery produces a change in the status of wealth which coincides with a change in the noble consciousness. Wealth "develops an *intrinsic being of its own*," (313) as the formerly noble consciousness confronts wealth as an alien object that holds power over it. Because wealth obtains an independent value—a value separate and distinct from the state authority—the noble consciousness no longer confronts either wealth or state power as forms of its own existence. Instead, the noble consciousness "sees self in the power of an alien will on which it is dependent for possession of its own self" (313). The dialectic between the noble and ignoble consciousness ends in the sublation of the two into what Hegel terms "disrupted consciousness" (314).

This historical account parallels the rise of a centralized monarchy in France under Louis XIV, and its decline after his death in 1715. In particular, Hegel's focus on the appearance of the intrinsic value of wealth ties the decline and fall of centralized monarchy with the rise of mercantilism and capitalism. These economic advances, in turn, determine a change in the subject's relation to the monarch. In the context of these historical changes, Hegel's description of disrupted consciousness is most important for understanding his reading of Diderot. There is no doubt that he reads Rameau's nephew as a clear example of this Enlightenment form of consciousness, which is determined by the change in status of both wealth and state power.[8]

According to Hegel's account, the changes in consciousness and wealth in turn produce a change in the language of flattery. The language of flattery becomes the language of base flattery, "for what it pronounces to be an essence, it knows to be expendable, to be without any *intrinsic* being" (315). Thus, the world becomes a place of inverted values:

> It is this absolute and universal inversion and alienation of the actual world and of thought; it is *pure culture*. What is learnt in this world is that neither the *actuality* of power and wealth, not their specific *Notions*, "good" and "bad," or the consciousness

of "good" and "bad" (the noble and ignoble consciousness),
possess truth; on the contrary, all these moments become
inverted, one changing into the other, and each is the opposite
of itself. [316]

The consciousness of the inversion of values is disrupted consciousness:

> The disrupted consciousness . . . is consciousness of the per-
> version, and, moreover, of the absolute perversion. What pre-
> vails in it is the Notion, which brings together in a unity the
> thoughts which, in the honest individual, lie far apart, and its
> language is therefore clever and witty.
>
> The content of what Spirit says about itself is thus the per-
> version of every Notion and reality, the universal deception of
> itself and others; and the shamelessness which gives utterance to
> this deception is just for that reason the greatest truth. [317]

For Hegel, Rameau's nephew best exemplifies the disrupted consciousness that voices the universal perversion of the world. He
writes:

> This kind of talk is the madness of the musician "who heaped
> up and mixed together thirty arias, Italian, French, tragic,
> comic, of every sort; now with a deep bass he descended into
> hell, then, contracting his throat, he rent the vaults of heaven
> with a falsetto tone, frantic and soothed, imperious and mock-
> ing, by turns." [317-18][9]

By contrast, the philosopher represents the ability to reconcile the
opposites of the disrupted consciousness. According to Hegel, the
philosopher as tranquil consciousness "restores Spirit to itself" and
looks ahead to the next stage of the dialectic characterized by what
Hegel terms pure insight:

> To the tranquil consciousness which, in its honest way, takes
> the melody of the Good and the True to consist in the evenness
> of the notes, i.e. in unison, this talk appears as a "rigamarole of
> wisdom and folly, as a medley of as much skill as baseness, of
> as many correct as false ideas, a mixture compounded of com-
> plete perversion of sentiment, of absolute shamefulness, and of
> perfect frankness and truth. It will be unable to refrain from

entering into all these tones and running up and down the entire scale of feelings from the profoundest contempt and dejection to the highest pitch of admiration and emotion; but blended with the latter will be a tinge of ridicule which spoils them." The former, however, will find in their very frankness a strain of reconciliation, will find in their subversive depths the all-powerful note which restores Spirit to itself. [318]

Thus, Hegel reads Diderot's dialogue as an example of the historical moment in which culture becomes *pure culture*, a moment characterized by the perversion of all values and the emergence of wit. The nephew's witty dialogue and pantomime, which mix styles and genres for effect, typify the truthful but perverted outlook of the disrupted consciousness. The tranquil consciousness—embodied by the philosopher—nonetheless is able to hear the grain of truth through the nephew's perversity.[10] He recognizes in the nephew an *original*, not overconcerned with conformity like the rest of the *individuals* in bourgeois society:

> I don't think much of these queer birds myself, though some people make boon companions of them, and even friends. They interest me once a year when I run into them because their characters contrast sharply with other people's and break the tedious uniformity that our social conventions and set politenesses have brought about. *If one of them appears in a company of people he is the speck of yeast that leavens the whole and restores to each of us a portion of his natural individuality. He stirs people up and gives them a shaking, makes them take sides, brings out the truth, shows who are really good and unmasks the villains. It is then that the wise man listens and sorts out people.* [72, 35, emphasis added][11]

The nephew "restores individuality" and "brings out the truth" precisely because as disrupted consciousness his "shamelessness" (Hegel's term) in reflecting the culture around him foregrounds everyone else's deception. An *individual* thoroughly mediated by the universal culture, the nephew stands out against a backdrop of conformity. Moreover, his shameless corruption and perversion only mirror the corruption and perversion around him, which are *masked* by manners.

Like Hegel, Diderot too points out that the corruption and perversity of *pure culture* extend throughout all levels of this society.

Diderot expresses the mutual dependence of everyone at every level—a dialectical dependence similar to the master/slave dialectic—in his extension of the nephew's behavior throughout society. The nephew is no different from anyone else, "simply more open, more consistent, and sometimes profound in his depravity" (176, 111, translation altered). According to the philosopher, no one is exempt from the often degrading role-playing of which Rameau's nephew is the master, not even the sovereign:

> I: But by your reckoning there are lots of beggars in this world, and I can't think of anybody who doesn't know a few steps of your dance.
> He: You are right. There is only one man in the whole of a realm who walks, and that is the sovereign. Everybody else takes up positions.
> I: The sovereign? But even then isn't there something else to be said? Do you think he doesn't find himself from time to time in the vicinity of a dainty foot, a little lock of hair, a little nose that makes him put on a bit of an act? Whoever needs someone else is necessitous and so takes up a position. The king takes up a position with his mistress and with God; he performs his pantomime step. The minister executes the movements of the courtier, flatterer, flunkey or beggar in front of his king. The mob of placeseekers dance your steps in a hundred ways, each more vile than the one before, in front of the minister. The abbé of noble birth puts on bands and long cassock at least once a week when he calls on the keeper of the list of benefices. Good heavens, what you call the beggars' pantomime is what makes the whole world go round. Everyone has his little Hus and his Bertin.
> He: That cheers me no end. [*190-91*, 121-22]

Consistent with Hegel's appraisal of the breakdown of the patronage system and the concomitant spread of the base language of flattery, both the philosopher's and the nephew's assessment of the world in which they live stress a kind of dependence that has alienated social relations. The nephew is consoled by the fact that he is no worse than anyone else. This is, in fact, how he rationalizes his behavior:

> There is nothing degrading in doing the same as everybody else. I didn't invent them [nasty little tricks], and I should be peculiar and incompetent if I didn't conform. Of course I well

know that if you start applying certain general principles of the sort of morality they all preach and nobody practices, it will work out that white is black and black white. But, Mr. Philosopher, there is such a thing as a standard conscience just as there is a standard grammar, and then exceptions in every language. [*109*, 61]

The disrupted consciousness merely reflects the base and vile depravity of a corrupt social order, which is characterized by a dialectical form of dependency and moral hypocrisy. The nephew's *nasty little tricks* are no different from the monarch's, the ministers' or even the philosopher's little ruses. The only difference is that the disrupted consciousness is no hypocrite.

In this alienated social order nothing remains but vanity. For Hegel:

> The consciousness that is aware of its disruption and openly declares it, derides existence and the universal confusion, and derides its own self as well; it is at the same time the fading, but still audible, sound of all this confusion. This vanity of all reality and every definite Notion, vanity which knows itself to be such, is the double reflection of the real world into itself. . . . In this aspect of the return into the self, the vanity of all *things* is its *own* vanity, it is *itself* vain. [319-20]

Fitting Hegel's description exactly, the nephew "derides existence . . . and [his] own self as well." Moreover, as Hegel describes, the nephew proclaims the vanity of all values save self-preservation and hedonistic enjoyment against the protests of the philosopher:

> You dignify this oddity with the name of virtue and you call it philosophy. But are virtue and philosophy made for everybody? Acquire them those who can, keep them those who are able. Imagine the universe good and philosophical, and admit that it would be devilishly dull. So long live philosophy and long live the wisdom of Solomon—drink good wine, blow yourself out with luscious food, have a tumble with lovely women, lie on soft beds. *Apart from that the rest is vanity.* [*114*, 65, translation altered, emphasis added]

In this disrupted world of alienated social relations, a question of value lies at the heart of the disagreement between the philosopher and the nephew. Both Diderot's dialogue and Hegel's account in the *Phenomenology* suggest that the breakdown of certain types of social relations that stabilized a feudal and monarchical system of values lead to a crisis in ethical life by mid-century.

Hegel's Reading of the Enlightenment

In the section of the *Phenomenology* entitled "The Enlightenment," which follows the section on self-alienated Spirit, Hegel discusses the dialectic between faith and pure insight. For Hegel, this dialectic characterizes the Enlightenment dispute between religious dogma and rational critiques of faith. According to Hegel, faith represents a form of thought that is not self-conscious, because it focuses on the transcendent qualities of the deity (324). Pure insight, on the other hand, is a self-conscious form of thought because its critiques of religious faith depend upon the rational capacities of the subject (324). Pure insight arises historically as a thought form out of the insights of disrupted consciousness.

As we saw in the preceding section, disrupted consciousness gains insight into the world of culture through its own character, which reflects the alienated social relations and perversion of values that attend the breakdown of monarchical authority and the appearance of wealth as a value. Disrupted consciousness, as Hegel defines it, is a self-centered form of consciousness because it reflects the real world back into itself (319-20). Pure insight—a philosophical extension of disrupted consciousness—signals the appearance of the subject-centered philosophies of the Enlightenment. Thus, pure insight opposes the transcendental perspective of religion in favor of the relativity of the subject.

Hegel also characterizes the dialectical relation between faith and insight as a dialectic between content and form. Whereas faith represents a predicative relation to the transcendent—a form of thought that attributes specific properties to the deity—pure insight, as critique, represents the purely formal capacity of reason to negate (329). Thus, faith or content struggles against pure insight or formal critique in a dialectic that pits the transcendental realm of God against the subject-centered relativity of reason.

For the purposes of understanding Hegel's citation of Diderot in the context of this dialectic of the Enlightenment, it will be necessary to recast the faith/insight dialectic in terms of a question of value. In the preceding section of the *Phenomenology*, which ended in the sublation of the noble and ignoble forms of consciousness into disrupted consciousness, the alienation of social values arose as a result of the appearance of the intrinsic value of wealth. The appearance of the intrinsic value of wealth aided the breakdown of monarchical authority and further determined the alienation of the noble subject.

In the context of such a crisis of value, the faith/insight dialectic may be understood as a further articulation of this ethical conflict. On the one hand, faith represents a transcendental ethic that relies upon a notion of ultimate good—independent of the subject— to ground moral action. Insight, on the other hand, represents a relativist ethic that assesses moral action from the perspective of the subject. Both the feudal order and the state under the authority of a divine monarch, represent social formations in which value resides in the transcendent authority of God. Social stability derives from the resemblance between the divine and human realms.[12] Once the authority of the king as representative of divine authority is challenged—as it is by the appearance of the value of wealth—a split develops between those who continue to believe in the transcendentally grounded authority of the social order and those who question this authority on the basis of the seemingly relative value of wealth. The disrupted consciousness, which no longer believes in state power or wealth, recognizes the vanity of all things and therewith the relativity of value.

Thus, the faith/insight dialectic may be recast in ethical terms as a dispute between an absolutist ethic, which relies upon a notion of ultimate or transcendent good, and a relativist ethic, which assesses moral actions contextually, without reference to a transcendent notion of the good. According to Hegel, the dialectic between faith and insight sublates into the value of utility (342). Consistent with the faith side of the dialectic, utility may be held as an ultimate or transcendent value. On the other hand, utility may also be understood as a relative value, consistent with pure insight. Thus, the sublation into utility preserves the dialectical dispute between the transcendental and the relative conceptions of the good by reproducing this dispute in the *value* of utility (342-43).

Historically, the sublation into utility marks the appearance of a distinctly bourgeois value. The decline of both monarchical and religious authority during the seventeenth and eighteenth centuries culminating in the French Revolution signals the rise of another set of values largely determined by the exigencies of capitalism.[13] Utility as a bourgeois value reconciles the competing interests of religious faith and rational calculation, which both play a formative role with respect to the bourgeoisie. As Max Weber astutely argues, the asceticism of Protestantism combined with the interests of capitalism to produce the Protestant work ethic, and further the economic and social goals of the emerging bourgeoisie. Utility as both ultimate good from the perspective of Protestantism, and relative good with respect to capitalism, allows for the reconciliation of seemingly opposite worldviews. Even in Catholic France it is evident that the same type of "utilitarianism" enabled the rise of a successful middle class. The strategic investment of capital and the exploitation of *resources* may be justified by the new value of utility as a relative good. Likewise, questions of the greater good to society, which led to the ultimate fall of the monarchy and the institution of democracy, find their justification in the value of utility.

Thus, Hegel's account of the faith/insight dialectic in the section of the *Phenomenology* on the Enlightenment may be understood as a further development of the ethical crisis that was raised at the end of the section on self-alienated Spirit. Specifically, the emergence of the bourgeois value of utility coincides historically with the breakdown of monarchical and ecclesiastical authority, and with the appearance of wealth as an independent value. Because utility necessarily reproduces the dialectic at a higher level, it only seemingly reconciles the conflict between faith conceived as a transcendental ethic and insight understood as a relativist ethic. As we will see in Diderot's articulation of the conflict in *Rameau's Nephew*, the appearance of the bourgeois value of utility merely masks the ethical conflict with the appearance of agreement. In fact, *utility* as both absolute and relative value only deepens the ethical crisis in bourgeois society.

Alienation and Ethical Crisis in *Le Neveu de Rameau*

Hegel's account of the Enlightenment in the *Phenomenology*, with its strategic citation of Diderot, raises many of the same issues found in *Rameau's Nephew*. But rather than a philosophical analysis, Diderot's text presents a staging of the dialectical conflicts of the eighteenth century identified by Hegel.[14] The desire to assign the absolutist and relativist positions (faith and insight) respectively to the two participants in Diderot's dialogue is almost overwhelmingly tempting. What could be simpler than a dialogical representation of the dialectical relation between the two opposing forms of pure consciousness identified by Hegel? Such a reading, however, would quickly fall short of the goal of demonstrating the dialectical implication between the positions.[15] As Hegel clearly observes, insight represents the negation of faith and vice versa. To steadfastly insist upon the separation and ultimately the clear distinction between the two positions would be to fail to recognize that insight becomes faith in its negation and that faith finds its negation in insight. Thus, the two participants in the dialogue do not each represent one form of consciousness, but rather their interaction demonstrates the mutual implication of their shifting positions. Alternately both absolutists and relativists, the philosopher and nephew represent the dialectical struggle between mutually implicating forms of consciousness.

In order to explore the dialectical relation between the philosopher and the nephew, and their respective philosophical positions, it will be necessary to follow one of their exchanges in which the two change sides in the debate.[16] In the opening discussion concerning men of genius, the philosopher and nephew switch positions depending upon the perspective being argued from. Following the shifts in argumentation, I will demonstrate the mutual implication of their arguments. Their discussion of men of genius highlights questions concerning judgment and value that run throughout the dialogue. Thus, it introduces the dialectical themes of truth/falsehood, right/wrong, sublime/mediocre. To open the discussion, the philosopher comments on the nephew's judgment, observing that he makes exception of men of genius:

> I: You are hard to please, and I see you tolerate only men of genius.
> He: Yes, in chess, in checkers, poetry, eloquence, music and other nonsense of that kind. What's the use of mediocrity in that sort of thing? [75, 36, translation altered]

The nephew's contempt for mediocrity and praise of sublimity accords with his aesthetic nature. His appreciation of fine music in particular typifies the aesthete side of his character. When the philosopher questions the nephew about his famous uncle, the musical genius, the nephew reveals that what he values most in men of genius is that, though they excel at one thing, they are usually miserable failures in other aspects of life:

> That is what I particularly value in men of genius. They are only good for one thing, and apart from that, nothing. They don't know what it means to be citizens, fathers, mothers,

brothers, relations, friends. Between us, we should resemble
them in every respect, but not wish the species to be too
numerous. [76, 37-38, translation altered]

Though he claims to value their gift for one thing and one thing
only, the nephew concedes that a nation of geniuses is far from desir-
able. In fact, as his elaboration of the negative side of genius continues, it becomes clear that he does not admire genius as he previously claimed, but in fact has come to hate it:

We need men, but not men of genius. My goodness no, them
we certainly don't want. . . . If I knew anything about history I
would show you that evil has always come here below through
some man of genius. . . . One day I was at the table of a Minis-
ter of the Crown who has brains enough for four. Well, he
demonstrated as clearly as one and one make two that nothing
was more useful to nations than lies and nothing more harmful
than truth. I don't recollect his proofs very well, but it obviously followed that men of genius are pernicious and that if a
child bore on his brow the mark of this dangerous gift of nature
he should be thrown to the wolves. . . .
I: So from then on you developed a terrible loathing for genius?
He: One I shall never get over. [76-78, 38]

The change in the nephew's appraisal of the value of men of genius is
motivated in part by a consideration of his uncle. The philosopher
chides the nephew that he ought to pick out a position and stick to it:

But I have seen the time when you were in despair at only
being an ordinary man. You will never be happy if you are
equally worried by the pros and the cons. You should make up
your mind and stick to it. [78, 38-39]

As the discussion continues and the philosopher questions the
nephew further, it becomes evident that the nephew's ultimate cri-
terion for judging the merit of men of genius compared with ordinary
men entails a pragmatic consideration: the nephew considers what
benefit he or people like him might derive from men of genius in
order to assess their worth. Although the philosopher reminds the
nephew that he despises his own mediocrity, this is not enough to
sway the nephew from his new position. Speaking about Racine,
the nephew proclaims:

Because all those fine things he created didn't bring him in as much as twenty thousand francs, whereas if he had been a worthy silk merchant in the Rue Saint-Denis or the Rue Saint-Honoré, a wholesale grocer or an apothecary with a good connexion, he would have amassed a huge fortune and while doing so would have enjoyed every possible kind of pleasure. From time to time he would have given a coin to some poor devil of a clown like me for making him laugh or for procuring, upon occasion, a girl to make a nice change from the eternal cohabitation with his wife. We should have had some excellent meals at his home, played for high stakes, drunk excellent liqueurs and coffee, gone for excursions in the country. You see I was perfectly aware of what I was saying. Yes, you can laugh. But let me tell you that it would have been better for everybody round him. [*81*, 40-41]

The nephew's argument finally rests on the extension of his own self-interest into a pragmatist ethic: if he or someone like him would benefit, the situation is good. The philosopher states his own position in an attempt to reorient the nephew's criteria for judgment toward future generations and another conception of the good. Speaking metaphorically, the philosopher defends the ultimate worth of men of genius even if they are not good human beings:

He is a tree which has stunted some others growing near by and smothered plants growing at its feet, but it has raised its head to the heavens and its branches have spread far and wide. It has given shade to all who came, come or are to come seeking rest round its majestic trunk. It has produced exquisite fruit in never-failing abundance. . . . Let us forget for a moment the point we occupy in time and space; let us cast our eyes over the centuries to come, the most distant lands and nations yet to be born. Let us think of the good of our race, and even if we are not generous enough ourselves let us at least forgive nature for having been wiser than we are. [*82-83*, 42, translation altered]

This discussion of the worth of men of genius ends in a stand-off. Whereas the nephew opens by defending men of genius and condemning mediocrity (specifically his own), he closes in a defense of the average man. The philosopher, on the other hand, never states his position until the end when he defends the value of the works of men of genius, which he maintains overrides the wrongs inflicted by particular individuals during their lifetimes. Assessing the arguments used by the nephew and philosopher in terms of the faith/insight opposition established by Hegel, it would seem that the nephew's opening statement concerning his appreciation for genius in chess, checkers, poetry, and the like involves an absolute standard or value that he has established for his judgments. His appraisals of various actors, chessplayers, and musicians throughout the dialogue are based on this absolute standard.

To the extent that the nephew exercises his discriminating aesthetic judgment, his position represents an absolutist aesthetic. The standard of judgment he maintains transcends the context of the work being judged. It is imposed from outside rather than being determined or limited by the work itself.[17] Moreover, he continually holds himself to this same standard of judgment. His self-hatred derives from his assessment of his life's achievements, which in his opinion fall woefully short of the mark of genius.

Returning at the end of the discussion to his initial position, the nephew proclaims, "So I have been and still am angry at being mediocre. Yes, yes, I am mediocre and angry" (*84*, 43). Furthermore, the nephew's appreciation for acts of villainy committed by other scoundrels exemplifies the extent to which his aesthetic sensibility extends into all realms of judgment. Rather than judge acts on the basis of a moral standard, the nephew appreciates immoral acts for their aesthetic qualities.[18] Insofar as he judges almost all situations according to an aesthetic standard, he may be considered an absolutist.

As regards aesthetic judgment, the philosopher does not discriminate to the same degree as the nephew. Although he clearly appreciates the works of great actors and dramatists, his aesthetic judgment is not as finely tuned as the nephew's. He even comments that the nephew has an extremely fine aesthetic sensibility, although his moral sensibility seems to be lacking altogether (*172*, 107-08). Moreover, the philosopher has a keen appreciation for the nephew's acting abilities and finds himself being moved in spite of himself by the nephew's performances:

> As I was listening to him acting the scene of the pimp and the maiden he was procuring, I was torn between opposite impulses and did not know whether to give in to laughter or furious indignation. I was suffering [*je souffrais*]. A score of times a burst of laughter prevented a burst of rage, and a score of times

the anger rising from the depths of my heart ended in a burst of laughter. I was dumbfounded at such sagacity and such baseness, such alternately true and false notions, such absolute perversion of feeling and utter turpitude, and yet such uncommon candour. [95, 51, translation altered]

The philosopher is not an aesthetic purist, and to this extent is not an absolutist. What bothers him in the nephew's performance—in effect what clouds his aesthetic judgment—amounts to a moral judgment. To the extent to which he combines his judgments, he may be labeled more of a relativist. His aesthetic judgment depends upon contextual considerations such as the moral effects a work might have on an audience.[19] On the other hand, when the nephew reverses his position and defends the common man against the man of genius, the philosopher too shifts his position. Instead of the relativist approach taken with respect to aesthetic judgment, the philosopher argues in favor of the overall good to humanity done by men of genius. Defending an absolutist position against the nephew's relativist ethic, the philosophical position of the *moi* requires transcending the here and now ["let us forget for a moment the point we occupy in space and time"] in view of the greater good to humankind.

Thus, both the philosopher and nephew defend transcendental and relativist positions with respect to the question of men of genius. Over the course of the discussion the question of genius involves two distinct forms of judgment: aesthetic and moral. As we have seen, with regard to aesthetic judgment the nephew is an absolutist, whereas the philosopher is a relativist. With regard to moral judgment their positions are reversed.

Beyond the shifting positions over the course of their debate concerning men of genius, the philosopher's uneasiness with the nephew's performances further underscores the dialectical implication of their positions [*je souffrais*]. As Hegel describes it, the encounter with one's antithesis involves a painful process of self-awareness:

This tranquil consciousness, however, as we saw, has no *special insight* into the world of culture; this latter has itself rather the most painful feeling and the truest insight about itself: the feeling that all its defences have broken down, that every part of its being has been tortured on the rack and every bone broken. [328]

According to Hegel, engaging in argument with one's antithesis ultimately amounts to engaging in argument with oneself:

> It [pure insight] entangles itself in this contradiction through engagement in dispute, and imagines that what it is attacking is something other than itself. It only *imagines* this, for its essence as absolute negativity implies that it contains that otherness within itself. . . . This struggle with its antithesis, therefore, also has the significance of being the *actualization* of insight. For this consists precisely in the process of developing the moments and taking them back into the self. . . . Its result, however, will be neither the re-establishment of the errors it struggles against, nor merely its original Notion, but an insight which recognizes the absolute negation of itself to be its own actual existence, to be its own self, or an insight whose Notion recognizes its own self. [333]

For both the nephew and the philosopher, the pain of insight manifests itself in their shifting philosophical positions. By arguing with the negation of their own position (a mirrorlike reversal), they gain painful insight into the shortcomings of the positions they hold. Each comes to recognize himself in the other.[20] What is more, despite the philosopher's protestations, certain passages of the dialogue hint at an underlying resemblance between the philosopher and nephew. After the nephew explains how he gave music lessons without knowing anything about music, he forces the philosopher to acknowledge that he too gave lessons without knowing anything about the subject matter in order to survive:

> He: Now, Mr. Philosopher, put your hand on your heart and tell the truth. Time was when you weren't as well off as you are today.
> I: I'm not all that well off even now.
> He: But you wouldn't still be going to the Luxembourg in summer, you remember—
> I: That'll do, yes, I remember.
> He: In a grey plush coat.
> I: Yes, yes.
> He: Threadbare on one side, with a frayed cuff, and black woollen stockings darned up the back with white thread.
> I: All right, all right, have it your own way.
> He: What did you do in those days in the Allée des Soupirs?

I: Look pretty silly.

He: After that you used to trot along the road.

I: Quite right.

He: You used to give math lessons.

I: Without knowing a word about it myself—isn't that what you're driving at?

He: Exactly. [*100-101*, 55]

As Hegel's account of the encounter between faith and insight predicts, ultimately the underlying similarities outweigh the differences between the two positions. The philosopher and nephew are more similar than they are dissimilar, and as such reflect a society increasingly characterized by alienated social relations.

As we have already seen, for Hegel the dialectical struggle between faith and insight ultimately ends in the sublation into utility. Utility preserves both the transcendental and the relativist conceptions of the *good*, and thus replicates the conflict at the same time that the conflict is raised to a higher level. In Diderot's text, the dialectical opposition between philosopher and nephew with all its characteristic reversals also ultimately sublates in the agreement over utility. In their ethical judgments in particular, it is clear that both the nephew and the philosopher value utility. The nephew judges men of genius based on their utility to him and persons like him—representing a relativist approach—while the philosopher judges men of genius based on their overall utility to humanity—the transcendental perspective. Thus, the two positions are temporarily reconciled in the apparent agreement over utility.

Alienation and the Problem of Ethical Life

Hegel's analysis of the Enlightenment in the *Phenomenology* and his reading of *Rameau's Nephew* signal a crisis in ethical life, which is represented in Diderot's text. As we have seen, Hegel highlights the breakdown of feudal values and the emergence of the value of utility as catalysts for this ethical crisis. But his discussion of faith and insight does not go so far as to problematize ethical relations between individuals in bourgeois society as Diderot's text does. However, Hegel's appraisal of the role played by the changed status of wealth in the breakdown of centralized monarchy and the emergence of a disrupted form of social life suggests a direction for further analysis.

Hegel's underscoring of the moment when wealth obtains "an intrinsic being of its own" points in the direction of Marxist analyses of the importance of the rise of capitalism during the seventeenth and eighteenth centuries, and its effects on systems of value already in place. Diderot's text documents a crisis in ethical life, which historically coincides with the changed status of wealth and the breakdown of monarchical authority. Using analyses of bourgeois ideology by Adorno and Horkheimer, I would like to extend Hegel's reading beyond the philosophical problems already discussed to include the ethical problems that Diderot's text raises. More specifically, I will attempt to fill in the historical gaps with a more detailed discussion of the effects of a capitalist market on culture in general.

As we have already seen in Diderot's text, the disagreements between the philosopher and the nephew involve questions of aesthetic and moral judgment. Leaving aside the question of aesthetic judgment here, which I will address in detail in the following chapter, the dispute concerning moral judgment pits an absolutist ethic against a relativist ethic. The philosopher usually defends a transcendent ethical principle against the contextual considerations of the nephew. As we saw in the discussion of men of genius, the philosopher defended the men of genius's ultimate worth to humanity against the charge that their specific actions are harmful to those who come in contact with them. By contrast, the nephew extolled the *virtues* of the average man who graciously shares his wealth with those around him. To further underscore their differences, the nephew suggests that unlike philosophers who hold absolute standards, most people behave in the same way that he does (*113-14, 67-68*). The philosopher acknowledges that the nephew does represent a significant portion of the general population (*110, 62*).

But we have also seen an underlying similarity between the ethical absolutist philosopher and the relativist nephew. Motivated by the need to survive, both stooped to charlatanry: they both gave lessons without knowing the subject matter. Furthermore, the philosopher's acknowledgment that the nephew truthfully reflects the society around him emphasizes the degree to which the *old values* have crumbled, giving way to a *new ethic* of survival.[21] Thus, the ethical problems raised in *Rameau's Nephew* foreground social changes that have eroded earlier value systems and led to a crisis in ethical life.

The crisis in ethical life posed by Rameau's nephew involves the need to use calculating skill at others' expense in order to survive. The nephew admires villainous acts committed by other scoundrels, acts that sink to the depths of depravity. Like a connoisseur of fine wine, the nephew collects tales of immorality:

> I was beginning to bear with difficulty the presence of a man who discussed a horrible act, an execrable crime, like a connoisseur of painting or poetry examining the beauties of a work of art. [*156*, 97, translation altered]

He admires one man for having denounced his Jewish benefactor to the Inquisition in order to rob him of all his wealth, all the while pretending to protect him from the authorities (*153-56*, 93-97). The nephew admires the originality and the overwhelming atrocity of the action, which he characterizes as sublime. His own actions, while not at the level of *sublime immorality*, often enough involve minor moral infractions. He has made a career of pandering to the rich and is not above flattery, lying, swearing, or perjuring himself (*93*, 49). While not as sublime in his depravity as those he admires, the nephew has nonetheless made a career of immoral actions. He rationalizes his actions to himself and the philosopher by citing his natural gift for vice. Furthermore, he insists that virtue would be of no use to him in earning a living:

> And since I can achieve happiness through vices natural to me which I have acquired without toil and retain without effort, which fit in with the customs of my country, appeal to the tastes of my patrons and are more in harmony with their little personal requirements than some virtues which would cramp their style by nagging away at them from morn till eve, it would be strange indeed for me to torture myself like a soul in hell so as to mutilate myself into something quite different from what I am. I should give myself a character quite foreign to me and qualities most praiseworthy (I grant you that, so as to have no argument), but which would cost a lot to acquire and land me nowhere, or worse than nowhere, because I should be continually satirizing the rich from whom poor devils like me have to make a living. People laud virtue, but they hate and avoid it, for it freezes you to death, and in this world you have to keep your feet warm. [*118-19*, 68-69, translation altered]

Ultimately, the nephew justifies his actions with three arguments: (1) He is *naturally* gifted for vice; (2) vice suits the mores of his society; (3) virtue would only impede his ability to earn a living. One might conclude from the nephew's self-defense that using any available means to survive is justified. In other words, his ethic amounts to a self-preservation doctrine that justifies nearly all behavior in the name of survival. The name of his game is to exploit all situations to his own advantage.

Oddly enough, the nephew's self-justificatory doctrine resembles the logic of capitalism. Market relations dictate that capitalists exploit all available resources, including labor power (other human beings), in order to turn a profit. The means-ends calculation of the capitalist extends the logic of enlightenment into the economy, and from there into social relations. Thus, in *Dialectic of Enlightenment*, Horkheimer and Adorno attribute the growth of social domination to the spread of enlightenment, and specifically to the use of arithmetical properties to decide questions of social justice:

> The same equations dominate bourgeois justice and commodity exchange. "Is not the rule, '*Si inaesqualibus aequalia addas, omnia erunt inaequalia*,' an axiom of justice as well as of mathematics? And is there not a true coincidence between commutative and distributive justice, and arithmetical and geometrical proportion?" Bourgeois society is ruled by equivalence. It makes the dissimilar comparable by reducing it to abstract quantities. To the Enlightenment, that which does not reduce to numbers, and ultimately to the one, becomes illusion. [7][22]

The rule of equivalence accounts for the decline in moral values. Reducing everything to abstract quantities enables means-ends calculation that tends to ignore qualitative questions of value.[23] This type of thinking supports the rationalization of, for example, cutting social programs for reasons of cost effectiveness. But already during the Enlightenment period, as evidenced in *Rameau's Nephew*, the effects of alienated social relations due to economic developments are making themselves felt in the form of nagging ethical problems such as those raised by the nephew's behavior. In *The Grundrisse* Marx dubs this stage of development "universal prostitution," and ties it directly to the appearance of both utility as a value and exchange value:

> Universal prostitution appears as a necessary phase of the development of the social character of personal talents, abilities, capacities and activities. This could be more delicately expressed as the general condition of serviceability and useful-

ness. It is the bringing to a common level of different things, which is the significance that Shakespeare already gave to money. [71]

For Marx, as for Hegel, the introduction of the intrinsic value of wealth leads to alienated social relations due to the appearance of exchange value and the new universal value of utility.[24] Using means-ends calculation to earn a living without regard for who or what suffers as a consequence, merely represents an extension of capitalist logic into the realm of social relations.

Ultimately, the conflict in bourgeois values that produces the crisis in ethical life reduces to a struggle between what Horkheimer calls in *Eclipse of Reason* "the subjectivistic principle of self-interest and the idea of reason that it is alleged to express."[25] According to Horkheimer, although the idea of reason originally referred to an objective claim—a transcendental category—reason eventually came to refer to a subjective claim—one concerned with means and ends (3-5). Coupled during the Enlightenment with the bourgeois value of self-interest, reason became "an instrument" (21). Thus, instrumental reason or means-ends calculation furthers the goals of individual self-interest without regard for broader questions of social justice and equality, which remain beyond the scope of a subjectivist concept. Consistent with the argument in *Dialectic of Enlightenment*, Horkheimer asserts in "Means and Ends":

> Concepts have been reduced to summaries of the characteristics that several specimens have in common. By denoting a similarity, concepts eliminate the bother of enumerating qualities and thus serve better to organize the material of knowledge. They are thought of as mere abbreviations of the items to which they refer. Any use of transcending auxiliary, technical summarization of factual data has been eliminated as a last trace of superstition. Concepts have become "streamlined," rationalized labor-saving devices. It is as if thinking itself had been reduced to the level of industrial processes, subjected to a close schedule—in short, made part and parcel of production. [21]

With the *streamlining* of concepts also comes the elimination of considerations of value, which clearly *transcend* the subjective realm of instrumental reason. Thus, in *Rameau's Nephew*, the nephew *reasonably* rationalizes his behavior because questions of value do not concern instrumental reason. His calculating skill in earning a living at others' expense goes unchallenged by the new subjectivistic (relativist) conception of reason. Instead, his skill in means-ends calculation—although not in the service of capitalism—nevertheless epitomizes the goals and aspirations of the self-interested and rational bourgeois individual.[26]

Thus, Hegel's reading of *Rameau's Nephew*, although it does not cite capitalism by name for historical reasons—the word was not yet coined—nevertheless points in the direction of such an analysis. His emphasis upon the changed status of wealth and the concomitant change in social relations—the use of base flattery and the collapse of the noble and ignoble forms of consciousness—suggests that economic and social developments led to a crisis of value during the Enlightenment.[27] More specifically, Diderot's text hints that the crisis extends to the level of ethical life. Wealth and the language of base flattery are both clearly central to the nephew's life. Moreover, Diderot's text suggests that the philosopher is not so different from the nephew as he might wish to believe. Both on the margins of society, the philosopher and nephew earn their livings with whatever means they find at their disposal.[28]

As Hegel painstakingly demonstrates in the section of the *Phenomenology* on the Enlightenment, opposed forms of consciousness such as faith and insight are in fact mirror reflections of one another.[29] The philosopher and the nephew, thus, reflect the dialectical implication of their respective positions. Both find their actions determined by changing social relations. Their interaction only confirms the extent to which broad social changes impinge upon both the philosopher and the nephew, even in the ethical realm. With the advent of capitalism and, most especially in the French context, the extension of market relations into the social realm, the bourgeois individual emerges only to find that its existence is determined by the universal culture of the capitalist market.

6 The Public/Private Dialectic Revisited: Diderot's Art Criticism

The preceding chapters on Diderot's materialist epistemology and his critique of ethical life under early capitalism highlight changes occurring in the public sphere that we have already seen diagnosed in the work of Rousseau. My analyses have underscored the appearance of alienated social relations as a result of the expansion of capitalist modes of reasoning into the realm of social life. Turning once again to the dialectical relation between the public and private spheres, the following analysis of Diderot's art criticism will examine the alienating effects of the new trend toward a capitalist consumer culture as it influences private life. In particular, Diderot's *Salons* as well as his suggestions for rethinking the theater acknowledge a problematic relationship between the public and private spheres.[1]

In the public sphere of cultural production, bourgeois ideology has several important effects. The eighteenth century saw the blurring of boundaries separating "official high culture, unofficial high culture and popular culture"[2] consistent with the bourgeoisie's general belief in equality and the claims of its ideology to represent universal interests. This blurring of boundaries contributes to the appearance of *mass culture* precisely because the failure to draw distinctions allows for the emergence of culture with a relatively broad appeal. This is not to say that the mass culture of the eighteenth century already appeared in the engineered form of the culture industry analyzed by Horkheimer and Adorno. The homogenizing effects of mass culture are strikingly absent in the art world of eighteenth-century France. Nonetheless, the public sphere has undergone a radical shift that entails a broadening of the audience for both *public* and *private* forms of art. As we shall see, changes in the system of patronage and the growth of a market for art have significant effects on the content of art, its distribution, reception, and consumption. The emergence of public and private art culture may be read as symptomatic of the influence of capitalism in public culture of the period.

The reestablishment of the Salons held in the Louvre on a regular basis after 1737 marks the historical beginning of the move toward a broader art public.[3] Thomas Crow describes the phenomenon as "the first regularly repeated, open, and free display of contemporary art in Europe to be offered in a completely secular setting and for the purpose of encouraging a primarily aesthetic response in large numbers of people" (3). But the Salon *public* seriously threatened the stability of meaning in the cultural realm precisely because of its heterogeneous nature. The word *secular* in Crow's description signals the absence of an official institution to regulate art's reception.[4] Recalling Lyotard's distinction between classical authors who know the tastes and expectations of their audience and modern authors who send a message in a bottle, the broadening of the art public with the advent of the Salons marked just such a break.

Crow quotes a description of a Salon from 1777 that underscores the heterogeneity of the *crowd*. While Crow questions whether such a crowd could be termed a public, due to the distinct lack of "meaningful degree of coherence in attitudes and expectations" that it represents (ibid.), I would suggest that the description is quite typical of a modern audience for mass culture:

> You emerge through a stairwell like a trapdoor, which is always choked despite its considerable width. Having escaped that painful gauntlet, you cannot catch your breath before being plunged into an abyss of heat and a whirlpool of dust. Air so pestilential and impregnated with the exhalation of so many unhealthy persons should in the end produce either lightning or plague. Finally you are deafened by a continuous noise like that of the crashing waves in an angry sea. But here nevertheless is a thing to delight the eye of an Englishman: the mixing, men and women together, of all orders and all the ranks of state. . . . This is perhaps the only public place in France where he could find that precious liberty visible everywhere in London. This enchanting spectacle pleases me even more than the works displayed in this temple of the arts. Here the Savoyard odd-job man rubs shoulders with the great noble in his *cordon bleu*; the fishwife trades perfumes with those of a lady of qual-

ity, making the latter resort to holding her nose to combat the strong odor of cheap brandy drifting her way; the rough artisan, guided only by natural feeling, comes out with a just observation, at which an inept wit nearby bursts out laughing only because of the comical accent in which it was expressed; while an artist hiding in the crowd unravels the meaning of it all and turns it to his profit.[5]

The juxtaposition of social classes—with all that it implies—prevents a predictable reception for the art on display. Instead, art in the Salons is subject to the varied opinions of a general audience.

The confusion wrought by the broadening of the art public coincides historically with an increase in the number and influence of private collectors. The same historical moment that inaugurates *free* public culture in the Salons, also marks the beginning of a significant number of private collections viewed in part as financial investments. The last line of the description of the Salon of 1777 underscores the financial concerns of artists subject to the opinions of the new *public*. But artists are less concerned with the opinions of the general public than they are with those of wealthy connoisseurs. Beginning with the death of Louis XIV and continuing throughout the eighteenth century, there is a steady increase in the market for rococo paintings and other genres that can be produced on a smaller scale suitable for decorating private homes.[6] Connoisseurs interested in purchasing works of art have a direct effect on what type of art is produced. But these collectors are driven less by aesthetic interest than by capitalist investment strategies or concerns with social standing (no longer purely based on genealogy). Thus, both financial and social considerations begin indirectly to determine cultural production.

Simultaneous with the historical development of a broader art public and a consumer market for art is the paradoxical turn toward the *private* consumption of art and of culture in general. Competing with the public Salons, connoisseurs establish private collections, removing art from the public realm.[7] The private consumption of art raises questions concerning aesthetic reception and lay judgment in the eighteenth-century context, which parallel concerns with the broader public's ability to judge art. In other words, there is a similarity between the concerns critics express over art's reception by the general public and its consumption by connoisseurs. In both cases the lack of institutional guidance for art's reception disturbs established patterns of interpretation and consumption.

I read both the trend toward a broader art public and toward private consumption as results of changes wrought by the bourgeoisie.[8] As I have already suggested, public exhibitions answer the bourgeois call for equality by making art accessible to "everyone." But the private consumption of art also fits the interests of the bourgeoisie. The emphasis placed on the home in bourgeois ideology as the site of moral development determines and reinforces the move toward the private sphere. As I have already noted in conjunction with Rousseau, the bourgeois home represents a haven from the rigors of alienated public life. According to the ideology, while at home, the family enjoys the fulfillment and joy that only the moral values associated with the family can provide. From the perspective of art and culture, the new emphasis upon the home and family means the development of new art forms and forms of consumption that ideologically reinforce bourgeois values.

To understand the implications of art's movement between the public and private spheres, it will be necessary to recall Weber's account of the spread of rationalization, which documents the advent of specialization in various realms of culture. In the eighteenth-century French context, Weber's thesis explains the appearance of *professional art dealers* and *expert* collectors who aspire to noble status through specialized knowledge at the precise historical moment at which art becomes more readily accessible to the general public.[9]

The Aesthetic and the Public Sphere

Max Weber's theory of rationalization documents the breakdown of the religious-metaphysical worldview that prevailed in Europe through the seventeenth century. According to Weber, the eighteenth century marks a significant moment in the process of rationalization, which entails the separation of domains of knowledge no longer dominated by the church and court. Instead, experts use their rational capacities in specific fields of knowledge.[10] Weber distinguished three domains of knowledge: science, morality and law, and art. Each one of these domains corresponds to a specific value: science to truth, law and morality to rightness, and art to beauty. Habermas has further identified these three domains or value spheres with specific forms of rationality. He dubs the type of rationality associated with scientific reasoning cognitive-instrumental. The second type he calls moral-practical. In the realm of art, he recognizes aesthetic-expressive rationality.[11]

According to Weber's theory, already with the discoveries of Copernicus and Galileo, the church's claim to privileged access to the truth in cognitive matters was disrupted. Scientific discoveries fueled the establishment of a separate domain of knowledge with its own specialists. Nature was no longer the realm of God, but instead an object to be dominated by reason.[12] In the eighteenth century, capitalism added incentive for scientific advances: a disenchanted nature considered as an object to be dominated can be exploited to turn a profit. Thus, by the eighteenth century science was already well established as a separate domain with its own scientific experts who used cognitive-instrumental reason to understand and dominate nature.[13]

The domain of law and morality escaped the hold of the church and court during the eighteenth century. Kant's *Critique of Practical Reason* clearly establishes the individual conscience as the origin of moral value. It insists that the individual freely submits to the categorical imperative that Kant derives from the individual's own innate faculty of reason.[14] Kant writes in the *Second Critique*, "The stage of morality on which man (and, so far as we know, every rational creature) stands is respect for the moral law" (87). Thus, for Kant and many thinkers of the French Enlightenment the compulsion to act morally comes from reason, and not from the divinity.

Finally, according to Weber, the aesthetic does not become a distinct realm with a specific value of its own until the nineteenth century and the *l'art pour l'art* movement.[15] Thus, for Weber and Habermas, the complete separation of the aesthetic realm entails the recognition of the aesthetic as a separate value in a form of art that privileges expression over all other values.

In the French eighteenth-century context, it seems clear that the aesthetic realm had become rationalized to the extent that a consumer market increased dramatically after 1750.[16] Krzysztof Pomian has argued that the shift in emphasis in sales catalogues from aesthetic appreciation toward a concern with correct attribution of paintings testifies to the importance of the consumer art market. Moreover, he finds that before 1750 art dealers were largely constrained by the opinions of collectors—in spite of their own often considerable knowledge and experience—while after mid-century they are considered to be the true experts, based on their technical ability to determine attribution. Coinciding with this shift Pomian cites a dramatic increase in the number of collectors, the number of public sales, and a rise in prices. The simultaneous appearance of these phenomena after 1750 indicate a correlation between rationalization and capitalist practices in the world of art collecting. Expert knowledge—in this case cognitive-instrumental rationality used to make correct attributions and determine the monetary value of paintings—appears in a form characteristic of capitalist modes of reasoning. According to this instrumental rationality, the value of art is dependent on both technical considerations in evaluating paintings and on the fluctuations of the market.

But within the eighteenth-century French context there is another aesthetic discourse, which runs counter to the expert knowledge of connoisseurs and dealers, linking the value of art to another sphere. The rift between the rococo and antirococo camps bears witness to two different ways of relating to art. Whereas the connoisseurs of rococo art were largely interested in art as an investment and a sign of status, antirococo critics, such as Diderot, see art as the expression of moral value—thus, from a moral-practical perspective.[17] The latter position is consistent with Weber's and Habermas's readings, according to which art, despite being already divorced from the institutions of the court and church during the eighteenth century, was still dependent upon the moral sphere for its value. Even Kant, in his *Critique of Judgment*, suggests that the beautiful ultimately serves the good: "it appears plain that the true propaedeutic for the foundation of taste is the development of moral ideas and the culture of the moral feeling, because it is only when sensibility is brought into agreement with this that genuine taste can assume a definite invariable form" (202).[18] Thus, consistent with Weber's and Habermas's accounts, neither rococo nor antirococo collectors and critics judge art according to purely *aesthetic* criteria. The aesthetic realm has been rationalized to a degree but is not yet fully separated from the moral sphere.

In addition to outlining the progressive separation of the three value spheres, Weber's theory of rationalization also highlights the concomitant rise of a division between specialist and layperson. His theory recognizes the average person's difficulty in mastering all forms of knowledge as a specific feature of modernity. Rationalization entails specialization and the layperson requires the explanations of experts in the fields of science, law, and art. The expansion of the art public beyond an educated elite necessitated critical guidance for the general public.

The revival of the Salons sparked considerable art criticism consistent with Weber's analysis.[19] The connoisseurs, collectors before 1750 and especially dealers after 1750 qualified as experts. However, it remains open to question what type of expert knowledge these art professionals had. There is no doubt that they had *expert* knowledge of art. But there is a significant difference between technical knowledge of art, knowledge of art's economic value and its investment potential, knowledge based on purely aesthetic criteria, and knowledge of the moral worth of art. I will return to these distinctions in my discussion of Diderot's *Salons*. Suffice it to say that art collectors and especially dealers were *specialists* according to Weber's theory of rationalization, at least from the standpoint of cognitive-instrumental rationality.

Diderot and the Judgment of Connoisseurs

Weber's theory of rationalization accounts for the appearance of specialists in the realm of art. But these specialists—both art dealers but especially the collectors—are clearly interested in elevating their social status and financial worth through the acquisition of art. Though the works may ultimately hang in private rooms of private homes, and thus be considered to be consumed *privately*, the connoisseurs' interest in acquiring art remains public. Connoisseurs interested in increasing their social standing by demonstrating that they have *good taste* use art as a sign in a market where value is equated with status. In other words, not only do connoisseurs invest financial capital in art in hopes of a return on their investment, they also invest social and cultural capital in hopes of a return in the form of a rise in social standing.[20]

In the *Salon* of 1767 Diderot already laments the appearance of financial interest in the art world:

> Here is how most of the wealthy men who employ great artists reason: The amount that I am going to put into drawings by Boucher, paintings by Vernet, by Casanove, by Loutherbourg, is invested at the highest interest rate. I will enjoy looking at an excellent piece all my life. The artist will die, and my children and I will get out of this piece twenty times the price we first paid for it. And this is very well-reasoned, the heirs are not distressed to see the riches they covet put to such use. [1767:58]

Already by 1767 art has become a commodity.[21] Investors are purchasing paintings in the hopes that they will appreciate in economic value after the painters' death. These purchases, according to Diderot, are made without regard for the paintings' aesthetic value.

Worse still, the selling of their paintings makes or breaks artists. The connoisseurs—ignorant of what *good* art is from Diderot's perspective—are setting artistic standards by controlling the purse strings. Amateurs are determining the content and production of art:

> Ah! my friend, the damnable race of connoisseurs! . . . It is those people who decide reputations without rhyme or reason, who made Greuze die of pain and hunger, who have galleries that hardly cost them anything, who have some knowledge [*lumières*] or more likely some pretentions that cost them nothing, who position themselves between the wealthy man and the indigent artist, who make talent pay for the protection they grant it, who open or close doors, who take advantage of the needs the artist has of them to dispose of their time, who lay claim to him, who rip his best productions from him at vile prices . . . who discredit and ruin the painter and the sculptor, if he has standing and he disdains their protection and counsel; who bother him, trouble him in his workshop, through the importunity of their presence and the ineptitude of their advice; who discourage him, who extinguish him, and who hold him, for as long as they can in the cruel alternative of sacrificing his genius, or his status, or his fortune. [1767:60-61]

According to Diderot, the decline in historical paintings and the increase in libertine paintings like those of Boucher and Baudouin is a direct result of the economic control connoisseurs have over artists. Destitute artists are not to be blamed for being manipulated by connoisseurs who offer them the comfort of money. Sounding much like the Rousseau of the *First Discourse* and *Project of Constitution for Corsica*, Diderot condemns luxury as the cause of the corruption of the taste and morals of the French. Diderot blames the decadence of eighteenth-century art on the false luxury of the French nation, which hides the true poverty of the people:

> Another kind of luxury, and it is this one that degrades and annihilates the fine arts. Because the fine arts, their progress and their lasting quality, demand real wealth, and this luxury here is only the fatal mask of an almost general poverty that it accelerates and worsens. It is under the tyranny of this luxury that talents remain hidden or are led astray. It is under such a constitution that the fine arts have only the waste of subal-

tern conditions; it is under an order of things so extraordinary, so perverse, that the fine arts are either subordinated to the whims and caprices of a handful of rich, bored, dull, men whose taste is as corrupt as their morals, or they are abandoned to the mercy of the indigent multitude that strives, through bad productions in all genres, to give itself the reputation and distinction of riches [*le crédit et le relief de la richesse*]. It is in this century and under this reign that the exhausted nation forms not one entreprise, no great works, nothing that sustains spirits and elevates souls. Thus it is that no great artists are born, or they are obliged to debase themselves under threat of dying of hunger. Thus it is that there are one hundred easel paintings for one great composition, one thousand portraits for a piece of history; that mediocre artists abound and the nation overflows with them. [*1767:167-68*]

Swarms of mediocre painters overrun the nation because the ignorant rich encourage their work. Deserving painters like Greuze die in poverty because of the nation's *poor taste*. Morals corrupted by the influence of money in turn corrupt the arts: "If morals [*les moeurs*] are corrupt, do you believe that taste can remain pure? No, no, that cannot be" [*1767:124*].[22]

Ultimately for Diderot, money is controlling the content of art and the reputations of artists. Art has become commodified to the extent that the art world's interest lies in buying and selling it. For Diderot, however, commodified art is without value. Precisely because of its economic value (its exchange value to the ignorant rich), art is without moral value, which Diderot equates with aesthetic value.[23] The growth of specialization and expertise in art has led to the commodification of art based on an ignorant public's economic interest. It has not led to the moral edification that Diderot sees as the proper function of art.[24]

Diderot's antirococo taste in art links his dual concerns with the commodification of art and its proper moral function. In the eighteenth-century context, these two concerns are conflated in the one word, *taste*. Taste is absolutely central to eighteenth-century aesthetic theory, but also reflects the social standing conferred by well-informed purchases. In the circle of connoisseurs, *good taste* means a number of things: it signals wise economic investments and an appreciation for a particular type of art, which is defined by a cultural elite of which one is or aspires to become a member. Clearly, for Diderot, *good taste* means something quite different.

Diderot's condemnations of particular painters—most of them rococo—on moral grounds indicates what *good taste* means to him. Not surprisingly, Diderot's judgments of many painters depend upon his evaluation of the moral worth of their paintings. For example, Boucher's paintings represent the height of *bad taste* for Diderot precisely because of the moral values they reflect.[25] In the *Salon* of 1765 he writes:

> I do not know what to say about this man here. The degrada-
> tion of taste, of color, of composition, of features, of expres-
> sion, of design, have followed step by step the depravity of
> morals. What do you want this artist to throw on the canvas?
> what he has in his imagination. And what can a man who
> spends his life with prostitutes of the lowest rank have in his
> imagination? . . . I dare say that this man does not really know
> what grace is, I dare say that he has never known truth, I dare
> say that the notions of delicacy, honesty, innocence and sim-
> plicity have become almost alien to him, I dare say that he has
> not for one instant seen nature, at least the nature that interests
> my soul, yours, that of a well-born child, that of a woman that
> feels, I dare say that he is without taste. [75-76]

Boucher's moral depravity is reflected in every detail of his paint-
ings.[26] More importantly for Diderot, his paintings have nothing to offer *people of quality*, here defined in contrast to the class of connoisseurs.

In addition to producing bad art, Boucher and painters like him present a danger to the general public. Though Diderot hates their paintings for their lack of artistic or moral worth, he is even more concerned that they may corrupt the morals of others. These *bad* paintings could seduce young women in particular with their titil-
lating depictions of bad morals. Diderot writes of paintings by Bau-
douin in the *Salon* of 1765:

> There was in the Salon a quantity of little paintings by Bau-
> douin, and all the young women, after having promenaded their
> glances distractedly over some paintings, finished their tours at
> the spot where one saw *la Paysanne querellée par sa Mère*, and
> *le Cueilleur de Cerises*; it was for this area that they had
> reserved all their attention. At a certain age a libertine work
> [*ouvrage libre*] is read rather than a good work, one would
> rather stop at a lewd painting than a good painting. There are

even old men who are punished for their continuous debauchery by the sterile taste that they retain from it. Some of these old men dragged along too, crutch in hand, hunched back, glasses on the nose, at the little infamies of Baudouin. [*137*]

In contrast to Boucher and Baudouin, Diderot admires the paintings of Greuze precisely for the moral lessons they evoke. In praise of Greuze, Diderot proclaims, "Here is your painter and mine, the first one among us who took it upon himself to give morals to art, and to link events so that it would be easy to write a novel from them" [*1765:144*]. No doubt he has a novel like one of Richardson's in mind, for these genre paintings represent the type of domestic scenes that celebrate bourgeois virtues.

In response to one of Greuze's sketches entitled *la Mère bien-aimée* Diderot extols the virtues of bourgeois domestic life:

That is excellent, both for the talent and the morals. It preaches population, and depicts with great pathos the happiness and inestimable value of domestic peace. It says to every man who has a soul and some sense: "Keep your family in comfort, give your wife children, give her as many as you can, give them only to her, and be sure to be well at home [*bien chez toi*]." [*1765:155*]

Diderot even laments the fact that he does not have enough money to commission Greuze to execute the painting. "Oh, if I were but rich enough to commission this painting, so that placed in my home it would ceaselessly reproach me for the unhappiness of not being a father of a family, and pain my eyes with the spectacle of happiness that I am not allowed to taste" [*1765:155*].

Diderot's lament may be read as part of a strategy to distinguish himself from the class of connoisseurs who do commission works of art. His *inability* to finance the work calls attention to the fact that he is not a member of the *cultural elite*. For Diderot, lack of financial means signals membership in another *class* of connoisseurs—those who appreciate *good* paintings for the *good* (read bourgeois) moral values they reinforce.

The Public/Private Dialectic and the Problem of Judgment

As I have already suggested, Diderot's equation of *good art* with moral art represents a reaction to the connoisseurs' conception of *good taste.*[27] In order to protect art from the degrading effects of a consumer market, Diderot's assessment turns away from the public toward the private sphere. As we have seen elsewhere, bourgeois ideology portrays the private sphere as a haven from alienated social relations. His insistence on judging art according to its moral worth effectively moves it out of the realm of consumer commodities and into the private sphere of bourgeois moral value. His attempt to shield art from the effects of a consumer market indicates a further step in the rationalization of the aesthetic realm.[28]

But the move toward the private sphere presents several difficulties. As Diderot himself recognizes, one of the effects of a consumer market is precisely this turn toward the private. Investors display art in their homes as a sign of their social position. In the *Salon* of 1769 Diderot makes an observation that sheds light on the move from public to private. While lamenting the lack of interesting paintings on display at the Salon, Diderot again blames individual collectors:

> The poor Salon that we have had this year! . . . It is not that our artists have been unemployed, they worked and quite a lot, but either their works went to foreign countries, or they were kept in the collections of apprentice connoisseurs who are still in the first throes of a passion that they are not willing to share with anyone.
> Vernet had executed eight large paintings for M. de la Borde. Due to a whim that cannot be understood, the rich man, in commissioning them from him, required that once the paintings were placed in his gallery, they would never leave it again. [1769:571]

To the extent that connoisseurs display paintings in their homes, they illustrate one of the two opposing general trends characteristic of the bourgeoisie: to consume art privately rather than publicly.[29] Though their ultimate aim may be to improve their social standing—an aim tied to the public sphere and its forms of representation—they nonetheless use the private sphere to further this goal.

The connoisseurs' *private* consumption of art highlights the difficulty of moving culture into the private sphere, especially in view of improving one's public standing. The use of the private sphere for public ends seemingly destroys the *private* nature of the private sphere. Diderot's suggestions for reforming the theater further illustrate the problematic nature of the move toward *private* consumption of art. Clearly the most public of all the arts, theater requires a *public* performance. Nonetheless, in the *Entretiens sur le Fils naturel* Diderot advocates moving theater into the salon. His conception of bourgeois drama replaces public spectacle with private spectacle: plays will be performed in living rooms rather than in large halls.

To attenuate the difficulties presented by the idea of *private* theater, Diderot suggests changes in performance to adapt bourgeois drama to the salon environment. Diderot's preference for *tableaux* over *coups de théâtre* serves this end as do his recommendations to actors: exaggerated speechmaking will be replaced by the pantomime and gestures, which he finds to be more *natural* and better suited to the salon environment.

Along with changes in performance, bourgeois drama also requires an important shift in subject matter. Diderot advocates choosing subjects for plays that are closer to the spectators' personal experience:

> It is the representation [*tableau*] of the misfortunes that surround us. What! you cannot imagine what the effect on you would be of a realistic setting, real clothes, words in proportion to actions, simple actions, dangers that it is impossible that you have not feared for your parents, your friends, yourself? A reversal of fortune, the fear of ignomiy, the effects of poverty, a passion that leads man to his ruin, from his ruin to despair, from despair to a violent death, these are not rare events, and you do not believe that they wouldn't affect you as much as the fabulous death of a tyrant or the sacrifice of a child on the altars of the gods of Athens or Rome? [*X:140-41*]

Reversing the traditional argument for portraying royalty, Diderot suggests that putting peasant characters on the stage allows for identification on the part of a wide array of spectators from different classes and backgrounds. The move from royalty to average person also allows for subjects that are common to all by virtue of their more *private* nature. The shift in subject matter from the public toward the private also reinforces the moral aim of art: domestic scenes and real life situations allow for didactic art geared to the bourgeois moral sensibility. The move away from historical and mythical subjects gives this art a broader appeal. Thus, the moral lessons of his *drame bourgeois* apply to a very broad segment of the public.

The move toward private consumption dialectically promotes changes in production as art increasingly reflects the influence of bourgeois ideology in the realm of taste. Not only Diderot's bourgeois drama, but paintings of the period reflect the turn toward the private sphere. Landscapes, still lifes, portraits, and genre paintings gain in popularity as historical and mythical subjects are less often represented due in part to the constraints of displaying art in private *hôtels* (Crow, 11).

Ultimately, it is this shift toward *moral art* that distinguishes Diderot's understanding of *private* consumption from the connoisseurs' use of the private sphere for public ends. While the connoisseurs seek to demonstrate their *good* taste by buying and displaying certain types of art, Diderot encourages another form of *good* taste in a more strictly private form of consumption. I will argue that the paintings admired by antirococo critics invite the type of *private* consumption that Diderot has in mind, and moreover discourage the type of cultural consumption practiced by connoisseurs.

Michael Fried's study of eighteenth-century aesthetics and art criticism details the close affinity between the subject matter of paintings and their reception, or more precisely, their positioning of the spectator. In *Absorption and Theatricality*, Fried argues that the paintings preferred by antirococo critics of the second half of the eighteenth century tend to depict scenes in which people are intensely absorbed in a particular activity. According to Fried, absorption is a characteristic of both historical and genre paintings, and often even of portraiture of the period. The figures' absorption within the painting in turn determines the position of the beholder. Fried writes:

> We have seen that for French painters of the early and mid-1750s the persuasive representation of absorption entailed evoking the perfect obliviousness of a figure or group of figures to everything but the objects of their absorption. Those objects did not include the beholder standing before the painting. Hence the figure or figures had to seem oblivious to the beholder's presence if the illusion of absorption was to be sustained. [66]

Absorption within the painting creates what Fried holds is the "supreme fiction" of late eighteenth-century painting: the negation of the beholder's presence before the painting [104-5]. In other words, the paintings preferred by antirococo critics do not present themselves to the beholder as art, because they do not acknowledge the beholder's presence at all. Rather they maintain their *naturalness* through the absorption of the figures presented.

Consistent with the bourgeois preference for epistolary novels, diaries, and travelogues—even if they are elaborate fictions—Fried finds that critics like Diderot prefer paintings that *naturalize* their own existence by negating the beholder's presence. Like the literary forms popular in the eighteenth century, paintings that depict absorption call for an act of voyeurism on the part of the spectator. None of these forms depend upon the *artifice* of presenting themselves to their audience as art.[30] Instead they rely upon the figures' disregard for the beholder to draw him/her into the painting. The beholder becomes absorbed in the painting to the degree that the painted figures are unaware of his/her presence.

Fried's reading of the preference for paintings that depict absorption and the attendant negation of the beholder's presence is consistent with the turn toward the private realm as a locus of moral value that I have outlined in response to the growth of a consumer market. On the one hand, the highly absorptive activities depicted arc often ones that take place within the private sphere. Genre paintings in particular, but also portraits and still lifes often represent the private sphere of the bourgeois individual. On the other hand, the negation of the beholder promotes private viewings rather than public exhibitions of these paintings within the framework of cultural institutions. Absorption even works against the use of paintings to further one's public social standing for two reasons. First, the moralizing scenes preach against social climbing and other financially oriented aspects of bourgeois life. And second, absorption with the painting tends to work against any awareness on the part of the beholder of the context in which the painting hangs. In other words, both the content and the style of these paintings discourage their reinsertion into the realm of public life. Instead both absorption of the spectator with the painting and the absorption of the figures depicted in the painting dictate that these works find their way into private collections where they remain displayed within the private realm.

The shift from public to private places a double burden on the beholder. In the first place, the reception of art in the private sphere is less easily guided and controlled by experts. In the second place, *moral art* requires a spectator who is educated enough to appreciate and learn from art. Thus, the move to the private sphere necessitates a spectator capable of forming judgments concerning the aesthetic and moral value of works of art. Changes in the production and dissemination of art require attendant changes in its reception.

These changes in production, dissemination, and specifically reception are reflected in the shift from aesthetic theories that emphasize taste—such as those of Shaftesbury and Burke—to those that emphasize judgment—like those of Kant and later philosophers. Taste, although at one level a private matter, is nonetheless shaped and cultivated by education, social standing, national origin, and the like, as evidenced by its importance among connoisseurs. Judgment, on the other hand, is private in the sense that it depends upon the individual's rational capacities. Although judgment may be aided by education, social standing, and so on, in Kant's formulation it represents an a priori subjective experience that is private in the strictest sense of the word—it requires no contact with the outside world.[31] For Kant, any representation made by the subject to consciousness, even dreams or hallucinations, may be beautiful.

Thus, one of the most striking features in the shift from aesthetic theories based on taste to aesthetic theories of judgment is the new emphasis placed upon the subject. Ancient philosophy located the beautiful in an aesthetic ideal outside both the subject and the work of art. Aesthetic theories prior to Kant tend to retain the objective notion of the beautiful and combine it with a subjective conception of taste. Taste in these theories, however, remains mediated by social and cultural norms. Kant's aesthetics breaks with both the objective conception of the beautiful and the socially mediated conception of taste by introducing a notion of aesthetic judgment that identifies an aesthetic attitude. Kant thus articulates an aesthetic theory that responds to the changes in art as a result of the move toward the private realm. An analysis of Kant's aesthetics of judgment will shed further light on the changes in art in the late eighteenth century, in particular in relation to Diderot's own aesthetics.

Aesthetic judgment, for Kant, depends first and foremost on the subject's distance from the work being judged:

> Everyone must admit that a judgment about beauty, in which the least interest mingles, is very partial and is not a pure judgment of taste. We must not be in the least prejudiced in favor of the existence of things, but be quite indifferent in this respect, in order to play the judgment in things of taste. [39]

Disinterestedness with regard to even the object's existence is the proper aesthetic attitude for judgments of taste. Returning to Fried's discussion of the representation of absorption in eighteenth-century art and the positioning of the beholder, we see a parallel between the represented figure's indifference to the beholder and the beholder's disinterested attitude with regard to the work of art. The absorption depicted in the painting and the attendant disregard for the beholder's presence serve as models for the beholder's own disinterested attitude with respect to the painting. Aesthetic judgment, according to Kant, requires precisely the kind of intense absorption that is depicted in the paintings—absorption that remains indifferent to any outside interest. Kant forbids interest in the object being judged—emanating from either the senses or reason—because such interest changes the character of the judgment. Sensory interest in an object arouses desire for the object, according to Kant, which colors the subject's attitude toward it. Likewise, rational interest in an object's use also changes the nature of the judgment from aesthetic to cognitive or moral. (This retrospectively explains Diderot's admonishments to collectors and investors for taking an economic rather than an aesthetic interest in art.) Aesthetic judgment relies upon the subject's pure disinterestedness with respect to even the existence of the object being judged. Like the represented figures, the beholder too must be intensely absorbed, and thus indifferent to any outside interest.

Beyond disinterestedness, Kant's aesthetics identifies and analyzes the mental processes of aesthetic judgment. For Kant, aesthetic judgments are reflective as opposed to determinant (15). By this Kant means that they do not involve the subsumption of a particular (the object of cognition) under a given universal, but instead involve a particular "for which the universal has to be found" (15). Reflective judgments, thus, do not involve the use of concepts. Rather, the subject considers an object and judges it to be beautiful without preconceived notions concerning the object, its potential use, and so forth. In judgments of the beautiful, the subject perceives an object and in the subject's presentation of that object to consciousness feels a pleasurable sensation from the spontaneous *free play* between the faculties that ensues. For Kant, the spontaneous free play between the faculties of the imagination and understanding arises from the perception of what Kant terms purposiveness without a purpose or form. In other words, the subject feels pleasure when it perceives form in an object because the perception of form produces a spontaneous play between the subject's own faculties of the imagination and understanding.

Thus, judgments of the beautiful for Kant entail a free play between the faculties of the imagination and understanding when the subject adopts a disinterested attitude with respect to an object and perceives form in that object. Ultimately, Kant's aesthetics has nothing to say about art itself. Strictly speaking, his aesthetics analyzes mental processes that could occur in a dream state or as a result of a hallucination. When the judgment of the beautiful arises as a result of a work of art, it produces a state of self-absorption because of the free play between the faculties. As Jean-Luc Nancy has argued about the Kantian sublime, the feeling of satisfaction that accompanies judgments of the beautiful has more to do with the subject itself than the object perceived.[32]

The Kantian account of judgments of the beautiful coincides perfectly not only with Fried's analysis of the primacy of absorption in paintings of the late eighteenth century, but also with Diderot's understanding of the nature of aesthetic experience. As part of the extended commentary on several landscape paintings by Vernet in the *Salon* of 1767, Diderot characterizes the pleasure of aesthetic experience as the subject's own enjoyment of itself. Diderot writes:

> I was there in my reverie, nonchalantly stretched out in an armchair, letting my mind roam at its will, a delicious state in which the soul is honest without reflection, the mind just and delicate without effort, where ideas and feelings seem to be born in us of themselves as if in some happy soil; my eyes were attached to an admirable landscape, and I was saying: the abbot is right, our artists do not understand this at all, since the sight of their most beautiful productions has never made me feel *the delirium that I feel, the pleasure of being with myself [d'être à moi], the pleasure of recognizing the good in myself, the pleasure of seeing myself and of pleasing myself, the even sweeter pleasure of forgetting myself: where am I in this moment? what surrounds me? I do not know, I am unaware of it. What do I need? Nothing. What do I desire? Nothing. If there is a God, this is how he is, he enjoys himself [il jouit de lui-même].* [*191-92*, my emphasis]

Although Diderot claims to be enjoying nature and not art, he later reveals that his reverie was in fact inspired by one of Vernet's landscapes. More importantly, the description he gives of the pleasure that these landscapes occasion is one that involves intense self-absorption. Consistent with Kant's account of aesthetic judgment, he is disinterested with respect to the scene before him. Moreover, the pleasure he derives remains centered on the self. His description highlights a loss of self ironically coupled with supreme self-satisfaction. Likening himself to God, Diderot maintains that his feeling of self-sufficiency and contentment goes hand in hand with his lack of awareness of himself. Wholly complete within himself, he has no desires or needs. Coincident with this perfect self-sufficiency and lack of self-awareness is a state of perfect enjoyment of the self.

Diderot's description of aesthetic pleasure—perhaps because of his familiarity with Shaftesbury—anticipates Kant's account in the *Third Critique*. As we have seen, the free play between the understanding and the imagination occasioned by the beautiful ultimately locates the pleasure of aesthetic experience in a priori subjective experience. For Kant and the Diderot of the *Salon* of 1767, the pleasure of the beautiful is really the pleasure of subjective experience, or the pleasure of the faculties. Thus, judgment remains a matter of private experience in the strictest possible sense. Whether occasioned by art or merely reverie, judgments of the beautiful involve the subjective pleasure of the faculties.

Reading Diderot in the light of Kant's aesthetics and Fried's analysis of eighteenth-century art criticism it is clear that both the representation of absorption and the attendant privatization of aesthetic reception spurred art's move from the public to the private realm. Thus, in spite of the growth of a consumer market for art and the broadening of the public in the Salons, changes in the production, dissemination, and reception of eighteenth-century art ultimately led to its privatization. This move constitutes an important stage in the progressive rationalization of the aesthetic sphere. In particular, the development of an aesthetics of judgment lays the groundwork for the eventual appearance of an aesthetic-expressive form of rationality in the nineteenth century. Diderot's aesthetics testifies to the importance of the influence of the market and bourgeois ideology concerning the private sphere in relation to the rationalization of the aesthetic sphere.

The Public/Private Dialectic Revisited

In the preceding chapters we have seen the public/private dialectic at work in bourgeois ideology in various ways. I argued in chapter 1 that in Rousseau's *Discourse on the Origin of Inequality* the attempt to shield against the nefarious effects of the public sphere led to the privileging of domestic life to the detriment of the bourgeois individual. Rather than protect the individual, the private sphere as conceived by Rousseau ironically stifles individual expression under the burden of subsistence. In Rousseau's utopia, identical bourgeois individuals pursue identical goals under the guise of individuality. Likewise in the *Project of Constitution for Corsica* and the *Considerations on the Government of Poland*, Rousseau again sacrifices the bourgeois individual by instituting a prototetalitarian state designed to protect individuals, but which ultimately serves to maintain uniformity of expression and therewith a supreme lack of individuality. Finally, Rousseau's autobiographical works—a tribute to his overriding concern with individuality—in the final analysis, point to the inexpressibility of individuality. Following Adorno's analysis of the subject/object dialectic, I demonstrated the impossibility of the project of autobiography: to write the private self. Instead, Rousseau is doomed to commodify himself for mass consumption in the public sphere.

Overall, my analyses have demonstrated Rousseau's failure to recognize the dialectical relation between the public and private spheres, and therefore his inability to secure the private sphere for individual expression of any kind. Rousseau's failure in this regard may be read as part of a general failure in bourgeois theory to come to terms with the problematic nature of the private sphere. Instead, theory remains harnessed to bourgeois ideology, unable to critically examine its own assumptions about the relation between the two spheres.

The present chapter returns to the dialectical relation between the bourgeois public and private spheres. Following Weber's rationalization thesis, I documented the simultaneous appearance of a general public and a new cultural elite composed of experts as art begins to break free from the institutions of church and court. In particular, the growth of a consumer market for art prompts critics such as Diderot to advocate *moral art* destined for consumption in the private sphere to counteract the degradation of art's commodification. Posing as another type of *expert*, distinct from art dealers and collectors, Diderot attempts to guide the lay judgment of art within the bourgeois private sphere. Responding to the move toward the private sphere, both artistic production and reception responded to the exigencies of private experience: artists depicted scenes of intense absorption and aesthetic theories moved away from taste toward judgment.

Diderot's art criticism and aesthetics document the commodification of art due to changes in the public sphere. His *Salons* attempt to stem the tide of commodification by theorizing a proper aesthetic attitude that will not admit of financial interest or sensory desire. In response both to the influence of connoisseurs and to the broadening of the art public, his aesthetics begins to address the problem of judgment rather than the issue of taste. Art's move into the private realm requires just such an aesthetic, which establishes the primacy of subjective judgment. Thus, as we have seen, Kant's conception of disinterestedness as the proper aesthetic attitude guards against viewing art as merely a financial investment, while his analysis of the a priori nature of aesthetic experience responds to the needs of spectators who have moved art into the private realm of moral values.[33]

The move toward the private realm in the case of art parallels the general tendency for bourgeois theorists to seek solace from the alienation of public life in the domestic sphere. As the public sphere becomes more commodified and alienated due to the expansion of capitalism, the myth of individuality requires the haven of the domestic space for its expression. As we have seen in the foregoing chapters, the private sphere offers no protection against the threats of mass culture. Instead the private haven becomes a prison in which bourgeois individuals express their *individuality* by means of cultural products provided by the public sphere.

Even art of the eighteenth century—designed to provide the supreme pleasure of self-absorption—is highly culturally mediated. Although clearly not as powerful as television for determining *private* experience, bourgeois art nonetheless provides *escape* for individuals through the consumption of images that promote the myth of bourgeois domestic bliss. Through paintings and especially engravings, artists paid by the new bourgeois patrons help the public sphere reach in and mediate *private* experience. Even more so, bourgeois literature promotes these same values and even appeals to the reader through the transgressive act of penetrating the private space. In this regard, both connoisseurs and antirococo critics like Diderot are part of a general *bourgeoisification* of art. The investment in art for the purposes of social climbing is as much a part of bourgeois ideology as its private consumption for moral edification.

Read in this light, Diderot's art criticism bears witness to the spread of a consumer market in art during the second half of the eighteenth century. Its concerns are consistent with issues raised by the blurring of boundaries between high and popular culture associated with the rise of the bourgeoisie. Paradoxically bourgeois ideology not only allows for the spread of consumer culture, but actually encourages the homogenization of culture in the interests of equality. The negative side of this phenomenon entails a perceived loss of value as each sphere is separated and rationalized. The reaction to the spread of a consumer market expressed in Diderot's *Salons* parallels the concern over the loss of moral value in *Rameau's Nephew* as social relations are influenced by instrumental reason. As we have seen, these effects of the dialectic of enlightenment are also diagnosed and continuously lamented by Rousseau.

Conclusion

In the preceding chapters I have argued for dialectical readings of works by Rousseau and Diderot that highlight the tension and anxiety associated with the rise of a capitalist consumer market. I have maintained that their works bear the traces of the changes taking place in the public sphere and attest to the alienation arising from the commodification of literature and culture in general. I have also suggested that the works of Diderot and Rousseau are exemplary in this respect—that they speak for a generation of French writers and readers. In this sense, Diderot and Rousseau are *modern* authors. Their textual practices testify to the changes in production and dissemination that ushered in the modern era of mass culture.

The texts of Diderot and Rousseau are also exemplary in the range and variety of subjects and genres they cover. As director of the *Encyclopédie*, Diderot authored hundreds of articles on incredibly diverse topics in addition to his own literary-philosophical output. Likewise, Rousseau's corpus includes literary, philosophical, sociological, and autobiographical works. In the foregoing analyses I have focused primarily on the philosophical works of both of these authors, but have attempted to take account of other aspects of their works as well. In concluding this study I would like to return to the question of *mass culture* during the latter half of the eighteenth century to bring together themes of the individual analyses.

In the introduction I distinguished between the *bourgeoisie*, as defined as a capitalist economic class, and the much broader applicability of the notion of *bourgeois sensibility*. I maintained that bourgeois ideology extended beyond the *middle class* to include members of both the aristocracy and the artisan classes. In keeping with Marx's conception of ascendant class ideology, these bourgeois values were touted as representing universal interests or the interests of the *whole of society* against the ideology of the dominant class. In effect, the empirical existence of the *bourgeoisie* here is less important than the articulation of the theoretical concept.[1] In other words, as long as theoretical works define, represent, and reflect a *bourgeois sensibility* that cuts across economic class boundaries and upholds values with *universal* appeal, then in some sense *mass culture* has already begun.

To put the argument another way, *mass culture* entails a perspectival change rather than a quantitative empirical leap. As soon as authors believe that they address their works to a *mass audience*—no matter how numerically restricted that audience happens to be—they have created the cultural space for mass culture. In reviewing the specific analyses presented in the foregoing chapters, I would like to construct an argument for thinking about the eighteenth century as the beginning of modern mass culture.

To pose the question in the most general terms, the problem of mass culture arises as part of the individual's changing relation to the social order. In Rousseau's social and political theory, I have highlighted the tension between individual identity and autonomy against the power of the social order or state. Focusing on the problem of individuation in the *Discours sur l'origine de l'inégalité*, I argued that Rousseau's conception of individual identity ultimately sacrifices moral development in favor of self-sufficiency. Reading the *Second Discourse* in light of Horkheimer and Adorno's analyses of the detrimental effects of reason in *Dialectic of Enlightenment*, reveals not only the common concern with reason's alienating effects but also the prototalitarian impulses in Rousseau's social theory. According to this reading, Rousseau attempts to shield individuals against the alienation of the public sphere, but ultimately members of his model society are atomized into self-sufficient but identical family units. Atomization comes about as a result of market relations that foster competition and work against cooperation and community. In other words, the phenomenon of mass culture works to isolate and separate identical individuals into easily malleable social units.

Continuing with the question of community from the perspective of Rousseau's political agenda for Poland and Corsica, I diagnosed a similar problem of individual identity in relation to the state. I maintained that both social programs bear a striking resemblance to totalitarian social practices specifically with respect to questions concerning individual and national identity. Adorno's Freudian analysis of fascist propaganda highlights precisely these problems of identity, which subtend the mob psychology of the fascist state. Reading Rousseau's *Projet de constitution pour la Corse* and *Considérations sur le gouvernement de Pologne* in conjunction with Adorno's analysis revealed the points of similarity between Rousseau's vision for social programs aimed at fostering political legitimacy and the programs of fascist regimes. Whereas in the *Second Discourse* an overemphasis on the individual led to a prototo-talitarian social existence, in *Corsica* and *Poland* individual identity is predicated on national identity that is imposed from without. In a more classic form of totalitarian social control than in the *Second Discourse*, the state plays a normalizing role with respect to the individual who in turn identifies strongly with the state. Individual identity is nothing but national identity because *public education* produces adults who rely upon the state for their sense of self.

The applicability of Adorno's analysis of fascist propaganda and specifically his use of Freud's work on mob psychology to Rousseau's suggestions for Poland and Corsica indicate that mecha-nisms of mass culture are again at work. Mob psychology is only possible when the population is addressed as a *mass*. Again, the question of numbers here is far less important than the shift in per-spective. Rousseau's attempts to control individual identity through imposed national identity indicate that he already thinks in terms of *mass culture*.

The problem of the individual in relation to the social order is recast in Diderot's work in view of his materialism. As I argue in chapter 4, Diderot's peculiar form of dynamic materialism implies a form of fallibilistic hermeneutic holism that not only undermines the stability of the material world, but of the subject as well. The subject's identity as well as the subject's interpretation of the world require constant revision in order to keep up with the constant flux of matter. The distinction between the individual and the universal thus breaks down in Diderot's version of hermeneutic holism.

The ethical implications of Diderot's materialism become apparent in *Le Neveu de Rameau*. Following Hegel's reading of this dialogue from the *Phenomenology of Spirit*, I analyzed Diderot's problematization of the nature of the individual's relation to the social order in the context of the breakdown of value systems during the second half of the eighteenth century. The rise of a capitalist market and the increasing importance of instrumental reason inform the nephew's arguments against absolutist moral positions. Despite the fact that the nephew is clearly not a capitalist nor even a member of the bourgeoisie, his ethical practices are modeled after rational cal-culations used by the bourgeoisie in economics. It is precisely the extension of instrumental reason into the realm of human relations that Adorno and Horkheimer credit with the spread of domination.

Most importantly for my argument concerning mass culture, the spread of instrumental rationality and market practices in general into other areas of social life and into the practices of other social classes signals the hegemony of bourgeois culture. In other words, the nephew's adoption of bourgeois practices indicates that he has a stake in *bourgeois ideology*. Both Diderot's text and Hegel's reading of it diagnose the spread of the alienation characteristic of the rise of capitalism and the increasing hegemony of bourgeois ideology.

The problematic relation of the individual to the social order is echoed in the work of Diderot and Rousseau in their articulation of the relation between the public and private spheres. Chapters 3 and 6 concentrate on the dialectical nature of this relation in Rousseau's autobiographies and in Diderot's *Salons*. These very different types of texts both signal the extent to which the private sphere is necessarily mediated by the public. In the case of Rousseau's autobiographies I have argued that the project of writing the private self is doomed to failure on several accounts. Most importantly, Rousseau's very insistence on autobiography testifies to the alienating effects of the bourgeois public sphere even in the *private* realm of the self.

In the case of Diderot, I have suggested that his art criticism responds to changes in art's reception brought about by the reestablishment of the Salon exhibitions and the growth of a consumer market for art. Contemporary descriptions of the Salon public bear witness to the heterogeneity characteristic of a public for mass culture. The simultaneous appearance of art *critics* and other experts to help guide the lay judgment of art demonstrates the extent to which the aesthetic realm has become rationalized in the French eighteenth-century context. More importantly, Diderot's concerns both with the lay judgment of art and connoisseurs' *misuse* of art are characteristic of the threat posed by an everwidening public. As public access to art expands and the influence of institutionally controlled interpretation diminishes, the reception of art becomes more difficult to control. The dialectical interdependence between the public and private spheres only adds to the difficulty as art moves from public exhibitions to private collections. Ultimately, Diderot's aesthetics, which attempts to guide the private consumption of art, implies a penetration of the public sphere into the private sphere.

The determining of individual relations even in the private sphere is characteristic of mass culture. As a remedy to atomization and problems of individuation in the public sphere that I diagnosed in Rousseau's social theory as well as Diderot's depiction of ethical relations, bourgeois ideology represents the private sphere as a haven from the alienation of public life. But bourgeois art forms and patterns of consumption in general only exacerbate the problem by imposing a homogenizing form of culture that increases alienation by further atomizing the bourgeois individual.

Rousseau's experience of alienation as a result of his celebrity, which he attempts to remedy with recourse to the private self, illustrates the public/private dialectic at work. His attempts to *publish* the private self as autobiography only deepen the dialectical implications between the two realms. Likewise, Diderot's art criticism with its shift toward reflective judgment and private consumption also reveals the fundamental interdependence between the bourgeois public and private spheres. Ultimately, the private sphere attests to the spread of alienation in the form of *mass culture.*

The preceding analyses all raise questions concerning the connections between Rousseau and Diderot, and the philosophical tradition that extends from German idealism through the Frankfurt School. I have argued that Rousseau and Diderot's works already identify to a certain extent the tensions and contradictions associated with capitalism, and specifically bourgeois ideology, that dominate nineteenth- and twentieth-century critical theory. I have also acknowledged to what extent their theories rely upon and even fall prey to other aspects of bourgeois ideology.

Rousseau's blind spot concerning independence and Diderot's insistence on the private nature of moral relations both signal the degree to which they are entangled in the ideology they critique. Nonetheless, I would like to consider Rousseau and Diderot as the first critical theorists. Their works already put into question assumptions concerning the value of enlightenment, the effects of mass culture, the meaning of community, and the nature of individual autonomy developed fully by the tradition that follows them.

I would hope that this line of inquiry will not only spark continued philosophical debate around these issues, but that the intersection of various disciplines in the questions raised here will promote a greater understanding of the complexity of the problems that faced Rousseau and Diderot, and continue to face us today.

Notes

Critical Introduction

1. Though it may be argued that both Rousseau and Diderot were supported financially by wealthy, aristrocratic patrons, I would maintain that there are significant differences between Racine's or Molière's relationship to Louis XIV's court and, for example, Diderot's relationship to Catherine the Great. For one thing, the politics of privilege during the seventeenth century determined which plays and operas were performed and by whom (see Isherwood, pp. 81-97). Thus, writers of the seventeenth century found the content of their literary output being largely determined by their patron(s), while the eighteenth-century writer seeks financial support in order to ensure a certain degree of independence. As Elizabeth Eisenstein points out, there is a dialectic here between financial dependence and intellectual independence. She writes, "When their work came off the presses, Voltaire and Rousseau often made a point of having dozens of copies specially printed on fine 'papier de Hollande' and sent to powerful personages who would in turn assure them of support and protection. 'Few people have made themselves so dependent in order to become independent'—the remark was made not about Erasmus but, by Goethe, about Voltaire." See Eisenstein, *Print Culture and Enlightenment Thought*, p. 15.

2. Darnton is careful to establish a comparative context for the cost of the *Encyclopédie*: "The 'democratization' of the *Encyclopédie* had limits, however, because even the cheapest edition would have seemed expensive to the common people. One can see how far beyond their reach it remained by translating its price into bread, the basic element of their diet. A first folio was worth 2,450 loaves of bread, a quarto 960 loaves, and an octavo 563 loaves, the standards of measurement being the subscription prices of the book and the 'normal' price of 8 sous for a four-pound loaf of ordinary bread in prerevolutionary Paris. An unskilled laborer with a wife and three children would have had to buy 12 loaves a week to keep his family alive and would have earned about a livre a day, when he could find work. Even in good times and even when the wife or children had jobs, half the family's income would have gone for bread. A 'cheap' octavo represented almost a year of this precarious food budget, a quarto a year and a half, a folio four

years. It would have been as likely for a laborer to buy an *Encyclopédie*—even if he could read it—as for him to purchase a palace. Skilled artisans—locksmiths, carpenters, and compositors—made 15 livres in a good week. Judging from the signatures on marriage certificates and from *inventaires après décès*, they often managed not only to read books but also to buy them. But they could not have bought any *Encyclopédies*, for a first folio represented sixty-five weeks of labor, a quarto twenty-six weeks, and an octavo seventeen weeks. Diderot's work remained beyond the purchasing power of the 'labor aristocracy,' including the men who printed it" (274-75, emphasis added). See also Chartier, *Cultural Uses of Print*, on the increasing accessibility of books.

3. Roger Chartier states that "the century, generally speaking, that separated the 1660s and the 1780s incontestably saw a broadening of the various reading publics. In the cities, . . . more people owned books and more books were owned by their owners. This advance is particularly noticeable among readers at the lower end of the social scale" (*Cultural Uses of Print*, p. 238).

4. As David A. Bell argues, part of the difficulty is relating this new group of people to an established category or class of persons. He writes, "there was clearly something innovative, and even subversive, about what was happening, for the new reading 'public' corresponded to none of the traditional social categories of the *ancien régime*: no *corps*, no *ordre*, no *état*" (914).

5. Ironically, this is also the period in which the public began to respond personally to authors, feeling that they "knew" them. The broadening of the reading public and the expansion in terms of types of literature elicited fan mail addressed to authors for the first time. Although at first glance this appears to be a lessening of the distance that separates reader from author, it is nonetheless a wider gap than previously experienced. Rousseau in particular became paranoid about the public's perception of him—a reaction that indicates the distance separating him from his readers. See Darnton, "Readers Respond to Rousseau: The Fabrication of Romantic Sensitivity" in *The Great Cat Massacre* and my discussion of Rousseau's autobiographies in chapter 3.

6. Elizabeth Eisenstein, *Printing Revolution*, p. 100.

7. I am grateful to Roxanne Lin for pointing this out to me in reference to the Superbowl. The selling of advertising time at exorbitant rates during the Superbowl is based on the projection of the number of households it will reach. The "reality" of mass culture—that is to say, the number of actual viewers or readers—must always be determined after the fact. No one would dispute that the Superbowl represents a mass cultural event, even if no one watched it. The creation of the cultural possibility identifies it as a mass cultural event and not the actual number of viewers.

8. Peter Widdowson has coined the expression *critical time-machine* to discuss the problematic nature of any attempt to overcome our own historical positioning in the interpretation of texts. Cited in Bennett, *Outside Literature*.

9. See Max Weber, "Science as a Vocation" in *From Max Weber*. For my discussion of rationalization, see chapter 6.

10. In Diderot's defense, it must be acknowledged that the *Encyclopédie* included a system of *renvois* (cross-references) that tied the articles together in provocative ways. The *renvois* work against the alphabetical organization of the *Encyclopédie* to establish a dialogue between different subjects.

11. See Darnton's reading of Rousseau's fan mail, "Readers Respond to Rousseau: The Fabrication of Romantic Sensitivity" in *The Great Cat Massacre*.

12. Adorno makes a distinction between the culture industry and mass culture. The latter refers to something like popular culture, while the former, used in *Dialectic of Enlightenment*, entails culture engineered for market consumption. As Martin Jay points out, his conception of the culture industry is deeply indebted to Marx's analysis of commodity fetishism (*Adorno*, 122). For my purposes here, mass culture refers to a phenomenon in the bourgeois public sphere related to both a broadening of the audience for culture—although culture does not spring from the masses—and the appearance of the market. I choose the term *mass culture* as opposed to *public culture* to stress both the "universal" appeal of these cultural forms consistent with liberal bourgeois ideology and to underline the importance of the capitalist market in determining cultural forms. The move away from court or church patronage and toward a capitalist market must be underscored in the eighteenth-century context. For an extended discussion of Adorno's problematic relationship to "high" and "popular" culture, see Jay, pp. 111-60.

13. In a recent addition to the debate around Habermas's account of the public sphere in France (*French Historical Studies*, Fall 1992), Daniel Gordon challenges the notion that public opinion was unified or political. Rather, he maintains that public opinion represented a "field for the play of diverse interests" (898), specifically those particular interests arising from the private sphere. Thus, he contends that public opinion was varied and was an "expression of will from the private sphere" (899). Gordon mistakenly understands consensus in the Habermasian model as a feature of the bourgeois public sphere rather than as a regulative ideal underlying rational discourse. Conflating Habermas's theory of communicative action with his historical account of the public sphere, Gordon charges Habermas with believing that "modern societies have only one possible normative basis or

self-justification" (884). Against Habermas, Gordon ironically insists on the importance of commerce and the press, which he seems to think are missing from Habermas's account. Moreover, his insistence on the interconnection between the public and private spheres, presumably overlooked by Habermas's analysis, demonstrates his failure to appreciate the dialectical implications of Marxist criticism. For the purposes of my argument here, it is significant that critics of Habermas and Marxist versions of French history highlight the importance of commerce and the interconnection between the public and private spheres. These features of Enlightenment culture are essential in Habermas's account of the bourgeois public sphere. Moreover, it seems difficult, if not impossible, to deny that a culture marked by commerce, consumerism, and deep connections between the public and private spheres is anything but bourgeois.

14. In particular, one could point to the publication of legal briefs and the growing importance of public opinion in the judicial realm as an example of public culture relatively independent of profit motives. But as David Bell points out, legal culture in prerevolutionary France is part of judicial culture and is strictly speaking part of the government and therefore not part of the public sphere. Nonetheless, the case can certainly be made that many of the disputes adjudicated by the courts arose within the corporatist framework and involved negotiating settlements between parties not unlike contract disputes, antitrust suits, and the like today. Even for Habermas, legal culture in the twentieth century occupies a special position between the public sphere and the state. If one considers legal culture to be part of the public sphere of critical debate, it is still not certain that this debate went on independently of financial interests. It is certainly true that these paper wars were directly fueled by political interests. Printers and booksellers were in the business to make money and the circulation of briefs was no doubt motivated as much by political and economic interests on their part as by more "altruistic" beliefs in the public's critical role. On the importance of public opinion in the legal realm, see Bell, Maza, and Ozouf. Compare Warner's discussion of the Zenger case in colonial America and his contention that it helped establish the "supervisory" and critical role of the public in questions of interpretation (58-63).

15. See especially Marin, pp. 130-40. Burke points out that the "public" did not yet exist during Louis XIV's reign: "Who then was, or were, the public? The question is a good deal more difficult to answer than it may look. For one thing, the concept of the 'public' was only just coming into existence at this time. The French used phrases such as 'the public good,' 'to preach in public,' and so on, but not 'the public' *tout court*. The concept of *'public opinion'* was not yet known—the first reference to *l'opinion du peuple* dates from the last year of the reign, 1715. . . . It might be argued that the signifier was lacking because the signified was also lacking. The public might be defined as a social group, which, like a social class, needs self-

consciousness in order to exist. This self-consciousness was encouraged by the growth in the media of communication. The official fabricators of the image of Louis XIV thus made an important contribution to the creation of public opinion in France" (152). Cf. Joan Landes's discussion of the public sphere in seventeenth-century France, pp. 18-21.

16. The course of economic development in France clearly problematizes certain aspects of the classical Marxist account. See my discussion of these difficulties below.

17. Interestingly, the Toquevillian analysis of changing social relations in the old regime is being revived to counter Marxist accounts of political change. David Bell summarizes the argument: "A possible 'revised Tocquevillian' argument along these lines might proceed as follows. Over the course of the seventeenth and eighteenth centuries the crown did much to build up national lines of communication. The *intendants* and *subdélégués*, even if they often served principally as conduits of information rather than as governors, nonetheless brought vast numbers of Frenchmen into direct contact with the central administration for the first time. The monarchy itself—rather than the capitalist interests described by Habermas—first sponsored a national press in France, with the institution of the *Gazette de France*, followed by the *Mercure* and the *Journal des Savants*. Under Louis XIV the monarchy bound members of ruling elites around France into large, and increasingly bureaucratized patronage networks" (917).

18. As I shall argue, the bourgeoisie must be broadly conceived and does include members with some social and political power, specifically lawyers. For an account of the importance of legal briefs on public opinion, see Bell, Maza, and Ozouf.

19. A recent visit to the St. Louis Zoo served as a useful reminder that public culture still inhabits a problematic realm between the free market and patronage. Corporate patrons exchange their financial support for certain privileges. This fact is evident upon entering the zoo and noting the Anheuser-Busch name on several buildings and signs, and the fact that Busch beer is the only beer sold at the St. Louis Zoo. The zoo obviously also receives support from other sources—I myself contribute to the "Friends of the St. Louis Zoo." Likewise, the zoo promotes programs to "adopt" animals on its maps. Although it does not charge for admission, the zoo does charge fees for riding the railroad, entering the children's zoo, and parking in the zoo lot. In these respects the zoo is typical of other forms of public culture in the twentieth century—still dependent on patrons (both private and corporate) and engaged in a business in a market. I am indebted to George Trey for a lively and enlightening conversation on this topic.

20. Although the first goal of this book is to offer a reading of eighteenth-century texts, it nonetheless also implies certain theoretical posi-

tions with respect to the Frankfurt School. In particular, in areas of dispute between individual theorists, I often "take sides" in order to suit the purposes of my argument. I have attempted to provide indications of such theoretical disputes in the endnotes. However, I apologize in advance for weaving theories together, often abandoning one in favor of another in the course of analyzing an eighteenth-century text. Perhaps the theoretical implications of my argument for the Frankfurt School will be fully developed by me in later work.

21. The main point of contention revolves around rigid or static economic definitions of classes and the relations between them. The central thesis of the revisionists maintains that a revolutionary "elite" of enlightened persons led the revolution composed of aristocrats and bourgeois. See Alfred Cobban, Elizabeth Eisenstein, "Who Intervened in 1788?"; William Doyle, George V. Taylor, Colin Lucas, Guy Chaussinand-Nogaret, and Denis Richet. For an excellent overview of the debate between revisionist and Marxist historians, see George C. Comninel.

22. This is not to say that the emergence of capitalism itself is unimportant. On the contrary, the Frankfurt School analyses blame the appearance of alienation and commodification on the rise of a capitalist market and more specifically on the spread of market relations to other areas of life. Although it may be difficult to distinguish nobles from bourgeois, and even some artisans during the second half of the eighteenth century, it seems clear that they all engage in capitalist practices to the extent that they manage their money "efficiently" according to bourgeois criteria.

23. See Maza, "Women, the Bourgeoisie, and the Public Sphere," p. 941. She continues: "Such a definition might include some of the following: that bourgeois values were articulated . . . primarily by professionals and administrators and by men of letters closely connected to such groups, and were in some instances shaped . . . by the experience of religious dissent; that bourgeois culture grew in importance thanks to increasing commercialism and consumerism, particularly with respect to printed matter and iconography; that its central thrust lay in demonstrating the exemplary nature of private experience among the non-elite segments of society . . . that such private experience could be given normative public status through the medium of both letters and law . . . and that the core of beliefs making up French bourgeois culture were, as historians like Georges Lefebvre and Patrice Higonnet have long since pointed out, universalistic rather than individualistic" (941).

24. I do not have the 1992 Bush/Quayle Republican platform in mind here, but rather a way of life associated with the rise of the nuclear family.

25. See Georges Snyders, pp. 257-352, and Philippe Ariès.

26. See Robert Darnton, "A Bourgeois Puts His World in Order," *The Great Cat Massacre.*

27. Many of these criticisms involving historical accuracy have been leveled against Habermas's account of the rise of the bourgeois public sphere in France. Critics have argued that the French context was significantly different from the English one that seems to serve as his model. In defense of Habermas, recent historical work into issues concerning public opinion in eighteenth-century France has borne out his assessment of the importance of the public sphere. See Keith Michael Baker and Sarah Maza's reply to Gordon and Bell.

28. Robert Darnton, "A Bourgeois Puts his World in Order," *The Great Cat Massacre*, pp. 274-75, note 9.

29. Marx and Engels specifically cite the work of Helvétius and Holbach in this context to show that the appeal of the value of utility extended beyond the "bourgeoisie" in precisely this way. See *The German Ideology*, pp. 111-12. See also my discussion of the value of utility in connection with Hegel's discussion of it in the *Phenomenology of Spirit* in chapter 5.

30. It should be clear that the liberal political claims concerning the universal rational foundation for individual freedom, liberty, and autonomy play a central role in the appeal of bourgeois liberal ideology.

31. *Apostrophes* was a weekly French television program that invited authors of recent books on a similar theme to discuss their works together. It clearly served a number of functions: advertisement for recent books, information for the public, book review in an interesting format, and general encouragement of reading and critical thinking.

32. See Darnton, "A Police Inspector Sorts His Files: The Anatomy of the Republic of Letters," in *The Great Cat Massacre*.

33. See *Surveiller et punir* and *Histoire de la sexualité: La volonté de savoir*, esp. "Droit de mort et pouvoir sur la vie," pp. 177-211.

34. Case/folio/FRC/10268 "Sentence de police" (Rennes), 30 mai 1788, pp. 3-4, emphasis added.

35. Darnton points out in "Philosophy under the Cloak," in *Revolution in Print* that most of the pamphlets burned were not even real: "When the public hangman lacerated and burned forbidden books in the courtyard of the Palais de Justice in Paris, he paid tribute to the power of the printed word. But he often destroyed dummy copies, while the magistrates kept the originals—and they were less profligate with their auto-da-fé than is generally believed" (27).

36. Case/FRC/6213/ "Siège royal de la police—Rennes," 30 juin et 1er juillet 1788, p. 3.

37. I will address objections to the use of the term 'totalitarianism' in the eighteenth-century context in the individual chapters.

Chapter 1

1. Cf. Herbert Marcuse's discussion in *Eros and Civilization* and *One-Dimensional Man*. Following Freud, Marcuse maintains that repressive society demands the sublimation of the sexual instincts or the replacement of the pleasure principle with the reality principle (*Eros and Civilization*, 12-16). The repression is never complete, however. The unconscious of both the individual and society continually struggles to return and disrupt rational domination. Marcuse contends that Freud's entire vision of culture is framed by "unfreedom" and "constraint" (18) and represents a rationalization of repression (17). In *One-Dimensional Man*, his analysis of what he dubs the "new conformism" highlights the way in which the system appears to gratify individual needs (84-94). In fact, mass culture serves to integrate and absorb opposition in advanced technological society through rationality. Individuals believe that their needs are being satisfied because they believe that the system satisfies their needs. Similarly, Horkheimer and Adorno read mass culture as a form of "mass deception," which attempts to overcome the opposition between universal and particular (an opposition that might produce a challenge to the system) by rendering them identical. See *Dialectic of Enlightenment*, 120-67.

2. See Max Weber's thesis in *The Protestant Ethic and the Spirit of Capitalism*, in which he argues that the demands of ascetic Protestantism combined with the the exigencies of capitalism to produce "sober, conscientious, and unusually industrious workmen, who clung to their work as to a life purpose willed by God" (177). By doing without certain material comforts, ascetic Protestants were able to amass more capital to reinvest in the system. Their visible prosperity was interpreted as a sign of Divine Providence (177).

3. My choice to read the *Second Discourse* as opposed to the *Social Contract* in connection with Horkheimer and Adorno's analysis is designed to emphasize the dialectical implications of both enlightenment and individuation. Many commentators have focused on what they have seen as the totalitarian implications of the *Social Contract*, in particular the subsumption of particular interests under the general will, which results in the absolute sovereignty of the state. Many of these analyses argue for an "individualist" reading of the *Second Discourse* in contrast to the "collectivist" *Social Contract*. My own reading attempts to demonstrate the "totalitarian" implications of "individualist" theory, given the dialectical framework that Rousseau establishes in both the *Discourses*. For an excellent review of the the secondary literature concerning the individualist/collectivist debate, see Peter Gay's introduction to Cassirer.

4. Italicized parenthetical references are to Jean-Jacques Rousseau, *Oeuvres complètes*, ed. B. Gagnebin and M. Raymond, 4 vols., Paris: Gallimard, Bibliothèque de la Pléiade, 1959; translation references are to Jean-

Jacques Rousseau, *The Social Contract and Discourse on the Origin of Inequality*, trans. Lester G. Crocker, New York: Simon and Schuster, 1967.

5. Throughout this chapter I will use the noun *man* and the masculine pronoun to refer to individuals in the state of nature. Although the state of nature is *supposed* to refer to both men and women, I find this assertion highly questionable at best. Clearly women with small children do not live in the extreme isolation that Rousseau describes. He tacitly acknowledges this in his account of the origin of language (146-47, 192-93). For a discussion of gender differences in Rousseau and their implications for his political theory, see Joel Schwartz and my "Expanding the Social Contract."

6. In *Rousseau Judge of Jean-Jacques* and certain passages of the *Confessions* and *The Reveries of the Solitary Walker*, it is evident that the alienating effects of public opinion in the case of Rousseau led to paranoia. In the Eighth Walk of *The Reveries* he writes: "I was never much given to self-love [*l'amour-propre*]; but in the world this artificial passion has been exacerbated in me, particularly when I was a writer; I may perhaps have had less of it than my fellow-authors, but it was still excessive. The terrible lessons I received quickly reduced it to its original proportions. At first it rebelled against injustice, but in the end it came to treat it with contempt; falling back on my own soul, severing the external links which make it so demanding, and giving up all ideas of comparison or precedence, it was content that I be good in my own eyes. And so, becoming once again the proper love of self [*amour de moi même*], it returned to the true natural order and freed me from the tyranny of public opinion" (1001, 129). From this passage, it would seem that some forms of reflection are not dangerous, but are in fact healthy. In Rousseau's attempt to return to a state resembling the state of nature, his self-imposed exiles afforded him the luxury of contemplation and reverie. He claims that the state of reverie freed him from the nefarious effects of public opinion. But his late autobiographical writings are clearly haunted by the specter of what others thought of him despite his attempts to deny being affected by it. For an illuminating discussion of the relationship between *amour propre* and alienation in Rousseau, see Bronislaw Baczko, esp. 13-56. Jean Starobinski's analysis of Rousseau's desire for transparency would also be relevant in this context, see *Jean-Jacques Rousseau.*

7. It is important to distinguish between the conception of freedom in the state of nature and the conception of freedom in civil society. Rousseau maintains that in the social contract man loses his natural liberty, but gains civil liberty and moral freedom (364-65, 22-23). Furthermore, in both the *Social Contract* and *Profession of Faith of the Savoyard Vicar* it is clear that freedom implies an act of will in the form of adherence to law, "the impulse of mere appetite is slavery, while *obedience to a self-prescribed law is liberty*" (*CS* 365, 23, my emphasis); see *Emile*, 600 (*Emile*, trans. Barbara Foxley, London: Everyman's Library, 1911, p. 243). For a clear discussion of the concept of freedom in Rousseau and its implications for Kant, see Cassirer, 78ff.

8. According to Rousseau man in the state of nature is naturally good (202, *note IX*, 248, note i), but because his capacity to reason is limited, he is not moral. His needs are basic and there is no scarcity in the state of nature; therefore the questions of right, obligation, and duty are avoided, and thus the problems of self-domination and alienation. A "good" action under such conditions would most likely entail self-satisfaction, and a "bad" action would probably amount to self-inflicted suffering. Interestingly, his account of self-satisfaction with regard to moral behavior in the *Profession of Faith* does not differ significantly from this account and implies that self-satisfaction is necessary for any conception of self. "If there existed a man so miserable that in his entire life he never did anything the memory of which made him content with himself and comforted to have lived, that man would be incapable of ever knowing himself" (601).

9. Rousseau's ambivalence on the question of man's *natural* sociability is well-known. In the *Profession of Faith* he writes, "man is sociable by his nature, *or at least made in such a way to become so*, he can only be that way because of other innate sentiments relative to his species; *for, to consider only the question of physical need, it would certainly require dispersing men, instead of bringing them together*" (600, my emphasis). In the *Discourse on the Origin of Inequality* the social impulse would seem to be a function of convenience (see *164-66, 214-16*), and closer to other social contractarian conceptions of the practical advantages of social life in terms of promoting happiness. On the question of sociability, see Jan Marejko's discussion of pity in the state of nature, pp. 83-84, and Roger D. Masters's thorough analysis of pity and self-love, pp. 136-46.

10. See Suzanne Gearhart's intriguing discussion of this passage in her examination of the problematic use of theatricality by Rousseau in *The Open Boundary of History and Fiction* (261-71). As Gearhart points out, the scene is "staged" for *natural* man. In similar passages from the *Letter to d'Alembert* and the *Discourse* she demonstrates that "the same examples, the same characters . . . even the same phrases can be used to illustrate both the irresistible power of *natural* pity over men *and* the sterility and perversity of pity, because pity itself represents both the natural foundation of morality and the last stage of depravity" (269). Compare David Marshall's reading of pity and its relation to spectacle in "Rousseau and the State of Theater."

11. In the *Essai sur l'origine des langues*, Rousseau is clearer about the process of identification, the level of reflection, the cognitive ability, and the judgment that pity requires than he is in the *Second Discourse*. There he writes: "How do we allow ourselves to be moved by pity? In transporting ourselves out of ourselves; in identifying with the suffering being. We only suffer in as much as we *judge* that he suffers. . . . When one thinks about *how much acquired knowledge* this transport presupposes! [*qu'on songe combien ce transport suppose de connoissances acquises!*]" (92, my emphasis).

12. Ironically, although the natural law grounded on the capacity for pity "obligates" the subject who feels pity not to harm other feeling beings (*126*, 171), the example given by Rousseau does not allow for moral action. The conception of natural law in general in Rousseau would seem to be problematic given the fact that any *law* entails a restriction of freedom and thus a degree of self-domination. I would argue against Cassirer's Kantian reading of Rousseau on this point insofar as *natural* freedom does not seem to entail willed adherence to a self-prescribed law as does moral or civil liberty. See Cassirer, 78ff.

13. It may be objected that even the idea of choice in the state of nature is problematic given the fact that *natural* man has no sense of the future (*166-67*, 190). What exactly would free choice entail if the one who chooses has only a dim awareness of himself as an agent and has no conception of the future? Would these "choices" be meaningful in any sense of the word? Could they constitute a ground for the claim that natural man is free? Ultimately, the attempt to ground freedom in choice rather than self-domination or determinism renders the conception of natural law highly problematic, if not altogether meaningless. Thus, the opening sentence of the citation from Adorno above, "the identity of the self and its alienation are companions from the beginning; this is why the concept of self-alienation is poorly romanticist," clearly applies to Rousseau.

14. John Charvet argues that it is Rousseau's attempt to redefine social relations without "freedom-destroying and corrupting dependence," which leads to "a paradox which lies at the centre of Rousseau's ultimate incoherence" (2). His reading of Rousseau's *Discourse on the Origin of Inequality*, *Emile*, and *Social Contract* stresses, likes Talmon's, what he perceives to be "the systematic abolition of the other" (145). He concludes, "the absurdity and incoherence of Rousseau's theory lies precisely in the elaboration of a social ideal founded on a rejection of the right of individuals to live and value each other in their particularity" (146). Consistent with Iris Marion Young's reading, and to a certain extent Cassirer's Kantian interpretation of Rousseau, these analyses focus on the notion of independence in the *Second Discourse* and of autonomy in the *Social Contract* to read Rousseau as a precursor of Kant. I would like to distinguish between the notion of independence in the state of nature, and even in the period of the *first revolution*, and the concept of autonomy that one finds in the *Social Contract*. It is my contention that the notion of independence, clearly an extension of the *amour de soi*, provides for rudimentary self-consciousness without the alienating effects of adherence to self-prescribed limits, which would constitute *moral* autonomy. Cf. Zev Trachtenberg's analysis of the transformation of *amour de soi* and *amour propre* in social life, pp. 76-103, 120-23.

15. See Trachtenberg's discussion of the development of economic interdependence, the division of labor—which he relates to perfectability—and the transformation of needs, pp. 108-11.

16. Cf. Rousseau, *Discourse on the Arts and Sciences*: "Today, now that subtler research and more delicate taste have reduced the art of pleasing to principles, there reigns in our manners a vile and deceptive uniformity, and all minds seem to have been made in the same mold. Without fail politesse requires, propriety [*bienséance*] commands: without fail we follow customs, never our own genius [*génie*]. We dare not appear anymore what we are; and under this perpetual constraint, the men that form this flock called society, placed in the same circumstances, will all do the same things if stronger motives do not divert them from it" (8).

17. I do not wish to invoke the criticisms of J.L. Talmon in this context. Talmon argues that Rousseau's political philosophy, in particular the social contract, leads to a totalitarian form of democracy. While I would agree that certain aspects of Rousseau's social contract demonstrate his preference for social unanimity (386, 390-91, 405, 49, 70-71, 111), I would not agree that the fostering of civic celebrations, for example, represents a totalitarian impulse in Rousseau (Talmon, 47). Talmon maintains that a sovereign people without any form of representation would inevitably lead to dictatorship (46) and that the general will functions as a kind of ideological goal, or "preordained will" (48) in the service of totalitarianism. I would suggest that Rousseau's utopia issues in a weaker form of totalitarianism characterized by social conformism and suppression of the individual similar to Horkheimer and Adorno's portrait of rational life under late capitalism. Furthermore, Talmon's reading, like many interpretations of Rousseau, addresses the individualist/collectivist debate in political theory, but fails to recognize their mutual implication. Dialectical criticism has the advantage of recognizing this mutual implication.

18. See Rousseau's account of Clarens in *Julie ou la nouvelle Héloïse*, quatrième partie, Lettre X; cinquième partie, Lettre I. The description of Clarens in *Julie*, although it provides many of the specifics necessary to fill in Rousseau's conception of ideal family life, ultimately poses some very serious practical problems for his conception of utopia. Foremost among these is the problem of self-sufficiency: Clarens resembles a feudal domain more than it does a *typical* bourgeois family. It would seem to be impossible for a small family, or even an extended family, to produce the requisite food, clothing, tools, shelter necessary for a fairly comfortable life, and still have time to devote to moral and spiritual development.

19. See Iris Marion Young's argument that the exclusion of considerations of affectivity, need, and desire from the public realm tends to lead to a conception of the state that homogenizes difference. Cf. also Stephen Ellenberg's description of the ideal citizen in "Rousseau and Kant: Principles of Political Right": "The virtuous citizen is a versatile, active amateur and devout patriot. He performs useful manual labor for the economic subsistence of his family. He rushes to attend legislative assemblies. He serves in the citizens' militia and does not shrink from risking his life in defence of

his homeland. He performs corvées of public service with patriotic zeal. He participates in public celebrations and outdoor festivals of civic piety. He obeys the ancient laws of his state, and he honours the memory of the wise legislator who founded his state. *He carries in his heart affection for his fellow citizens, and cannot conceive his own interests diverging from their interests"* (9, emphasis added).

20. One might argue that the general will fulfills this function. But Rousseau fails to recognize that the general will in its function as a *universal* will necessarily be experienced as "extraneous and heteronomous," as Adorno points out, and if not, can only serve an ideological function.

21. Robert Elbaz blames the lack of a temporal and dialectical conception of the social order for the lack of a notion of integration in Rousseau. He reads the positing of an origin in the state of nature as indicative of the atemporal tendency in eighteenth-century political theory. He relates this reading to aspects of Rousseau's autobiography. See "Autobiography and Political Theory in Rousseau," *Neohelicon*, 1985, vol. 12(2):9-33.

22. See p. 8 and also the *Considérations sur le gouvernement de Pologne*, pp. 960-62.

Chapter 2

1. This definition of totalitarianism is consistent with Claude Lefort's, "The economic, legal and cultural dimensions are, as it were, woven into the political. This phenomenon is characteristic of totalitarianism" (280). Furthermore, N.S. Timasheff argues that there are at least two workable definitions of totalitarianism: "The term 'totalitarian society' is applied in two closely related but nevertheless distinct meanings. In the first meaning it connotes a *type* of society characterized by a number of traits such as concentration of power in the hands of a few; the absence of rights ascribed to the individuals *vs.* the collectivity; and an unlimited extension of the functions of the state making the state almost tantamount to society. . . . In another meaning the term connotes one definite *trait*, namely the unlimited extension of state functions, then, the term designates not a concrete type of society, but a trait isolated by means of abstraction and apt to appear in societies of various types" (39). Timasheff goes on to argue that the second, more abstract definition is both plausible and fruitful for analytic purposes (40). In keeping with these definitions, Jan Marejko argues that Rousseau collapses the distinction between governors and governed [*gouvernants et gouvernés*], a symptom of totalitarianism (23).

2. Hannah Arendt's influential study cites anti-Semitism and imperialism as necessary conditions for totalitarianism, which she takes to mean the form of government under Hitler and Stalin. My definition of totalitari-

anism is slightly broader and includes any state that exhibits the phenomenon of total social control and the breakdown of the distinction between the state (or the political) and civil society. I would reserve the term fascist for the regimes of Hitler, Stalin, and Mussolini.

3. In the *First Discourse* Rousseau writes, "Today, now that subtler research and more delicate taste have reduced the art of pleasing to principles, there reigns in our manners a vile and deceptive uniformity, and all minds seem to have been made in the same mold" (8). He further laments in the *Considerations*, "Today there are no more Frenchmen, Germans, Spaniards, Englishmen even, despite what people say; there are only Europeans. All have the same tastes, the same passions, the same manners [*moeurs*], because not one received a national form from a particular institution" (960). Therefore, he exhorts the Poles to maintain a distinct cultural identity and not to follow "the general trend [*pente*] in Europe to adopt the tastes and manners of the French" (962).

4. Totalitarian and fascist leaders are idealists in a sense. Their efforts to prevent social disintegration by creating mythically cohesive societies stems from an idealistic impulse despite the horrific end results. Rousseau shares the concern over social disintegration and, as I seek to demonstrate, attempts to engineer social cohesion in ways similar to those employed by twentieth-century fascist leaders, for similarly idealistic reasons.

5. Cf. Cobban's assertion that Rousseau navigates the transition "from the classical ideal of patriotism to the modern ideal of nationality" (*Rousseau and the Modern State*, p. 104).

6. This difficulty has been pointed out by numerous critics. For a clear discussion of the problem of the motivation for community in Rousseau, see Stephen Ellenburg.

7. All italicized parenthetical references to works by Rousseau are to the *Oeuvres complètes*, ed. B. Gagnebin and M. Raymond, 4 vols, Paris: Gallimard, Bibliothèque de la Pléiade, 1959. All references to translations of the *Social Contract* are to Jean-Jacques Rousseau, *The Social Contract and Discourse on the Origin of Inequality*, trans. Lester G. Crocker, New York: Simon and Schuster, 1967. References to the *Discourse on Political Economy* are to Jean-Jacques Rousseau, *On the Social Contract with Geneva Manuscript and Political Economy*, ed. Roger D. Masters, trans. Judith R. Masters, New York: St. Martin's Press, 1978. Where no page reference is provided, translations are my own.

8. Rational instrumental calculation as a motive for social life runs counter to the line of argument I developed in the preceding chapter. Clearly, Rousseau is opposed to instrumental reason in general, and would deny it as a motive for social existence because of its alienating effects, which could potentially inhibit full moral development. One could render his argument

consistent by maintaining that in the state of nature, rudimentary instrumental calculation motivates some social activity, but that the lack of moral and psychological development prohibits real social existence. Thus, true social life would be characterized by moral ties that would be motivated by sentiment rather than reason. Cf. Marejko's discussion of the problem of the origin of the social pact, pp. 88-89. He points out that a first manuscript version suggested the divine origin of society.

9. For Hobbes, clearly no community exists prior to the social compact, because he characterizes the state of nature as a "war of all men against all men" (29). Rousseau seems to follow Hobbes in the *Discourse on the Origin of Inequality*, at least insofar as he maintains that there is no distinction between right and wrong, good and bad in the state of nature (202-8, 248-54, note i). Thus, for Rousseau, there is no moral law in the state of nature. However, Rousseau also maintains some principles from Locke's version of the social contract. Locke posits the existence of a community of sorts, governed by natural law, before the social contract; see pp. 7-12. He maintains that private property precedes and motivates the contract that is designed to settle disputes in a just manner (19, 56). According to Locke, the social contract empowers a third party judge ("umpire") to adjudicate disputes, thus instantiating civil society. Rousseau retains from Locke the existence of private property prior to the social contract in the *Second Discourse*, borrowing his theory of property acquisition (208, 223). Thus, Rousseau would seem to fall between Hobbes and Locke, retaining the lack of moral law in the state of nature from Hobbes, but allowing for private property like Locke. I would argue that this position necessitates at least a rudimentary conception of community prior to the social compact itself.

10. Althusser maintains that the first party of the contract consists of each individual contracting individually with the second party of the contract—the community. Thus, his reading emphasizes that the second party does not *exist* until the contract is concluded. My reading differs from Althusser's in suggesting that the *first party* of the contract consists, not of each individual contracting separately, but of the group as yet not unified by any *explicit* bond of community.

11. In Chapter VII of Book 1 Rousseau writes, "We see from this formula that the act of association contains a reciprocal engagement between the public and individuals, and that every individual, contracting so to speak with himself, is engaged in a double relation, viz., as a member of the sovereign towards individuals, and as a member of the State towards the sovereign" (362, 20). This formulation of the contract is often cited to justify the reading according to which the sum of individuals contracting separately constitutes the first party to the contract. On my reading this interpretation again begs the question of community. For, although the *original* force of the contract may derive from each individual—who in this sense *contracts with himself*—it is evident that a form of community already

binds these individuals together, albeit loosely, before the contract is executed. In other words, only the individual may decide to freely give over his individual liberty to the community—the community can never force him to do so. But the individuals who decide to enter into the contract, nevertheless, are already bound to one another in their common project to form an official and explicit bond.

12. Timasheff uses Jefferson and Mussolini as extremes on the continuum from liberal society to totalitarian society. Compare his quotation of Mussolini to Rousseau's conception of the relation of individuals to the state: "Mussolini declares that everything must be done within the nation (in the meaning of the state), nothing against the nation or outside the nation; *the individuals are related to each other through the medium of the whole*, or one of its spheres (political, economic, and so on)" (43, emphasis added).

13. In Kant's *Critique of Judgment* he maintains that ideally rational beings would agree about matters of taste because all rational beings have the same faculties. Kant argues, "The judgment of taste requires the agreement of everyone, and he who describes anything as beautiful claims that everyone *ought* to give his approval to the object in question and also describe it as beautiful. . . . We ask for the agreement of everyone else, because we have for it a ground that is common to all; and we could count on this agreement, provided we were always sure that the case was correctly subsumed under that ground as rule of assent" (74). Thus, it is because of this tacit assumption of agreement that we argue over judgments concerning taste according to Kant's account. In the case of Rousseau, interpreting the general will as a form of *sensus communis* entails that its regulative force derives from the same ideal ground of common faculties not clouded by private interest.

14. One cannot help but think of the Nazi *Blut und Boden* propaganda in this context. Although the translation of *patrie* as fatherland may make the parallels between Rousseau and fascism more evident, I have nonetheless chosen to translate *patrie* as mother country to preserve the gender of *patrie*. The non-French-speaking reader should bear in mind that *patrie* comes from the Latin *patria* and resonates with *pater*. Although it is a feminine noun in Latin and French, it also serves as the root of patriot, patriotic, and patriotism, bearing a strong masculine connotation as well. In defense of Rousseau, Cobban maintains that attachment to the land represents a defensive and conservative form of patriotism rather than an aggressive and imperialistic one (*Rousseau and the Modern State*, p. 121).

15. Money—an *artificial* value—lies at the heart of Rousseau's critique of commerce because of the *false* values it ushers in. Throughout the two texts on Corsica and Poland, Rousseau warns of the dangers not only of commerce, but of money itself. He advocates barter systems even for taxes and approves of the establishment of corvées (*Corsica, 932; Poland, 1009*).

This suspicious attitude concerning money is also evident in passages of the *Confessions*—in which he claims that money never allowed him any personal satisfaction—and in the "Neuvième Promenade" of the *Reveries*— in which he maintains that he desired money only for the pleasures it could buy. I would interpret Rousseau's wariness concerning money as a proto-Marxist aspect of his general analysis of the alienation of modern society. His critiques in the *Project for Corsica* and *Considerations on Poland* point to an awareness of the distinction between use value and exchange value (*Corsica, 921, 923; Poland, 1008*), and the possibility of exploiting this distinction by capitalists. This reading is also consistent with passages from the *Discourse on the Origin of Inequality* in which he identifies the effects of alienated labor and suggests that society often enables the strong to exploit the weak (*175*).

16. Some would consider these types of controls already characteristic of totalitarianism. Waldemar Gurian argues that "the totalitarian system differs from old fashioned despotism and autocracy in its use of economic and techonological pressures and manifestations of so-called public opinion" (122). We will see in the work on Poland the degree to which *public opinion* is determined by the state.

17. Compare Rousseau's forceful statement in the *Social Contract*: "In order, then, that the social pact may not be in a vain formulary, it tacitly includes this engagement, which alone can give force to the others—that whoever refuses to obey the general will shall be constrained to do so by the whole body; *which means nothing else than that he shall be forced to be free*" (364, 22, my emphasis).

18. Determining the public's *needs*—and by extension its desires— corresponds precisely to Marcuse's definition of totalitarianism. He writes in *One-Dimensional Man*, "'totalitarian' is not only a terroristic political coordination of society, but also a non-terroristic economic-technical coordination which operates through the manipulation of needs by vested interests. It thus precludes the emergence of an effective opposition against the whole" (3).

19. See Zev Trachtenberg's thorough and illuminating dicussion of the relation between *amour de soi, amour propre*, civic virtue, and patriotism (131-43). It is his contention that the legislator's job is to help citizens displace their self-love onto the country in the form of civic virtue. Thus, the *amour de soi* becomes subordinate to the *moi commun*.

20. In this vein Rousseau cites Moses, Lycurgus, and Numa as exemplary lawgivers who established customs for their peoples, thereby infusing them with a strong sense of identity (*Poland, 956*).

21. Cf. Judith Shklar's discussion of the legislator and his role in imposing a national character from above, pp. 150-64.

22. I do not have in mind here Talmon's evaluation of the role of the general will in the *Social Contract*. Although I would agree with him that Rousseau's conception of the general will serves an ideological function, I would not agree that it is necessarily "a preordained goal" (48). As I have already argued, there are two contradictory conceptions of the general will, neither of which in my mind is teleological. I also differ from Talmon on the issue of dictatorship, whereas he reads the expectation of unanimity in Rousseau's democracy as a recipe for dictatorship, I stress other elements of his political theory as protototalitarian or even protofascist without the presence of a dictator (46). For a defense of Rousseau's conception of the general will, and in particular the conception of freedom that emerges from the *Social Contract*, see Alessandro Ferrara, *Modernity and Authenticity*, esp. pp. 61-65.

23. Joseph Pestieau similarly argues that Rousseau avoids the need for a state in his "conservative anarchism." Pestieau maintains that for Rousseau, "The law ought to be so well internalized, so well inscribed in the functioning of the social body and in the mentalities, that we would be dealing with a society where the State would tend to disappear as a distinct social body. Constraint guarantees peace, the defense and unity of this body would be essentially moral and ideological. Legitimate authority would dictate that to which all consent [*L'authorité légitime dirait ce à quoi tous consentent*]. Thus, it would maintain its own prestige, the order and unity of the nation. The pressure of opinion would replace the police. Citizens would be patriotic "out of inclination, out of passion, out of necessity" because they would be nothing outside of the role that they received in the mother country [*patrie*]" (479).

24. Lester Crocker's reading of Rousseau's political theory as well as *La Nouvelle Héloïse* and *Emile* stresses the engineered aspects of community and citizens' identity in what he terms Rousseau's preference for an "invisible hand." Striking in this analysis is the overlapping of the totalitarian tendencies that he perceives in Rousseau and Adam Smith's invisible hand of liberal capitalism. See *Jean-Jacques Rousseau*, esp. vol. 2, pp. 132-66.

25. Cf. F.M. Barnard's reading of Rousseau in comparison with Herder. He sees the emphasis on nationalism in both writers' works as the result of the collapsing of three levels of questioning concerning political legitimacy, "political legitimacy generally involves at least three levels of applicability: the who, how and where of government. By tending to focus on the third level of political legitimacy—the ethnic composition of the population and its territorial boundaries—it [the doctrine of national self-determination] either disregards the first two levels (who should properly rule and in what manner) or views them as necessary entailments of the third, thus collapsing the three levels of political legitimacy into one" (253).

26. See Immanuel Kant, *Critique of Practical Reason*, esp. pp. 85-88.

27. In the eighteenth-century context, this proposition is one possible logical conclusion of Montesquieu's style of relativism. See my discussion of Diderot's relativism in chapters 4 and 5.

28. *Emile or on Education* testifies to the complexity of Rousseau's conception of the development of human faculties. Although he maintains throughout the treatise that the education he proposes is *natural*, designed to foster and aid what was already given by God, there is little doubt that the primary role of the preceptor is to create situations in which *nature* may take its course. As Suzanne Gearhart adeptly points out, the preceptor functions as a *metteur en scène* of Emile's *natural* education; see *The Open Boundary of History and Fiction*. Likewise, Thomas Kavanagh demonstrates the extent to which nature and artifice are blurred in *Julie or the New Heloïse*, in the creation of the *bosquets* and open-air aviary of the gardens at Clarens, see *Writing the Truth*, pp. 16-17.

29. Citizens with improperly cultivated reason or unguided reason could possibly be viewed as detrimental to the community, and hence justifiably exiled due to the danger they pose to the welfare of society. But Rousseau is clear, in some texts at least, that he does not approve of torturing or executing people because of the risk to the legitimacy of the state if one innocent individual is punished or killed. In *On Political Economy* he states, "One must not believe that one may harm or cut off an arm, and that the pain does not reach the head. And it is not believable that the general will would agree that a member of the state, whoever he may be, harm or destroy another, anymore than a man using his reason would use his fingers to poke out his eyes. Individual safety is so tied to the public confederation that without the respect owing to human weakness, this convention would be dissolved by right, if one single citizen of the state perished who might have been saved, if one single citizen were wrongly detained in prison, and if one single case were lost with evident injustice. For, the fundamental conventions having been broken, it is no longer clear what right or what interest could maintain the people in social union, unless it is retained by the unique force that constitutes the dissolution of the civil state" (256). But a rather different case is made in the *Social Contract* with regard to civil religion. In Book IV, chapter viii, he writes, "There is, however, a purely civil profession of faith, the articles of which it is the duty of the sovereign to determine, not exactly as dogmas of religion, but as sentiments of sociability, without which it is impossible to be a good citizen or a faithful subject. Without having power to compel any one to believe them, *the sovereign may banish from the State whoever does not believe them; it may banish him not as impious, but as unsociable, as incapable of loving law and justice and of sacrificing at need his life and his duty. But if any one, after publicly acknowledging these dogmas, behaves like an unbeliever in them, he should be punished with death; he has committed the greatest of crimes, he has lied before the*

laws" (145-46). Along the lines of Plato's Republic, one can imagine a Rousseauian state expelling individuals based on their "lack of public reason" and the consequent threat they pose to "public safety," and even putting to death those who violate the principles of the civil religion they profess, as Robespierre did citing Rousseau as theoretical justification. See Cobban's discussion of civil religion in *Rousseau and the Modern State*, pp. 51-53 and Judith Shklar's analysis of the potential for xenophobia in *Men and Citizens*, p. 16.

30. Cf. Rousseau's justification for giving up his children to the foundling home in Book 8 of the *Confessions*: "I believed that I was acting as a Citizen and as a father, and I regarded myself as a member of Plato's Republic" (357).

31. Shklar compares this process of identity formation to the soldierly ideal. She writes: "In Poland the choice between man and citizen is to be clearcut. A young Polish adult is not a man, he is a Pole. He may dislike and shun all foreigners as long as he is at one with his fellow-citizens. What is needed is national soul. For, sensibly enough, Rousseau knew that Polish survival would be salvaged in the minds of the Poles, not on the battlefield. The soldierly ideal finds its justification here. *For the military life is the most perfect model of public service. Here, as in no other form of social endeavor, the individual loses his personal identity and becomes a part of a purposive social unit. Here alone the group absorbs all his resources, emotional as well as physical*" (15, my emphasis). Cf. Trachtenberg's assertion that public education serves to found political legitimacy and provide models for emulation, but does not train future citizens to recognize the common good (232-83).

32. Waldemar Gurian in fact maintains that the totalitarian state functions as a politico-social secularized religion (122). He writes: "What is the formal structure of the totalitarian ideocracy or socio-political religion? Essential is the belief; . . . it must embrace the whole of life and society. It must determine all realms of individual and social existence. There can be no private life outside. Passive acceptance is insufficient. Enthusiastic, active acclamation and support are necessary" (125-26). Cf. Shklar's contention that ceremonies and even political assemblies serve to reinforce the "civic self" (20).

33. All references are to Theodor Adorno, "Freudian Theory and the Pattern of Fascist Propaganda," *Critical Theory: The Essential Readings*, ed. David Ingram and Julia Simon-Ingram, New York: Paragon House, 1991:84-102.

34. Some commentators have argued that Rousseau's conception of the legislator represents a charismatic leader with a magnetic personality. See Shklar, pp. 150-64.

35. Marejko argues that the mediation of relations between citizens by the state effectively suppresses alterity, a characteristic of totalitarian regimes. See pp. 23, 83-119, and my discussion of the problem of mediation in Rousseau's autobiographies in chapter 3.

36. See Hunt's reading of Robespierre's views on terror as an "emanation of virtue" (*Politics*, 46). She cites the *Rapport sur les principes de morale politique qui doivent guider la Convention nationale dans l'administration intérieure de la République* (5 February 1794) in support of her contention: "in this situation the first maxim of your policy must be to guide the people with reason and the people's enemies with terror. . . . Terror is nothing other than justice, prompt, severe and inflexible, it is therefore an emanation of virtue. . . . Break the enemies of liberty with terror, and you will be justified as founders of the Republic. The government of the revolution is the despotism of liberty against tyranny" (*Oeuvres* 10: 356-57, cited in Hunt, 46). See also Marejko on the suppression of alterity and Shklar on xenophobia.

37. Adorno and Horkheimer present a convincing analysis of the relation between myth and reason in *Dialectic of Enlightenment* (see esp. "Odysseus or Myth and Enlightenment"). In particular, they establish that the notion of the bourgeois individual exhibits certain mythic traits, ones that they find even in Homer. My reading of the representation of the individual in the Enlightenment is consistent with their analysis insofar as it sees these representations as dialectical: mythic representations like that of Robinson Crusoe, for example, mask the relative loss of autonomy experienced by individuals in eighteenth-century society.

38. Much ink has been spilled over the totalitarian implications of Rousseau's conception of the legislator. Most germane to my discussion here is Shklar's characterization of the legislator as having "the sheer hypnotic power of a great personality" (161).

39. Hannah Arendt identifies these traits as necessary for fascism. Moreover, she maintains that imperialism as a political program results from the political empowerment of the bourgeoisie who are driven by economic interests (126). While I agree in principle with her analysis, I disagree with Arendt's characterization of eighteenth-century society. Whereas she contends that colonialism, venture capitalism, and the like, did not determine political policy during the eighteenth century, because the bourgeoisie was not directly involved in politics, I would disagree. The formation of the nation-state depends on precisely these economic developments. Nation-states encouraged economic development of this type for political reasons. She is right in maintaining that imperialism differs from colonialism because it is an official, state policy. However, the economic and the political are not so easily separated in the modern period. In short, colonialism is as much a political program motivated by economic interests as is

imperialism. The distinction may only amount to a question of degree. As a basis for distinguishing between the bourgeoisie of the eighteenth century and those of the nineteenth century, Arendt argues that bourgeois individuals of the eighteenth century are *private* people. It is not until they get involved directly with the politics of expansionism that they become *public* figures (138). I would disagree with this characterization. In the following chapter I argue that the private is always already mediated by the public and as such serves an ideological function. Moreover, I will demonstrate that the bourgeoisie are the first *public* figures because of their need to manipulate their own representations of themselves.

Chapter 3

1. The internal citation is from Kirchner, *Beiträge zur Geschichte des Begriffs*, 22.

2. The *positive* effects would include, but not be limited to, increased democratization. As the public develops its capacity to reason critically, it can begin to engage in the political process. This would necessitate increased information, and a further expansion of the conception of the public realm.

3. Compare Habermas's argument to Walter Benjamin's explanation of the loss of the aura in "Art in the Age of Mechanical Reproduction," in *Illuminations*. Both would seem to suggest that the loss of the aura can be interpreted both positively and negatively. On the one hand, the loss of the aura signals greater access to art both by artists and spectators, and therewith the possibility of broader-based social critique. On the other hand, the loss of the aura points to the profanation and degradation of art due to commodification. For the purposes of my argument, Habermas and Benjamin's positions signal an important dialectic during the Enlightenment period. The process of rationalization, as conceived by Weber, involves the separation of cultural value spheres of art, science, and morality. The separation of these spheres is necessary for increased rationality—that is to say, for the breakdown of the religious-metaphysical worldview that previously bound them together. In the case of art, the isolation of an aesthetic value sphere enables works of art to have a purely *aesthetic aura*. But the separation from the other value spheres also instantiates the breakdown of art works' *sacred aura*. The popularization of culture necessitated by the break from church and court ultimately contributes to the loss of the aura. Thus, the dialectic of specialization enables a purely aesthetic aura, while at the same time commences a process that leads to the loss of this aura. This account of the loss of the aura parallels the dialectical tension in the process of specialization generally. Specialization in any of the cultural value spheres leads to increased knowledge among a cultural elite, which furthers cultural progress. It also contributes to a widening gap between specialists and

laypersons, which fosters a sense of alienation and lack of knowledge in the general public. According to Habermas, the Enlightenment period used this dialectic to relink specialized spheres of knowledge to everyday life. Habermas cites bourgeois art as an example of this unique form of bridge: "Bourgeois art adresses *both* of these expectations to its public: on the one hand, the layperson who enjoyed art should educate himself to the level of the expert, and on the other hand, the layperson could act as a connoisseur who relates aesthetic experience to his own life-problems" ("Modernity: An Unfinished Project," p.352; cf. *Legitimation Crisis*, pp. 78-85). In this way art retains its status as a separate value sphere without becoming a degraded commodity, but is also able to be integrated into everyday praxis. One significant factor that may have enabled this phenomenon during the eighteenth century was the link between art and morality. In Habermas's account, the complete loss of the aura depends upon the development of capitalism. In turn, it may be argued that the development of capitalism entails the complete separation of the three value spheres. Nonetheless, it remains clear that the link between morality and art helped preserve both the link between art and everyday life, and the dialectical tension between specialization and popularization during the Enlightenment. I discuss this important relationship between art and morality in chapter 6. For a complete discussion of the importance of aesthetics in Habermas's work, see D. Ingram, "Habermas on Aesthetics and Rationality."

4. Habermas cites R. Williams, *Culture and Society 1870-1950*, London, 1958, xv, xvi.

5. Habermas's argument here follows Weber's theory of increased rationalization that both accompanies and helps breakdown the religious-metaphysical worldview. Rationalization also brings with it increased specialization and the separating of spheres of activity. Whereas Weber's account claimed that an adversarial relationship would obtain between the separate spheres as a result of the purposive nature of rationality, Habermas's work attributes the uncoupling of life world and system (his term for increased specialization and the attendant conflicts between the spheres) to the advance of capitalism. This contributes to the modern individual's sense of alienation in the face of technological specialization. See M. Weber, *The Protestant Ethic and the Spirit of Capitalism*. For a discussion of Weber's relation to Habermas, see D. Ingram, *Habermas and the Dialectic of Reason*, ch. 4.

6. See Darnton (*Underground*) on hack writers, and my discussion of art production in chapter 6.

7. See Peter Burke and Louis Marin on the representation of Louis XIV.

8. Others have pointed out the applicability of Habermas's study to the eighteenth-century French "Republic of Letters." See Dena Goodman, "The

Hume-Rousseau Affair: From Private *Querelle* to Public *Procès*"; and in the special issue of *Eighteenth-Century Studies*, The French Revolution in Culture, ed. Lynn Hunt, Daniel Gordon, "'Public Opinion' and the Civilizing Process in France: The Example of Morellet"; Goodman, "Enlightenment Salons: The Convergence of Female and Philosophic Ambitions"; Jeremy Popkin, "Pamphlet Journalism at the End of the Old Regime"; Bernadette Fort, "The Carnivalization of Salon Art in Prerevolutionary France." See also Mona Ozouf, "'Public Opinion' at the End of the Old Regime" and the Forum, "The Public Sphere in the Eighteenth Century."

9. In a sociopsychological study of Rousseau's autobiography, Roland Galle reads Rousseau's texts as "a reaction to the collapse of . . . central institutions" of the ancien régime—namely, social status, religion, and the family. In the *Confessions* Galle sees the beginning of modernity and specifically a creative response to an "epochal collapse."

10. Clearly there are numerous motives behind the autobiographical writings, conscious and otherwise. For a discussion of motives for autobiography, see Georges May, pp. 40-61.

11. All italicized parenthetical references are to Jean-Jacques Rousseau, *Oeuvres complètes*, ed. B. Gagnebin and M. Raymond, 4 vols., Paris: Gallimard, Bibliothèque de la Pléiade, 1959ff. Parenthetical page references are to the following translations: Jean-Jacques Rousseau, *Reveries of the Solitary Walker*, trans. Peter France, London: Penguin Books, 1979; *The Confessions*, trans. J.M. Cohen, London: Penguin Books, 1953; *Rousseau Judge of Jean-Jacques: Dialogues*, ed. Roger D. Masters and Christopher Kelly, trans. Judith R. Bush, Christopher Kelly, and Roger D. Masters, Hanover, N.H.: University Press of New England, 1990. Where no page reference is indicated, translations are my own.

12. His efforts to read his *Confessions* aloud to his friends, to which he makes reference at the end of volume 2, also indicate that there is an *intended* public to which these texts are destined.

13. Even in passages in which he clearly states his "intentions" in the *Reveries*, it is evident that he has an audience in mind: "Alone for the rest of my life, since it is only in myself that I find consolation, hope and peace of mind, my only remaining duty is towards myself and this is all I desire. This is my state of mind as I return to the rigorous and sincere self-examination that I formerly called my *Confessions*. I am devoting my last days to studying myself and preparing the account which I shall shortly have to render. *Let us give ourselves over* [*livrons-nous*] entirely to the pleasure of conversing with my soul, since this is the only pleasure that men cannot take away from me" (999, 32, translation altered, emphasis added). The use of the first person plural in the last sentence cited suggests that Rousseau does not write solely for himself. The imperative form suggests an

implied audience who will contemplate his soul with him. For discussions of the audience for autobiography, see Philippe Lejeune, Georges May, and Georges Gusdorf.

14. There have been numerous psychoanalytic readings of Rousseau. For a review of this literature, see E. Pierre Chanover, "Jean-Jacques Rousseau: A Psychoanalytic and Psychological Bibliography." I would argue that paranoid schizophrenia represents a type of mental illness that can arise only in a historical period marked by a particular kind of public sphere. The fear of being followed and watched arises because of Rousseau's *high profile*, and is thus a direct result of the changes in the public sphere.

15. In the eighth book of *Confessions*, he directly associates the rise of the conspiracy against him with his fame and success in the public realm: "So long as I lived unknown to the public, I was loved by all who knew me, and had not a single enemy. But as soon as I had a name I ceased to have friends. That was a very great misfortune. A still greater one was that I was surrounded by people who took the name of friend, and used the rights it gave them only to drag me to my undoing" (362, 338).

16. For an illuminating discussion of this same passage, and the contradictory reading practices that it raises, see Christie V. McDonald, *The Dialogue of Writing*.

17. Rather than publish works never intended for publication, the conspirators at other times either attempt to prevent Jean-Jacques from writing by watering down his ink, or they steal his manuscripts in order to prevent them from being published. "Frenchman: . . . We have recommended to all around him to be especially careful about what he can write. We even tried to remove all the means from him, and in the retreat where we drew him at Dauphiné we succeeded in removing all readable ink from him, so that all that he could find called ink was lightly tinted water, which in little time lost all its color. In spite of all these precautions the rascal still manages to write his memoires that he calls his confessions and that we call his lies: with Indian ink that we didn't think of. But if we cannot prevent him from scribbling on paper at his leisure, at least we prevent him from circulating his venom: for no scrap either little or big, not a note of two lines can leave his hands without falling right away into the hands of the people established to collect everything" (717).

18. See my argument in "Expanding the Social Contract: Rousseau, Gender and the Problem of Judgment," in which I maintain that reading Jean-Jacques requires having a sympathetic bond with the author. The sympathetic reader-judge is able to bond in sympathy with the *true* Jean-Jacques, because she has learned to penetrate false appearances, and to discern the hidden "truth." Cf. David Marshall's reading of the importance of sympathy in *The Surprising Effects of Sympathy*, and "Rousseau and the State of Theater."

19. According to the Frenchman, this sort of manipulation is easy to accomplish because of the nature of the public: "The Frenchman: Oh, the public does not put together ideas one is shrewd enough to present to it separately. It sees him as rich in order to reproach him for acting poor or to defraud him of the fruit of his labor by saying he does not need it. It sees him as poor in order to insult his poverty and treat him like a beggar. It sees him only on whichever side shows him to be most odious or most contemptible at the moment, even though that is incompatible with the other ways in which it sees him at other times" (722).

20. For an excellent detailed discussion of the feud between Hume and Rousseau, see Dena Goodman, "The Hume-Rousseau Affair: From Private *Querelle* to Public *Procès.*" Goodman points out that the progression from private letters to public *trial* by letters helps to define the *reading public* during the eighteenth century.

21. In commenting on Rousseau's claim in the opening of the *Confessions* that he will present himself to God on judgment day with this book in his hand, James Jones has noted the curious reversal of the Christian tradition by Rousseau here: "The work will be such a perfect representation of the man that the two may be viewed as co-equal as well as co-existent: not the 'Verbum factum est' of the Christian tradition manifested in the Gospel accounts of Christ embodying written prophecy, but rather the reverse. Not 'the Word made Flesh', but rather 'The Flesh made Word', a 'Corpus factus est', so to speak" (*Rousseau's Dialogues*, p. 22).

22. Cf. my discussion of Rousseau to Wilda Anderson's discussion of Diderot's criticism of Michel Van Loo's portrait of him in *Diderot's Dream*, pp. 180-82. She maintains that Diderot holds a version of the position that I will argue for—namely, that the *true self* is irreducible, and thus can never be *represented*.

23. For a persuasive reading of Rousseau's *Confessions* asserting that Rousseau both displays and hides himself in his writing, see David Marshall, "Rousseau and the State of Theater." Marshall reads an incident involving a botched experiment that temporarily blinded Rousseau while he was trying to make *sympathetic ink* as a key for reading the *Confessions* as a whole. Marshall writes: "Sympathetic ink provides the language of autobiography because it stands as the only language capable of representing the self. In other words, sympathetic ink not only reveals how the self must be read; it is itself a figure for the self: that which cannot be figured, that which can only be figured" (108). Compare Lejeune's reading of the spanking episode and Starobinski's reading of the broken comb incident for their insight into the dialectic of revealing and concealing.

24. It is not my intention to review all the literary questions posed by autobiography, nor to exhaust all the philosophical paradoxes this form of

writing raises: The task is far too great and excedes the limits established by the questions at hand. For excellent studies of autobiography, see Gusdorf, Lejeune, May, Olney, and Spengemann.

25. Huck Gutman makes a similar point in his Foucaultian reading of the *Confessions*. See "Rousseau's *Confessions*: A Technology of the Self."

26. Shierry Weber's reading of Rousseau's aesthetics ("The Aesthetics of Rousseau's *Pygmalion*") maintains that Rousseau is closer to Kant than Hegel in his conception of the self as finite, and consequently in his elaboration of a "phenomenology of the consciousness of the finite aesthetic subject" (67). More importantly, Weber contends that there is a negative moment within the self, in which "the self is not identical with itself" (69). Weber locates this moment in Pygmalion's desire for Galathée. She contends that in giving his self to Galathée, Pygmalion becomes the other, momentarily negating the self. In this moment of self-negation and union, Weber reads a crucial difference between Rousseau and the absolute subject of German idealism (74-77). Consistent with the moment in the aesthetics when the self is negated in the other, the moment I have located in the autobiographical writings, also entails the negation of the self in the other. In this case, however, the autobiographical representation confronts the self as the aesthetic object with which the self temporarily unites. The significant difference lies in the fact that the aesthetic object in the case of autobiography is clearly an objectification of the subject. Thus, reading Rousseau's autobiographical writings as aesthetic objects, one must conclude that they highlight the negative moment of self-awareness and criticism. Consistent with Weber's reading of Rousseau's "critical aesthetics" (her phrase), the autobiographical writings also exhibit a critique of the absolute subject of German idealism consistent with Adorno's insights.

27. I discuss the implications of this type of dialectic for epistemology and the constitution of subjectivity in the following chapter in conjunction with *D'Alembert's Dream*.

28. See the previous chapters for a discussion of Adorno's critique of the Kantian conception of freedom and its relevance to Rousseau's social theory, specifically with respect to Rousseau's problematic conception of self-consciousness in the state of nature.

29. This reading is consistent with Derrida's own reading of Rousseau in *Of Grammatology*, in which he identifies writing as the *dangerous supplement* that inevitably distances Rousseau from the full presence of self-immediacy. I would agree with Derrida's assertion that ultimately Rousseau realizes that at "the self's very origin" lies the corruption of the self by the other (53, *Jean-Jacques Rousseau*). In other words, that alterity or even mediation by the other is necessary for self-consciousness. However, I do want to distance my own analysis from Derrida's critique of the general

privileging of *presence* in the Western metaphysical tradition. Rather than provide a deconstruction of the metaphysics of consciousness, my analysis seeks to demonstrate the historical determination of Rousseau's specific aversion to the public realm. I would maintain that the difficulty of self-representation in Rousseau does not issue from a metaphysical problem of consciousness but rather from the rise of commodification and the attendant alienation experienced by writers and artists of the Enlightenment period.

30. Robert Elbaz identifies this ideological strain in both Rousseau's political thought and autobiography as a result of his insistence on an atemporal origin.

31. Macpherson links the conception of the possessive individual subject to its ability to acquire property for itself: "The individual, it was thought, is free inasmuch as he is proprietor of his person and capacities. The human essence is freedom from dependence on the wills of others, and freedom is a function of possession. Society consists of relations of exchange between proprietors. . . . It cannot be said that the seventeenth-century concepts of freedom, rights, obligation and justice are all entirely derived from this concept of possession, but it can be shown that they were powerfully shaped by it" (3). This characterization is consistent with Rousseau's insistence on protecting individual autonomy in the *Second Discourse* and clearly contributes to his understanding of the *private* self.

Transitional Interlude

1. In the *Essay on the Origin of Language*, Rousseau claims that the French language is ill suited to public speaking. He cites ancient Greek as an example of a language in which one could address a large audience from a public place (*144*). He even goes so far as to suggest that both the corrupted French language and the degenerate form of government with which it coincides are best adapted for saying "give money" (*143*). This goal is best served, he maintains, by keeping people apart. Thus, the public sphere as gathering place for critical liberal debate existed for Rousseau in ancient Greece and cannot be replicated without radical revolution, both linguistic and political.

2. Ironically, the formation of the public sphere was largely motivated by an interest in protecting private property from tyranny. However, it is necessary to note the difference between Locke and Rousseau on the issue of private property. Whereas Locke maintains that property precedes the social contract, and that the contract in fact protects property rights, Rousseau sees property as part of the corruption of society. As I have argued, the general will protects the public interest against private interests in the *Social Contract*. In this respect Rousseau seems to be aware of the tension between private property and hence private interest on the one hand, and the public good on the other.

3. See Darnton, *Literary Underground*, pp. 35-36.

4. For the booktrade in England, see, Ross. On France, see Darnton (1979, 1982), and Darnton and Roche.

5. I am grateful to Paul Benhamou for an insightful discussion of his current research into subscription libraries.

6. Darnton claims that, "*La Nouvelle Héloïse* was perhaps the biggest best-seller of the century" (*Cat Massacre*, p. 242).

Chapter 4

1. For a thorough and careful study of the emergence of Diderot's materialism out of Cartesian rationalism, see Aram Vartanian, *Diderot and Descartes*.

2. In *The Order of Things: An Archaeology of the Human Sciences*, Foucault distinguishes between mechanistic and vitalistic theories in the eighteenth century. The mechanistic theories he characterizes as closer to the "origins" of the classical age—Descartes and Malebranche—while the vitalistic theories look ahead toward developments in the nineteenth century. He generalizes: "the historians see the emergence, as though before their very eyes, of an opposition between those who believe in the immobility of nature—in the manner of Tournefort, and above all Linnaeus—and those who, with Bonnet, Benoît de Maillet, and Diderot, already have a presentiment of life's creative powers, of its inexhaustible power of transformation, of its plasticity, and of that movement by means of which it envelops all its productions, ourselves included, in a time of which no one is master. Long before Darwin and long before Lamarck, the great debate on evolution would appear to have been opened by the *Telliamed*, the *Palingénésie* and the *Rêve de d'Alembert*" (126-27). Wilda Anderson is careful to distinguish Diderot's *epistemology* from the "clean picture presented by Foucault" (12). Anderson insists that Diderot's work must be understood in context and therefore cautions against the use of terms such as *epistemology*, *science*, and *paradox* without careful definition (ibid.). She maintains that Diderot's materialism "openly combined parts of the sometimes contradictory works of Spinoza and Leibnitz and drew on Newton as well as Descartes. He revived components of Aristotle's theory of forms, linked his own work almost symbiotically with Condillac's, and owed much to Buffon, all the while engaging in close argument with the ideas of La Mettrie and Helvétius" (11).

3. Emmet Kennedy cites Diderot as a turning point in eighteenth-century scientific theory as well as philosophy. He writes: "In 1754 Diderot predicted that 'we are approaching the moment of a great revolution in the

sciences. . . . I would dare almost to assert that before one hundred years are up, we will not count three great geometricians in Europe.' This has often been interpreted as the clue to a change, around mid-century, when a mechanistic, natural philosophy like that of Laplace gave way to a vitalistic biology like that of Lamarck" (63-64). Diderot, nonetheless, owes a tremendous debt to his contemporaries. For a clear discussion of Maupertuis's influence on Diderot, especially on the important concept of *sensibilité*, see Aram Vartanian, "Diderot and Maupertuis." For a discussion of the productive relationship between Diderot and d'Holbach, see Josiane Boulad-Ayoub, "Diderot et d'Holbach: un système matérialiste de la nature."

4. Both Hegel's and Marx's admiration of Diderot is well known. Hegel cites Diderot's *Rameau's Nephew* by name on three occasions in the *Phenomenology of Spirit* as a text that represents the moment of disrupted consciousness; see my discussion of this reading in chapter 5. In a manuscript entitled "Confessions" by Marx's daughter Laura, she cites Diderot as Marx's favorite prose writer (reprinted in Erich Fromm, *Marx's Concept of Man*). Jean Varloot is a bit more guarded in his reading of *D'Alembert's Dream*, although he does recognize that key aspects of Diderot's materialism are indispensible for modern materialism (226-27). See Varloot's introduction to *D'Alembert's Dream*, in *Le Neveu de Rameau/Le Rêve de d'Alembert*. All italicized parenthetical references in chapters 4, 5, and 6 are to Denis Diderot, *Oeuvres complètes*, 19 vols., ed. H. Dieckmann et al., Paris: Hermann, 1990. All references to translations are to *Rameau's Nephew/ D'Alembert's Dream*, trans. Leonard Tancock, London: Penguin, 1966. Where no reference appears, translations are my own.

5. I use the terms *epistemology*, *hermeneutics*, and *critical* all in the modern sense. My project is to read Diderot's epistemology as a forerunner of critical theory. I acknowledge that in so-doing I sacrifice to a large extent a historically contextualized understanding of Diderot's work. I refer the reader to Wilda Anderson's *Diderot's Dream* for an excellent and thorough discussion of Diderot's epistemology in its historical context. While in the present study I lose a contextual appreciation for Diderot's work, I nonetheless gain an understanding of Diderot's importance for the tradition that follows. To cite Wilda Anderson: "What makes his [Diderot's] dream special is that he hoped to do this [teach] not by telling them what to do but by showing them how to figure it out for themselves. Yet surprisingly, his tradition has no intellectual sons, only nephews— only lateral descendents" (6). It is my contention that the German idealist and critical tradition from Kant through Habermas represents these *nephews*.

6. Leibnitz's influence on Diderot is apparent in numerous passages of the *Dream* in which he subscribes to a monadological conception of the universe replete with a nonteleological determinism. D'Alembert exclaims: "In this vast ocean of matter not a single molecule resembles any other, not a single molecule remains for a moment just like itself" (128, 174).

7. To anticipate my negative dialectical analysis comparing Diderot and Adorno at the end of this chapter, compare Jameson's use of the term

flux to characterize the problematization of identity that one finds in Adorno (*Late Marxism: Adorno, or, the Persistence of the Dialectic*). Jameson contrasts identity conceived as neurotic repetition and sameness with "the unrepresentable vision of the ceaseless flow of the absolutely new, the unrepetitive, the great stream which never comes twice and which Deleuze calls the 'flux' of perpetual change" (16) to introduce the question of identity as both one of philosophical concept and a concern with the ego.

8. Oddly, the form-matter distinction begins to breakdown in Diderot's version of materialism. He maintains that while every particular thing is subject to change, the whole nonetheless remains constant. Thus, although the whole may be composed of matter, one cannot consistently maintain that matter merely changes form. Matter changes as well as form, according to Diderot's formulation.

9. See Anderson's contention that Diderot's understanding of chemistry indicates that "his notion of matter excluded the notion of fixed chemical identity" (54).

10. This reading is consistent with Anderson's claim that Diderot prefers to demonstrate rather than explain (3). Her reading of the *Dream* also emphasizes the enactment of his epistemology through the use of literature (42-76). Jacques Proust suggests a similar line of analysis in his contention that early on in the *Encyclopédie* project, Diderot perceived "the fundamental inadequation between represented things and the discourse which was supposed to represent them," in "Diderot et le système des connaissances humaines" (122). Cf. Georges Benrekassa's reading of the article "*Encyclopédie*," "La Pratique philosophique de Diderot dans l'article 'Encyclopédie' de l'*Encyclopédie*." He argues that the organization and writing of the article itself demonstrate a new kind of philosophical writing that is paradigmatic for Diderot's understanding of the *Encyclopédie*. See also Huguette Cohen's and Jean Renaud's similar contentions concerning the limits of literary and/or artistic discourse in the *Salons*: Cohen, "Diderot's Awareness of the Limits of Literature in the *Salons*," and Renaud, "De la théorie à la fiction: les *Salons* de Diderot." Finally, Pierre Saint-Amand links the disputes with d'Alembert over the *Encyclopédie* with a fundamental disagreement concerning the conception of science and scientific truth. Saint-Amand argues that Diderot rejected the static idealism of mathematical models carried into physics, chemistry, and biology. In what pertains to the organization of the *Encyclopédie*, Saint-Amand reads the system of *renvois* as undermining any mathematical order or conception of truth. See *Diderot Le Labyrinthe de la relation*, pp. 24-49, 68-82.

11. Citing a passage from Diderot's correspondence, Elisabeth de Fontenay (*Diderot ou le matérialisme enchanté*) demonstrates how seriously Diderot took this doctrine, even where his own works were concerned: "The reader, the partner in such writings, is thus invited to take with it all possible liberties, 'Dispose of my work as you wish. You are the master to approve, contradict, to add, to subtract'" (231).

12. In this respect Diderot breaks significantly with his contemporaries. Wilda Anderson notes that d'Alembert's "Discours" marks *history* as the enemy. She writes: "The encyclopedia was d'Alembert's tool, therefore, to fight history. The only acceptable change was to be a change that is not really change: the accumulation and uncovering of what was already there, not the creation of something truly new" (91). She contrasts this to Diderot's *dynamic* conception of the project in his article "Encyclopédie," which remains consistent with his epistemological position that I am presenting here.

13. In the *Theses on Feuerbach*, Marx highlights what he perceives to be the missing element in all previous materialist theories. Singling out critical practice, Marx takes Feuerbach to task for emphasizing the theoretical attitude over and above critical-pratical activity. Marx writes: "Hence, in *Das Wesen des Christentums*, he regards the theoretical attitude as the only genuinely human attitude, while practice is conceived and fixed only in its dirty-judaical manifestation. Hence he does not grasp the significance of 'revolutionary,' of practical-critical activity" (143). As we shall see, Diderot's version of materialism does not suffer from this same deficiency. My analysis seeks to show that Diderot anticipates later dialectical materialism by including a critical-practical element in his formulation of the theory.

14. Sigmund Freud, *The Ego and the Id*, trans. James Strachey, New York: W.W. Norton, 1960, p. 44.

15. Freud later describes this same pleasure as the oceanic feeling (*Civilization and its Discontents*), which he recognizes in various religious practices. He ascribes the pleasures offered by religion to the temporary annihilation of self offered through fusion with the deity. In *Group Psychology and the Analysis of the Ego*, this same pleasure fuels the mob mentality. Mobs are formed when individual egos cathect on a charismatic leader, and form a group identity. In *Totem and Taboo*, the pleasure of group identification is explored in the context of *primitive* societies. Freud maintains that tribal identity is reinforced through the consumption of sacrificial totemic animals. The group cathects on the totem and then eats it to solidify the communal bond.

16. In *Beyond the Pleasure Principle*, Freud acknowledges that while the ego is the reservoir of the libido, it is also the seat of the ego instincts. Although they are seemingly at odds with each other, Freud ultimately collapses the distinction between the ego and libidinal instincts. Thus, Freud maintains that the self-preservation instincts have a libidinal character. In this respect, Freud approaches a dialectical understanding of the relationship between the life and death instincts in *Beyond the Pleasure Principle*. However, his account of primary narcissism remains undialectical in its articulation of the relationship between subject and object, as we shall see.

17. Hegel provides perhaps the clearest articulation of the importance of recognition in the dialectical relation between subject and object in the so-called master/slave dialectic. In the *Phenomenology of Spirit*, he succinctly expresses the necessity of the other for any self-consciousness: "Self-consciousness exists in and for itself when, and by the fact that, it so exists for another; that is, it exists only in being acknowledged" (111).

18. Strictly speaking, according to the dialectical theorists such as Hegel, the child subject does not exist either.

19. Anderson also stresses the material conception of thought in Diderot, see esp. her discussion of vibration and sensibility, and her understanding of the relation between intellectual and physical interaction in the dialogue, pp. 49-54 and 62ff. For a discussion of the important and subtle relationship between music and philosophy in Diderot, and particularly the metaphor of the clavichord, see Fontenay, pp. 196-205.

20. I borrow the term *fallibilistic* from Rorty's discussion of scientific models. See Richard Rorty, *Philosophy and the Mirror of Nature*, Princeton: Princeton University Press, 1979. Fallibilism in Diderot entails that there is no ultimate *telos* in his dialectical hermeneutic. In contrast to Hegel, there is no final point of ultimate knowledge for Diderot that would not be subject to revision. The term *hermeneutic holism* I borrow from contemporary discussions in hermeneutics to designate a position that does not allow for any knowledge outside interpretation. Thus, hermeneuticists from Gadamer to Derrida would be included under the general category of hermeneutic holists.

21. Diderot seems to imply something like Kant's synthetic a priori judgment in his analysis of this epistemological problem. Unlike Hume, who only allows for beliefs about matters of fact arising from associations between ideas and habit or custom, Diderot seems to maintain that the formerly blind person would form a synthetic judgment based on his previous conception (rational idea) of the sphere and cube, attained through the sense of touch. Diderot's insistence that tactile verification would not be necessary underscores the synthetic element in this act of judgment. This type of judgment cannot be accounted for by either habit or an association between ideas as Hume would have it, because it involves new sensory input. It does correspond perfectly to the type of transcendental act of judgment that Kant has in mind.

22. See Fontenay's insightful discussion of *La Lettre sur les aveugles*, pp. 157-61.

23. Cf. Andrea Calzolari's discussion of the dialectical hermeneutic in *Le Paradoxe sur le comédien* in "Les Interprétations du paradoxe et les paradoxes de l'interprétation."

24. On this point, Adorno's critique of identitarian thinking resembles many Derridean critiques of mimesis that disclose the nonidentity or difference that philosophical discourse often attempts to conceal. Cf. Nancy, "Le ventriloque," and Lacoue-Labarthe, "Typographie." Derrideans, and Adorno, are quick to forget that both Kant and Hegel recognized the nonidentity in relations of identity. As I have already mentioned, these judgments are synthetic for Kant, and not necessary. For Hegel, they require a dialectical relation between part and whole, individual and universal.

25. I have already used Adorno's critique of identitarian thinking to expose the contradictions inherent in Rousseau's conception of the private self in his autobiographical works. See chapter 3.

26. The distinction between identitarian and nonidentitarian thinking drawn by Adorno to critique idealism also characterizes the distinction between d'Alembert's and Diderot's conceptions of the *Encyclopédie*. Anderson maintains that d'Alembert's notion of *analysis* amounts to a form of reductionism that I would call identitarian. See Wilda Anderson, *Diderot's Dream*, esp. chapter 3.

27. Interestingly, Jacques Proust points out that the *Encyclopédie* was eclectic in its use of taxonomies. He maintains that Diderot's refusal of *tout esprit de système* led him to use various systems for classifying birds, quadrupeds, insects, shells, etc. (125).

28. See Fontenay's formulation: "Diderot, therefore, attempts to think alterity, unbearable to most of the men of his time, as an identity in difference" (96). See also her discussion of the difficulty of establishing and maintaining a conception of sexual difference in Diderot, pp. 101-10, 167-75. Pierre Saint-Amand's discussion of Diderot's critiques of mathematics and his preference for chemistry and biology also highlights the dialectical nature of Diderot's thought, although Saint-Amand does not characterize it in this way. In Diderot's debates with d'Alembert, Saint-Amand reads a critique of idealism and static truths in science. Saint-Amand stresses Diderot's preference for scientific models that reach beyond tautologies, consistent with the negative dialectical model I have established here. See *Diderot Le Labyrinthe de la relation*, pp. 24-49.

29. We have already seen the implications of dialectics in terms of the question of personal identity in the case of Rousseau (chapter 3). The difference between Diderot and Rousseau consists in Diderot's use of a negative dialectical framework, whereas Rousseau continues to deny the relation between the public and the private self. Diderot's position in *D'Alembert's Dream* as well as in other texts does not preclude the dissolution of the traditional subject of philosophy. Perhaps for this reason Lyotard includes him among the postmoderns, see *Au juste*, p. 26.

30. Cf. Jack Undank's reading of Diderot's use of citation and metaphor, *Diderot: Inside, Outside and In-Between*, esp. pp. 28-72.

31. In relation to the continuity/contiguity problem, metaphor represents a form of discontinuity that disrupts continuity in much the same way that the concept of contiguity disturbs a ready notion of continuity. In other words, metaphor works according to a paradigm of discontinuity insofar as it evokes absence and therefore disrupts linear patterns of thought. As the discussion of Diderot and Adorno suggests, metaphor in Diderot disrupts continuity in the same way that negative dialectics resists identitarian thinking and sublation for Adorno. I am especially grateful to Charles Oriel for a discussion of metonymy and metaphor, which brought this connection between metaphor and discontinuity to light.

32. The metaphors also succeed one another in an almost musical linearity that resists totalization in much the same way that melodies do. For a compelling discussion of the importance of music in Diderot's materialism, see Fontenay, and especially her discussion of *Le Neveu de Rameau*.

33. Christie McDonald ("Transforming Thought: Diderot's Displacements") also signals the literary as the site of Diderot's departure from traditional philosophy conceived as *esprit de système*. For McDonald, Diderot's use of literature "rais[es] the question of the very possibility of philosophy."

Chapter 5

1. Hegel's *use* of Diderot presents several interesting questions, among them, what constitutes *citation* in the *Phenomenology of Spirit*. I will not address these issues concerning citation, cooptation, or misrepresentation. For an interesting discussion of Hegel's use of Diderot, see James Hulbert, "Diderot in the Text of Hegel: A Question of Intertextuality." See also Christie McDonald's reading of *Le Neveu de Rameau* in *The Dialogue of Writing: Essays in Eighteenth-Century French Literature*, pp. 89-104, in which she treats the intertextual relation between Diderot and subsequent *interpreters*.

2. I refer the reader to Jean Hyppolite's masterful account of the same sections of the *Phenomenology* in *Genèse et structure de la Phénoménologie de l'esprit de Hegel*, II: 353-412.

3. In chapter 3 I characterized this same historical phenomenon as the emergence of the bourgeois public sphere, adopting and following Habermas's analysis. Habermas and Hegel would seem to be in agreement on this point.

4. Hegel's analysis here prefigures Adorno's insights in *Negative Dialectics*, which I used against Rousseau in chapter 3.

5. As I suggested in the chapters on Rousseau, particularly in my analyses of the *Second Discourse* and the autobiographical works, this dialectic is at work already in the political and social theory of the Enlightenment, even if Rousseau at some level refuses to acknowledge it.

6. The French reads: *de toutes les épithètes la plus redoutable, parce qu'elle marque la médiocrité et le dernier degré du mépris* (Denis Diderot, *Oeuvres complètes*, ed. H. Dieckmann and J. Varloot et al., Paris: Hermann, 1990, 173). All italicized parenthetical references are to this edition.

7. I have already noted Rousseau's concerns with preserving individuality in the face of a ubiquitous and homogeneous culture in the *Second Discourse* and in the autobiographical writings. As I have previously maintained, it is only in the context of a changed public sphere that *individuality* becomes a problem.

8. Wilda Anderson reads the Bertin-Hus household in a similar way. She writes: "The social contract in this minisociety is the following: those who eat pay in flattery and humiliating services for what they eat and spend" (*Diderot's Dream*, p. 214). Her detailed account of the role of money in the dialogue is consistent with Hegel's reading in the *Phenomenology*, see chapter 6. Likewise, Jean Starobinski reads the *pacte tacite* of the Bertin-Hus world as "sadistic and destructive" in "Sur l'emploi du chiasme dans 'Le Neveu de Rameau.'" In this sense, the nephew's worldview and sense of "morality" approach that of the libertines in the work of Sade.

9. The French reads: *Il entassait et brouillait ensemble trentes airs italiens, français, tragiques, comiques, de toutes sortes de caractères; tantôt avec une voix de basse-taille, il descendait jusqu'aux enfers; tantôt s'égosillant, et contrefaisant le fausset, il déchirait le haut des airs, imitant de la démarche, du maintien, du geste, les différents personnages chantants; successivement furieux, radouci, impérieux, ricaneur* (165).

10. Many have faulted Hegel for making a monologic text out of *Rameau's Nephew*. See James Hulbert and Suzanne Gearhart, "The Dialectic and its Aesthetic Other: Hegel and Diderot," and Hans Robert Jauss, "The Dialogical and the Dialectical *Neveu de Rameau*: How Diderot adopted Socrates and Hegel Adopted Diderot." I would agree with Lionel Trilling's asssessment that Hegel tends to overemphasize one side of an ambiguous text, "The Honest Soul and the Disintegrated Consciousness," in *Sincerity and Authenticity*. According to Trilling the text "passes a direct and comprehensively adverse moral judgement upon society," while at the same time suggesting "that moral judgement is not ultimate, that man's nature and destiny are not wholly comprehended within the narrow space between vice and virtue" (31-32). It is the second position that Hegel identifies with the nephew—and with the Enlightenment in general—and which he tends to overvalue at the expense of the first point. Cf. also Elisabeth de Fontenay's assessment that "this totalitarian, reductive, obsessive gloss succeeds in penetrating to the heart of the matter and makes of this text the moment of a decisive philosophico-historical intervention" (210).

11. All translations of Diderot not included within Hegel's text are from *Rameau's Nephew/D'Alembert's Dream*, trans. Leonard Tancock, London: Penguin, 1966.

12. See Jürgen Habermas, *The Structural Transformation of the Public Sphere: An Inquiry into a Category of Bourgeois Society*, and Michel Foucault, *The Order of Things: An Archaeology of the Human Sciences*.

13. Cf. Lukác's reading of the *Phenomenology* in *The Young Hegel: Studies in the Relations between Dialectics and Economics*.

14. Lukács points out that Hegel turns to eighteenth-century French culture in this section to fill a void in German culture, see p. 507.

15. On this point I disagree with Jauss's reading of Hegel's interpretation of Diderot. Jauss maintains that the nephew represents disrupted consciousness and the philosopher represents simple consciousness (25). Consequently, he claims that Hegel's dialectical reading of *Rameau's Nephew* closes off the dialogical openness of the text in favor of what he terms the *monologism* of dialectics (29). According to Jauss, from Hegel's historical vantage point he reconstructs the text in accordance with his own view of history. Similarly, James Hulbert also argues that Hegel's reading subsumes the dialogic into monologism.—I disagree with Jauss and Hulbert not only about the *monologism* of Hegel's reading of Diderot, but also about their reconstruction of the *Phenomenology*. I would maintain that Hegel's reading highlights the dialectical relation between the participants in the dialogue—a relation that implicates them in each other's arguments and positions. Consequently, I do not see the sublation of the dialectic as closure, but merely as a continuation of the struggle.

16. Jean Starobinski has detailed the use of chiasmus by Diderot in the dialogue to demonstrate the shifting positions of *Moi* and *Lui*. See "Sur l'emploi de chiasme dans 'Le Neveu de Rameau.'"

17. The nephew's high aesthetic standards correspond in large measure to Diderot's aesthetic in *Le Paradoxe sur le comédien*. In this work he defends an absolute aesthetic for actors whom he advises to construct an ideal model upon which they ought to base their performances. Responding to the audience or any other contextual variable only relativizes the artistry of the performance. The ideal dramatic performance must be able to be repeated in any context. Thus, good acting is not a question of swaying an audience or being *convincing*. Rather dramatic perfection consists in approaching an ideal model and being able to repeat it. See Andrea Calzolari, "Les Interprétations du paradoxe et les paradoxes de l'interprétation," and Wilda Anderson's discussion of the *modèle idéal* in *Diderot's Dream*, esp. pp. 200-10.

18. This aspect of the nephew's character prompts Suzanne Gearhart ("The Dialectic and its Aesthetic Other") to argue that he represents the aes-

thetic realm. According to her reading, the stand-off between the nephew and the philosopher represents the incommensurability between the aesthetic and ethical realms. This Kantian approach charges Hegel with subsuming the aesthetic into the ethical and finally into the philosophical. Similarly, James Creech allies the nephew with Nietzsche and Artaud in his Derridean reading of the dialogue. See *Diderot: Thresholds of Representation.* My reading emphasizes the ethical dispute between the philosopher and nephew. I would not agree that the nephew represents the purely aesthetic, but rather see the possiblity for his ethical position, albeit relativist, in conflict with the absolutist ethic of the philosopher. See also Starobinski, "Sur l'emploi du chiasme" on the ethical/aesthetic conflict in the dialogue.

19. In chapter 6 I discuss the relation between the moral and aesthetic value spheres during the eighteenth century in conjunction with my discussion of Diderot's *Salons.*

20. Elsewhere I have argued from a deconstructionist position that the two sides of the dialogue are, at some level, indistinguishable. The nephew represents the philosopher's double. See my "The Theatrics of Dialogue: Diderot and the Problem of Representation." Elisabeth de Fontenay even goes so far as to maintain a resemblance between the nephew and Diderot himself; see *Diderot ou le matérialisme enchanté,* p. 226.

21. It is clear that the survival ethic—or some version of an ethic based on self-preservation at all costs—has always existed. In the lower strata of society it was perhaps more common than it was in the upper social echelons. The change I would like to signal here involves the rationalization behind this survival ethic. Capitalism and market relations introduce new possibilities for explaining away exploitation of others. Cf. Fontenay's assertions concerning the importance of hunger and other basic needs for the nephew. She even suggests that he may suffer from tuberculosis, pp. 161-67.

22. The interior quotation is from Bacon, *Advancement of Learning, Works,* Vol. II, p. 126. The Latin reads: "If unequal things are added to equal things, then you have unequal things."

23. In *Negative Dialectics,* Adorno cites the "barter principle" as responsible for both promoting social justice *and* aiding the growth and development of monopolies and hence social injustice. "The barter principle, the reduction of human labor to the abstract universal concept of average working hours, is fundamentally akin to the principle of identification. Barter is the social model of the principle, and without the principle there would be no barter; it is through barter that non-identical individuals and performances become commensurable and identical. The spread of the principle imposes on the whole world an obligation to become identical, to become total. But if we denied the principle abstractly—if we proclaimed, to

the greater glory of the irreducibly qualitative that parity should no longer be the ideal rule—we would be creating excuses for recidivism into ancient injustice. From olden times, the main characteristic of the exchange of equivalents has been that unequal things would be exchanged in its name, that the surplus value of labor would be simply appropriated. If comparability as a category of measure were simply annulled, the rationality which is inherent in the barter principle—as ideology, of course, but also as a promise—would give way to direct appropriation, to force, and nowadays to the naked privilege of monopolies and cliques" (146-67).

24. Marx explains the appearance of exchange value as the commodification of money itself. He writes: "The process is thus simply that the product becomes a commodity, that is, *a pure element of exchange.* Commodities are converted into exchange value. So that it can be identified as exchange value, it is exchanged for a symbol, which represents it as exchange value properly so called. In this symbolic form it can again be exchanged, under certain conditions, for any other goods. When the product becomes a commodity, and the commodity becomes exchange value, it possesses (ideally at first) a double existence. This ideal dual identity necessarily means that the commodity appears in a dual form when actually exchanged: as a natural product on the one hand, as an exchange value on the other. In other words, its exchange value has a material existence, apart from the product. The definition of the product as exchange value necessarily entails that the exchange value leads a separate existence, severed from the product. This exchange value which is severed from the commodity and yet is itself a commodity is—*money*" (59). This account supplements Hegel's suggestive analysis of the relationship between the appearance of the intrinsic value of wealth and the breakdown of social relations during the seventeenth and eighteenth centuries.

25. Max Horkheimer, "Means and Ends," p. 20. Michel Foucault's reading of *Rameau's Nephew* contrasts with Horkheimer's distinction by placing the immediacy of need on the side of *déraison*. See *Histoire de la folie à l'âge classique,* pp. 363-69.

26. Cf. Jacques Proust's fascinating reading of *Rameau's Nephew* in conjunction with Diderot's article "Bas au métier" in the *Encyclopédie,* "De l'*Encyclopédie* au *Neveu de Rameau*: L'Objet et le texte." Proust maintains that the nephew understands the social mechanism and his place in it not unlike Diderot's understanding of the stocking industry from his perspective as author of an *Encyclopédie* article.

27. Fontenay maintains that Diderot diagnoses a crisis of reason that is not inconsistent with my reading here (195). However, I do not agree with her assessment that Hegel's reading sacrifices negativity in favor of positivity and reconciliation, which she does not see in the dialogue. See pp. 210-17.

28. I am grateful to Suzanne Gearhart for pointing out the marginality of the two figures. Robert Darnton's studies of the life on the Parisian equivalent of Grub Street bear out the marked resemblance between philosopher and nephew. Most hack writers—including Diderot—would write anything in order to survive. See "The High Enlightenment and the Low-Life of Literature," in *The Literary Underground of the Old Regime*.

29. In "Means and Ends," Horkheimer points out that the opposition between faith and reason in the Enlightenment led to the separation of the two into separate spheres. This separation of philosophy and religion negated religion's claim to "totality," or effectively *neutralized* its claim to objective truth. Horkheimer further points out that ultimately both philosophy and religion were affected by the conflict: "In reality the contents of both philosophy and religion have been deeply affected by this seemingly peaceful settlement of their original conflict. The philosophers of the Enlightenment attacked religion in the name of reason; in the end what they killed was not the church but metaphysics and the objective concept of reason itself, the source of power of their own efforts. Reason as an organ for perceiving the true nature of reality and determining the guiding principles of our lives has come to be regarded as obsolete. Speculation is synonymous with metaphysics, and metaphysics with mythology and superstition. We might say that the history of reason or enlightenment from its beginnings in Greece down to the present has led to a state of affairs in which even the word reason is suspected of connoting some mythological entity. Reason has liquidated itself as an agency of ethical, moral and religious insight" (17-18). Horkheimer's analysis of the emptying out of reason's objective content and therewith its ethical or moral agency is consistent with the ethical issues raised in *Rameau's Nephew*. As reason acquired a subjective meaning—essentially concerned with means-ends calculation according to Horkheimer—it lost its claim to decide questions of value. These questions of value remain largely unanswered in Diderot's text. But the fact that they remain unanswered signals a significant shift away from objective reason toward subjective reason.

Chapter 6

1. A dialectical relationship between the public and private spheres in the late eighteenth century and continuing through the revolution is also suggested by studies of the pamphlet literature concerning Marie Antoinette and specifically her sexual activities. Sarah Maza speaks of the "privatization of the king of France," beginning with the pamphlet literature linking Louis XV to Madame de Pompadour and Madame Du Barry ("The Diamond Necklace Affair Revisited (1785-86): The Case of the Missing Queen," in *Eroticism and the Body Politic*, p. 68). See also in the same volume Lynn Hunt, "The Many Bodies of Marie Antoinette: Political Pornography and the Problem of the Feminine in the French Revolution."

2. Julie Plax, "Gersaint's Biography of Antoine Watteau: Reading Between and Beyond the Lines," p. 557. For a detailed analysis of the rise of the art public, see Thomas Crow, *Painters and Public Life in Eighteenth-Century Paris*. See also Robert M. Isherwood, *Farce and Fantasy: Popular Entertainment in Eighteenth-Century Paris*, in which he argues that theatrical entertainment and in particular the *spectacles* of the Palais Royal appealed to a very broad audience representing a wide-spectrum of the population after the Duc de Chartres's renovations during the 1780s, pp. 217-49.

3. In *The Structural Transformation of the Public Sphere*, Habermas argues that in allowing for public viewings of paintings, museums tacitly authorize public judgment (40). He specifically cites Diderot's *Salons* as the "first and most significant representative" of "professional art criticism" (ibid.). Although strictly speaking, the Salons were not permanent collections on display, they nonetheless function under the old regime in the way that museums would after the revolution.

4. The problem is compounded by the numerous critics claiming to represent *public opinion* in *libelles* (Crow, pp. 13-14), and by the consequent lack of authority of the Academy to control reception and interpretation.

5. Pidansat de Mairobert, "Lettres sur l'Académie Royale de Sculpture et de Peinture et sur le Salon de 1777," from the *English Spy* news sheet, quoted in Crow, p. 4.

6. For an account of the decline of the state's ability to finance high art and the lucrative trade in the lower genres, see Crow 11-18, 39-44.

7. I would disagree with Pomian on this point concerning the distinction between public and private collections. Pomian hinges the distinction on public access; thus, for him church collections are public, while royal collections are private. I would like to suggest that it makes more sense to conceive the distinction between public and private art in the eighteenth-century context in terms of its consumption and reception. Therefore, for the purposes of my analysis, art that remains tied to public institutions—even if those institutions restrict the general public's access to art—resides in the public sphere. See Krzysztof Pomian, *Collectors and Curiosities: Paris and Venice, 1500-1800*, pp. 267-69.

8. Although I acknowledge the fact that connoisseurs did not come from the middle class, I will nonetheless argue that the practices of collectors are being determined by a capitalist market system. As for the influence of the middle class on the art world, Pomian argues that they are responsible for the eventual turn back to the public sphere. He writes in *Collectors and Curiosities* that "the people who had no access to the new semiophores were the members of the 'middle classes', whose lack of finance stood in the way of their ambitions to become fully-fledged collectors, and their number

increased in step with economic growth and the spread of schooling. It was they, or their spokesmen, and in particular scientists, writers, scholars and artists who had not yet gained the favour of the rich and powerful, who started to press for the opening up of the collections which housed the various different semiophores (books and manuscripts, historical sources, objects) they needed when exercising their professions. And it was to their request that private individuals and those in power responded, firstly by setting up public libraries in the seventeenth century, later by opening museums, even if a certain number of them were, in fact, motivated by religious considerations" (41).

9. See Plax, "Gersaint's Biography of Antoine Watteau," esp. 551-53. Plax describes a "nobility of esprit" composed of people who "collect[ed], appreciat[ed] and [knew] how to talk about art" (552). I would maintain that this aspiration to status through knowledge is one of the hallmark's of the nouveaux riches and most definitely associated with the social-climbing tendencies of the bourgeoisie. For a more general discussion of importance of art dealers in the eighteenth-century French art world, see Joseph Alsop, *The Rare Art Traditions*, and Krzysztof Pomian, *"Marchands, connaisseurs, curieux à Paris au XVIIIe siècle,"* translated and reprinted in *Collectors and Curiosities*, pp. 139-68.

10. According to Weber, specialization occasions the splitting off of domains of knowledge as well as specialization within specific fields. For example, in "Science as a Vocation," he notes that "science has entered a phase of specialization previously unknown and that this will forever remain the case" (134). Thus, the "modern" view of knowledge entails that it will necessarily always be surpassed and remains an extension of the Enlightenment belief in progress (138-39).

11. For Habermas's account of Weber, see "Modernity: An Unfinished Project." For a clear discussion of Habermas's use of Weber, see David Ingram, *Habermas and the Dialectic of Reason*, pp. 43-59.

12. We have already seen this thesis in the work of Adorno and Horkheimer as part of the dialectic of enlightenment. According to them, enlightenment entails the domination of nature by man and consequently the use of instrumental reason. They cite Bacon to mark the beginning of rationalization with respect to the domination of nature.

13. It is interesting to note that natural history collections increased in popularity during the eighteenth century. K. Pomian documents a decline in medal collecting and an increase in shell and other natural history collections. Pomian maintains that while the art collector generally tried to "use his collection as a means of foisting himself onto artists in the capacity of connoisseur, the owner of a natural history collection was seen as providing scholars with a useful aid" (*Collectors and Curiosities*, p. 138).

14. Immanuel Kant, *Critique of Practical Reason*, p. 79.

15. Weber maintains that until art represents a domain of separate values, it is not fully distinct from the moral sphere. He writes in "Religious Rejections of the World and their Directions": "The development of intellectualism and the rationalization of life change this situation. For under these conditions, art becomes a cosmos of more and more consciously grasped independent values which exist in their own right. Art takes over the function of this-worldly salvation, no matter how this may be interpreted. It provides a *salvation* from the routines of everyday life, and especially from the increasing pressures of theoretical and practical rationalism" (*From Max Weber*, p. 342). Following and expanding on Weber, Habermas recognizes four distinct stages in the progressive separation of the aesthetic realm that correspond to Weber's rationalization thesis. David Ingram ("Habermas on Aesthetics and Rationality: Completing the Project of Enlightenment") explains Habermas's account of the progression: "The Renaissance . . . marked the removal of art from the public domain of religious cult into markets for private consumption. The beautiful is now constituted as a distinct value; complex stringed and wind instruments are invented; and scientific and mathematical principles are deployed in the pictoral representation of linear and atmospheric perspective, the engineering and construction of new architectural forms, and in the development of musical notation and harmony. Next Habermas notes that toward the end of the eighteenth century, popular literature, music and other fine arts, were publically institutionalized—outside of courtly and religious life—in museums, theatres, concert halls, and literary magazines. . . . The next wave, late romanticism, gave birth to aestheticism (art for art's sake) and a corresponding hedonistic counterculture which encouraged the separation of artistic production and critique from the popular demands of the marketplace. This resulted in the redirection of artistic aims away from representation and moral enlightenment toward expression" (70).

16. See K. Pomian, *Collectors and Curiosities*, esp. pp. 159-61.

17. See Mary D. Sheriff, *Fragonard: Art and Eroticism*, pp. 5-9. This is also consistent with Pomian's thesis discussed above. Even during the second half of the century, Diderot's *Salons* represent the earlier *aesthetic* appreciation for art.

18. It may be argued that Kant's *Third Critique* presents two distinct and incompatible aesthetic theories. The one maintains that judgments of the beautiful serve the good, the other purely formal aesthetic theory allows for purely aesthetic judgments. Kant's formulation of the formalist theory, however, remains so formal to be nearly vacuous. According to this reading of Kant, the disinterested subject perceives "purposiveness without purpose" (55) in the object that produces the judgment of the beautiful. In fact, it is the free play between the faculties of the imagination and understand-

ing in the representation of the object to consciousness that produces the judgment of the beautiful. Kant maintains that a feeling of pleasure accompanies the judgment of the beautiful, which I would maintain resembles the "intellectual feeling" he describes in the *Second Critique* as respect for the moral law.

19. See Crow, *Painters and Public Life*, on the art criticism *industry* in pamphlets and other literature, esp. pp. 7-11, 79-103.

20. In this sense, although they aspire to noble rank, the connoisseurs use bourgeois means to get there. On this point I would disagree with Pomian's assessment that art in collections is by definition without exchange or use value. In the social game of one-upmanship, art clearly has a use value based in part on its exchange value, despite the fact that it remains out of circulation. See *Collectors and Curiosities*, esp. pp. 26-44.

21. According to Pomian, the growth in the number of collectors rose from 150 between 1700 and 1720 to 500 between 1750 and 1790. Coinciding with the rise in number of collectors is an increase in the number of public sales and a rise in prices. See *Collectors and Curiosities*, pp. 159-61. Thus, Diderot's complaints in 1767 are consistent with Pomian's dating of the shift.

22. This passage is reproduced in the Seznec and Adhémar edition only (Oxford: Clarendon Press, 1975).

23. For a fascinating discussion of the problem of *use value* with respect to objects in collections, see Pomian, *Collectors and Curiosities*, p. 10. Pomian maintains that objects in collections are by definition not usable since they are "permanently or temporarily out of the economic circuit," (11). He also distinguishes between objects possessing usefulness and those possessing meaning (30), characteristics he finds to be mutually exclusive. For Diderot, art seems to have a use value in relation to its moral value, but not a use value in the ordinary sense of the term.

24. Diderot himself was well acquainted with the art world of collectors and experts. Pomian cites Diderot's correspondence indicating that while negotiating the purchase of a well-known collection for Catherine II, he employed three experts to help establish the value of the works. See Pomian, *Collectors and Curiosities*, pp. 153-54.

25. For a fascinating discussion of Diderot's *obsession* with Boucher, see Jean Renaud, "De la théorie à la fiction: les *Salons* de Diderot."

26. Sheriff points out that Diderot's aesthetics ties mannered art to decadent art, thus reserving the possibility for nondecadent art in another style. His assessment of technique is directly related to his moral judgment of art. See *Fragonard: Art and Eroticism*, pp. 5-6.

27. Pomian uses the distinction between the mind and the hand to illuminate the shift in emphasis among collectors and dealers he dates at mid-century. Catalogues before 1750 emphasize aesthetic criteria over attribution and also privilege collectors' opinions over those of art dealers. After 1750, catalogues underscore attribution and equate expertise with ability to determine attribution, thus identifying dealers as experts. Writing specifically about Diderot and his efforts to negotiate a large purchase for Catherine II, Pomian explains, "even someone as competent as Diderot was shown to be incapable of verifying dealers' estimates, even though he was considerably better equipped for appreciating the merits of pictures and discussing them" (*Collectors and Curiosities*, p. 155). As I will demonstrate, Diderot's use of aesthetic and moral criteria to stem the tide of the commodification of art is a return to a notion of expertise defined by Pomian as ability to "talk cogently about paintings" [*tenir un discours*] (p. 154, "Marchands, connoisseurs, curieux," p. 29) characteristic of the first half of the century.

28. The tension between the commodification of art that effectively broadens the art public and thus serves the liberal and egalitarian interests of the bourgeoisie and the desire to preserve the value of art by linking it to the moral private sphere, anticipates the rift in the Frankfurt School over questions concerning popular culture, mass culture, high art, and the culture industry. On the one hand, Benjamin's ambivalent though largely positive reading of the deauraticization of art coincides with the positive effects of public and even mass culture. On the other hand, Adorno's extreme pessimism concerning the culture industry and his belief in the critical power of only "the most esoteric and incomprehensible works of art" (Jay, "Habermas and Modernism," p. 128) coincides with the attempt to preserve an autonomous aesthetic realm. For Jay, Habermas's attempt to suggest an eventual reintegration of the three value spheres creates a theoretical position somewhere between Benjamin and Adorno. My reading of the historical appearance of the aesthetic realm during the eighteenth century suggests that adjustments need to be made in contemporary theory, specifically with respect to the mode of separation of the spheres. If the rationalization of the aesthetic sphere was only possible through its successive rationalization in cognitive-instrumental and moral-practical terms, then perhaps the reintegration that Habermas calls for is already part of the process of its historical emergence. In other words, the aesthetic realm could only be understood as specifically aesthetic and expressive after it had been understood as both a commodity and as a source of moral value. The separation of the spheres may in fact be the dialectical reversal of their intimate historical connection.

29. Diderot's complaints here anticipate the establishment of public collections in museums due in part to pressure from the bourgeoisie. See Pomian, *Collectors and Curiosities*, esp. 34-44, 261-75. But he also seems wary, given the conditions in the Salons, of placing his trust in public exhibitions where judgment is as poorly guided as it is in collectors' homes.

30. Of course all these attempts to *naturalize* art appear to the twentieth-century audience as the height of artifice. Prologues that proclaim that a manuscript was found in a wall, maintain the authenticity of an exchange of letters, or insist that the "author" is merely a translator, are the literary equivalent of paintings that negate the spectator's presence.

31. Kant does say that aesthetic judgment may be cultivated to serve the good. Strictly speaking, however, his conception of aesthetic judgment as part of a priori subjective experience need not be influenced by any social norms.

32. Jean-Luc Nancy ("L'offrande sublime") argues that it is the infinite nature of the faculty of the imagination combined with reason's attempt to limit the perception of the sublime that results in the mingling of pleasure and pain in judgments of the sublime. For Nancy, it is the subject itself that is sublime and not the object perceived (90). Michel Delon also draws a parallel between the sublime and the creative artist in his reinterpretation of the religious sublime through materialism. See "Le Sublime et l'idée d'énergie: De la théologie au matérialisme."

33. In a broader sense, Kant links disinterestedness to moral autonomy in a classically bourgeois conception of a theory of right. In order to have the proper moral respect for human beings, Kant maintains that they must be viewed as ends in themselves and not means to an end.

Conclusion

1. The distinction between the class's empirical existence and its theoretical articulation parallels the double premise of Habermas's *Structural Transformation of the Public Sphere*. On the one hand, he asserts that the bourgeois public sphere actually did exist as an arena for rational, critical discussion. On the other hand, he maintains that this public sphere is a normative ideal of bourgeois liberal theory. See Keith Michael Baker, "Defining the Public Sphere in Eighteenth-Century France: Variations on a Theme by Habermas."

Selected Bibliography

Adorno, Theodor W. "Freudian Theory and the Pattern of Fascist Propaganda." *Critical Theory: The Essential Readings.* Ed. David Ingram and Julia Simon-Ingram. New York: Paragon House, 1991: 84-102.

——— . *Negative Dialectics.* Trans. E.B. Ashton. New York: Continuum, 1973.

Alsop, Joseph. *The Rare Art Traditions.* Bollingen Series 35. New York: Harper and Row, 1982.

Althusser, Louis. "*The Social Contract* (The Discrepancies)." *Jean-Jacques Rousseau.* Ed. Harold Bloom. New York: Chelsea House, 1988.

Anderson, Wilda. *Diderot's Dream.* Baltimore: Johns Hopkins University Press, 1990.

Arendt, Hannah. *The Origins of Totalitarianism.* San Diego: Harcourt, Brace Jovanovich, 1973.

Ariès, Philippe. *L'Enfant et la vie familiale sous l'Ancien Régime.* Paris: Seuil, 1973.

Attali, Jacques. *Noise: The Political Economy of Music.* Trans. Brian Massumi. Minneapolis: University of Minnesota Press, 1985.

Baczko, Bronislaw. *Rousseau: Solitude et communauté.* Trans. Claire Brendhel-Lamhout. Paris: Mouton, 1974.

Baker, Keith Michael. "Defining the Public Sphere in Eighteenth-Century France: Variations on a Theme by Habermas." *Habermas and the Public Sphere.* Ed. Craig Calhoun. Cambridge: MIT Press, 1992: 181-211.

Barnard, F.M. "National Culture and Political Legitimacy: Herder and Rousseau." *Journal of the History of Ideas.* 1983 Apr.-June, vol. 44(2): 231-53.

Bell, David A. "The 'Public Sphere,' the State, and the World of Law in Eighteenth-Century France." *French Historical Studies.* Vol. 17, no. 4. Fall 1992: 912-34.

Bellanger, Claude, Jacques Godechot, Pierre Guiral, and Fernand Terrou. *Histoire générale de la presse française*. 5 vols. Paris: Presses Universitaires de France, 1969.

Benjamin, Walter. *Illuminations*. Ed. Hannah Arendt. Trans. Harry Zohn. New York: Harcourt, Brace and World, 1968.

Bennett, Tony. *Outside Literature*. London: Routledge, 1990.

Benrekassa, Georges. "La Pratique philosophique de Diderot dans l'article 'Encyclopédie' de l'*Encyclopédie*." *Stanford French Review*. 1984 Fall. Vol. 8(2-3): 189-212.

Berger, John. *Ways of Seeing*. New York: Penguin, 1972.

Blum, Carol. *Rousseau and the Republic of Virtue: The Language of Politics in the French Revolution*. Ithaca: Cornell University Press, 1986.

Boulad-Ayoub, Josiane. "Diderot et d'Holbach: un système matérialiste de la nature." *Dialogue: Canadian Philosophical Review/Revue Canadienne de Philosophie*. 1985 Spring. Vol. 24(1): 59-89.

Bürger, Peter. *Theory of the Avant-Garde*. Trans. Michael Shaw. Minneapolis: University of Minnesota Press, 1984.

Burke, Peter. *The Fabrication of Louis XIV*. New Haven: Yale University Press, 1992.

Calzolari, Andrea. "Les Interprétations du paradoxe et les paradoxes de l'interprétation." *Interpreter Diderot aujourd'hui*. Ed. Elisabeth de Fontenay and Jacques Proust. Paris: Sycamore, 1984: 117-29.

Caplan, Jay. *Framed Narratives: Diderot's Genealogy of the Beholder*. Minneapolis: University of Minnesota Press, 1985.

Cassirer, Ernst. *The Question of Jean-Jacques Rousseau*. Ed. and trans. Peter Gay. 2d ed. New Haven: Yale University Press, 1989.

Chanover, E. Pierre. "Jean-Jacques Rousseau: A Psychoanalytic and Psychological Bibliography." *American Imago*. 31 (1974):95-100.

Chartier, Roger. *The Cultural Origins of the French Revolution*. Trans. Lydia G. Cochrane. Durham: Duke University Press, 1991.

———. *The Cultural Uses of Print in Early Modern France*. Trans. Lydia G. Cochrane. Princeton: Princeton University Press, 1987.

Charvet, John. *The Social Problem in the Philosophy of Rousseau*. Cambridge: Cambridge University Press, 1974.

Chaussinand-Nogaret, Guy. "Aux Origines de la révolution: noblesse et bourgeoisie." *Annales: Economies, Sociétés, Civilisations.* Vol. XXX, 1975: 265-78.

Cobban, Alfred. *Aspects of the French Revolution.* London: Paladin, 1971.

———. *Rousseau and the Modern State.* London: George Allen & Unwin, 1964.

Cohen, Huguette. "Diderot's Awareness of the Limits of Literature in the Salons." *Studies on Voltaire and the Eighteenth Century.* 1989. Vol. 264: 1172-74.

Comninel, George C. *Rethinking the French Revolution: Marxism and the Revisionist Challenge.* London: Verso, 1987.

Creech, James. *Diderot: Thresholds of Representation.* Columbus: Ohio State University Press, 1986.

Crocker, Lester G. *Jean-Jacques Rousseau.* 2 vols. New York: Macmillan, 1968.

Crow, Thomas. *Painters and Public Life in Eighteenth-Century Paris.* New Haven: Yale University Press, 1985.

Darnton, Robert. *The Business of Enlightenment: A Publishing History of the Encyclopédie 1775-1800.* Cambridge: Harvard University Press, 1979.

———. *The Great Cat Massacre and Other Episodes in French Cultural History.* New York: Vintage Books, 1984.

———. *The Literary Underground of the Old Regime.* Cambridge: Harvard University Press, 1982.

———, and Daniel Roche, Eds. *Revolution in Print: The Press in France 1775-1800.* Berkeley: University of California Press, 1989.

Davis, Natalie Zemon. *Society and Culture in Early Modern France.* Stanford: Stanford University Press, 1975.

Delon, Michel. "Le sublime et l'idée d'énergie: De la théologie au matérialisme." *Revue d'histoire littéraire de la France.* 1986. Vol. 86(1): 62-70.

Derrida, Jacques. *Dissemination.* Trans. Barbara Johnson. Chicago: University of Chicago Press, 1981.

———. *Of Grammatology.* Trans. Gayatri Spivak. Baltimore: Johns Hopkins University Press, 1976, ". . . That Dangerous Supplement . . ." reprinted in *Jean-Jacques Rousseau.* Ed. Harold Bloom. New York: Chelsea House, 1988.

Diderot, Denis. *Le Neveu de Rameau/Le Rêve de d'Alembert.* Ed. Roland Desné and Jean Varloot. Paris: Messidor/Editions sociales, 1984.

————. *Oeuvres complètes*. 19 vols. to date. Ed. H. Dieckmann and J. Varloot et al. Paris: Hermann, 1990.

————. *Rameau's Nephew/D'Alembert's Dream*. Trans. Leonard Tancock. London: Penguin, 1966.

————. *Salons*. Ed. Jean Seznec. Oxford: Clarendon Press, 1979.

Doyle, William. *Origins of the French Revolution*. Oxford: Oxford University Press, 1980.

Eisenstein, Elizabeth. *Print Culture and Enlightenment Thought*. Chapel Hill: University of North Carolina Press, 1986.

————. *The Printing Revolution in Early Modern Europe*. Cambridge: Cambridge University Press, 1983.

————. "Who Intervened in 1788?" *Annales: Economies, Sociétés, Civilisations*. Vol. LXXI, 1975: 77-103.

Elbaz, Robert. "Autobiography and Political Theory in Rousseau." *Neohelicon*, 1985. vol. 12(2):9-33.

Ellenburg, Stephen. "Rousseau and Kant: Principles of Political Right." *Rousseau after Two Hundred Years: Proceedings of the Cambridge Bicentennial Colloquium*. Ed. R.A. Leigh. Cambridge: Cambridge University Press, 1982:3-35.

Febvre, Lucien, and Henri-Jean Martin. *L'apparition du livre*. Paris: Albin Michel, 1971.

Ferrara, Alessandro. *Modernity and Authenticity: A Study of the Social and Ethical Thought of Jean-Jacques Rousseau*. Albany: State University of New York, 1993.

Fontenay, Elisabeth de. *Diderot ou le matérialisme enchanté*. Paris: Editions Grasset et Fasquelle, 1981.

Fort, Bernadette. "Voice of the Public: The Carnivalization of Salon Art in Prerevolutionary France." *Eighteenth-Century Studies*. Spring 1989. Vol. 22(3): 368-94.

Foucault, Michel. *Histoire de la folie à l'âge classique*. Paris: Gallimard, 1972.

————. *Histoire de la sexualité: La volonté de savoir*. Paris: Gallimard, 1976.

————. *The Order of Things: An Archaeology of the Human Sciences*. New York: Random House, 1970.

————. *Surveiller et punir: Naissance de la prison*. Paris: Gallimard, 1975.

Fraser, Nancy. "What's Critical About Critical Theory? The Case of Habermas and Gender." *Feminism as Critique*. Ed. Seyla Benhabib and Drucilla Cornell. Minneapolis: University of Minnesota Press, 1987.

Freud, Sigmund. *The Standard Edition of the Complete Psychological Works of Sigmund Freud*. 24 vols. Ed. and trans. James Strachey. London: Hogarth Press, 1955.

Fried, Michael. *Absorption and Theatricality: Painting and Beholder in the Age of Diderot*. Berkeley: University of California Press, 1980.

Fromm, Erich. *Marx's Concept of Man*. New York: Frederick Ungar: 1966.

Galle, Roland. "Sociopsychological Reflections on Rousseau's Autobiography." *New Literary History: A Journal of Theory and Interpretation*. 1986 Spring. Vol. 17(3):555-71.

Gearhart, Suzanne. "The Dialectic and its Aesthetic Other: Hegel and Diderot." *MLN*. Vol. 101/no. 5, Dec. 1986:1042-66.

————. *The Open Boundary of History and Fiction: A Critical Approach to the French Enlightenment*. Princeton: Princeton University Press, 1984.

Goodman, Dena. "Enlightenment Salons: The Convergence of Female and Philosophic Ambitions." *Eighteenth-Century Studies*. Spring 1989. Vol 22(3): 329-50.

————. "The Hume-Rousseau Affair: From Private *Querelle* to Public *Procès*." *Eighteenth-Century Studies*. Vol. 25/no. 2, Winter 1991-92:171-201.

————. "Pigalles's *Voltaire nu*: The Republic of Letters Represents Itself to the World." *Representations* 16 (Fall 1986): 86-109.

Gordon, Daniel. "Philosophy, Sociology, and Gender in the Enlightenment Conception of Public Opinion." *French Historical Studies*. Vol. 17, no. 4. Fall 1992: 882-911.

————. "'Public Opinion' and the Civilizing Process: The Example of Morellet." *Eighteenth-Century Studies*. Spring 1989. Vol. 22(3): 302-28.

Gurian, Waldemar. "Totalitarianism as Political Religion." *Totalitarianism*. Ed. Carl J. Friedrich. Cambridge: Harvard University Press, 1954: 119-29.

Gusdorf, Georges. *Auto-bio-graphie: Lignes de vie 2*. Paris: Editions Odile Jacob, 1991.

Gutman, Huck. "Rousseau's Confessions: A Technology of the Self." *Technologies of the Self: A Seminar with Michel Foucault*. Ed. Luther H. Martin, Huck Gutman, Patrick H. Hutton. Amherst: University of Massachusetts Press, 1988: 99-120.

Habermas, Jürgen. *Legitimation Crisis*. Trans. Thomas McCarthy. Boston: Beacon Press, 1975.

———. "Modernity: An Unfinished Project." *Critical Theory: The Essential Readings*. Ed. David Ingram and Julia Simon-Ingram. New York: Paragon House, 1991.

———. *The Structural Transformation of the Public Sphere: An Inquiry into a Category of Bourgeois Society*. Trans. Thomas Burger with the assistance of Frederick Lawrence. Cambridge: MIT Press, 1989.

———. *The Theory of Communicative Action*. Trans. Thomas McCarthy. 2 vols. Boston: Beacon Press, 1984.

Hegel, Georg Wilhelm Friedrich. *Phenomenology of Spirit*. Trans. A.V. Miller. Oxford: Oxford University Press, 1977.

Higonnet, Patrice. *Sister Republics: The Origins of French and American Republicanism*. Cambridge: Harvard University Press, 1988.

Hobbes, Thomas. *De Cive or The Citizen*. Ed. Sterling P. Lamprecht. New York: Appleton-Century-Crofts, 1949.

Horkheimer, Max. *Eclipse of Reason*. New York: Continuum, 1947.

Horkheimer, Max, and Theodor Adorno. *The Dialectic of Enlightenment*. Trans. John Cumming. New York: Continuum, 1972.

Hulbert, James. "Diderot in the Text of Hegel: A Question of Intertextuality." *Studies in Romanticism*. Vol. 22, No. 2, 1983 Summer: 267-91.

Hunt, Lynn. Ed. *Eroticism and the Body Politic*. Baltimore: Johns Hopkins University Press, 1991.

———. *Politics, Culture and Class in the French Revolution*. Berkeley: University of California Press, 1984.

Hyppolite, Jean. *Genèse et structure de la Phénoménologie de l'esprit de Hegel*. 2 vols. Paris: Aubier, Editions Montaigne, 1946.

Ingram, David. *Habermas and the Dialectic of Reason*. New Haven: Yale University Press, 1987.

———. "Habermas on Aesthetics and Rationality: Completing the Project of Enlightenment." *The Aesthetics of the Critical Theorists: Benjamin, Marcuse, Adorno and Habermas*. Lewiston, New York: Edwin Mellen Press, 1990. Reprinted in *New German Critique*. No. 53. Spring/Summer 1991: 67-103.

Isherwood, Robert M. *Farce and Fantasy: Popular Entertainment in Eighteenth-Century Paris*. Oxford: Oxford University Press, 1986.

Jameson, Fredric. *Late Marxism: Adorno, or, the Persistence of the Dialectic*. London: Verso, 1990.

Jauss, Hans Robert. "The Dialogical and the Dialectical *Neveu de Rameau*: How Diderot Adopted Socrates and Hegel Adopted Diderot." *Center for Hermeneutical Studies Berkeley Protocol of the Forty-fifth Colloquy*. 27 Feb. 1983. Ed. William R. Herzog II.

Jay, Martin. *Adorno*. Cambridge: Harvard University Press, 1984.

———. "Habermas and Modernism." *Habermas and Modernity*. Ed. Richard J. Bernstein. Cambridge: MIT Press, 1985: 125-39.

Jones, James F., Jr. *Rousseau's Dialogues: An Interpretive Essay*. Geneva: Droz, 1991.

Kant, Immanuel. *Critique of Judgement*. Trans. J.H. Bernard. New York: Hafner Press, 1951.

———. *Critique of Practical Reason*. Trans. Lewis White Beck. New York: Macmillan, 1985.

Kavanagh, Thomas M. *Writing the Truth: Authority and Desire in Rousseau*. Berkeley: University of California Press, 1987.

Kennedy, Emmet. *A Cultural History of the French Revolution*. New Haven: Yale University Press, 1989.

Labrosse, Claude, and Pierre Retat. *L'Instrument périodique: La fonction de la presse au XVIIIe siècle*. Lyon: Presses Universitaires de Lyon, 1985.

Lacoue-Labarthe, Philippe. "Typographie." *Mimesis des articulations*. Paris: Flammarion, 1975.

Landes, Joan. *Women and the Public Sphere in the Age of the French Revolution*. Ithaca: Cornell University Press, 1988.

Lefebvre, Georges. *The Coming of the French Revolution. 1789*. Princeton: Princeton University Press, 1947.

Lefort, Claude. *The Political Forms of Modern Society: Bureaucracy, Democracy, Totalitarianism*. Ed. and trans. John B. Thompson. Cambridge: MIT Press, 1986.

Lejeune, Philippe. *Le Pacte autobiographique*. Paris: Seuil, 1975.

Locke, John. *Treatise of Civil Government and A Letter Concerning Toleration*. Ed. Charles L. Sherman. New York: Appleton-Century-Crofts, 1937.

Lucas, Colin. "Nobles, Bourgeois and the Origins of the French Revolution." *Past and Present*. Vol. 60, 1973: 84-126.

Lukács, Georg. *The Young Hegel: Studies in the Relations between Dialectics and Economics*. Trans. Rodney Livingstone. Cambridge: MIT Press, 1975.

Lyotard, Jean-François, and Jean-Loup Thébaud. *Au juste*. Paris: Christian Bourgois, 1979.

Macpherson, C.B. *The Political Theory of Possessive Individualism: Hobbes to Locke*. Oxford: Oxford University Press, 1962.

Marcuse, Herbert. *Eros and Civilization: A Philosophical Inquiry into Freud*. Boston: Beacon Press, 1966.

———. *One-Dimensional Man*. Boston: Beacon Press, 1964.

Marejko, Jan. *Jean-Jacques Rousseau et la dérive totalitaire*. Lausanne: Editions L'Age d'Homme, 1984.

Marin, Louis. *Portrait of the King*. Trans. Martha M. Houle. Minneapolis: University of Minnesota Press, 1988.

Marshall, David. "Rousseau and the State of Theater." *Representations*. 1986 Winter. Vol. 13: 84-14.

———. *The Surprising Effects of Sympathy: Marivaux, Diderot, Rousseau and Mary Shelley*. Chicago: University of Chicago Press, 1988.

Marx, Karl. *The Grundrisse*. Ed. and trans. David McLellan. New York: Harper and Row, 1971.

———. *The Marx-Engels Reader*. Ed. Robert C. Tucker. 2nd ed. New York: W.W. Norton, 1978.

Marx, Karl, and Frederick Engels. *The German Ideology*. Ed. C.J. Arthur. New York: International Publishers, 1970.

Masters, Roger D. *The Political Philosophy of Rousseau*. Princeton: Princeton University Press, 1968.

May, Georges. *L'Autobiographie*. Paris: Presses Universitaires de France, 1979.

Maza, Sarah. "Le Tribunal de la nation: Les Mémoires judiciaires et l'opinion publique à la fin de l'Ancien Régime." *Annales Economies, Sociétés, Civilisations*. January-February 1987: 73-90.

———. "Women, the Bourgeoisie, and the Public Sphere: Response to Daniel Gordon and David Bell." *French Historical Studies*. Vol. 17, no. 4. Fall 1992: 935-50.

McDonald, Christie V. *The Dialogue of Writing: Essays in Eighteenth-Century French Literature.* Waterloo, Ontario: Wilfrid Laurier University Press, 1984.

————. "Transforming Thought: Diderot's Displacements." *Dilemmes du roman: Essays in Honor of Georges May.* Ed. Catherine Lafarge. Saratoga, Calif.: Anma Libri, 1990: 89-97.

Nancy, Jean-Luc. "L'offrande sublime." *Poésie.* 1984. No. 30: 76-103.

————. "Le ventriloque." *Mimesis des articulations.* Paris: Flammarion, 1975.

Olney, James. *Metaphors of Self: The Meaning of Autobiography.* Princeton: Princeton University Press, 1972.

Ozouf, Mona. "'Public Opinion' at the End of the Old Regime." *Journal of Modern History.* 60 (September 1988): S1-21.

Pappas, John. "Les Considérations sur Le gouvernement de Pologne et le Contrat social: contradiction ou adaptation?" *Rousseau et Voltaire en 1978: Actes du Colloque international de Nice.* (juin 1978). Geneva: Slatkine. 1981:127-32.

Pestieau. Joseph. "Peuples sans Etat et sans histoire; réflexions sur le conservatisme et sur Rousseau." *Dialogue: Canadian Philosophical Review/Revue Canadienne de Philosophie.* 1982 Sept. Vol. 21(3): 473-82.

Plax, Julie. "Gersaint's Biography of Antoine Watteau: Reading Between and Beyond the Lines." *Eighteenth-Century Studies.* Vol. 25, no. 4 (Summer 1992): 545-60.

Pomian, Krzysztof. *Collectors and Curiosities: Paris and Venice, 1500-1800.* Cambridge: Polity Press, 1990.

————. "Marchands, connaisseurs, curieux à Paris au XVIIIe siècle." *Revue de l'Art.* 43, 1979: 23-36.

Popkin, Jeremy. "Pamphlet Journalism at the End of the Old Regime." *Eighteenth-Century Studies.* Spring 1989. Vol. 22(3): 351-67.

Proust, Jacques. "De l'*Encyclopédie* au *Neveu de Rameau*: L'objet et le texte." *Recherches nouvelles sur quelques écrivains des Lumières.* Geneva: Droz, 1972.

————. "Diderot et le système des connaissances humaines." *Studies on Voltaire and the Eighteenth Century.* 1988. Vol. 256: 117-27.

Renaud, Jean. "De la théorie à la fiction: les *Salons* de Diderot." *Studies on Voltaire and the Eighteenth Century.* 1982. Vol. 201: 143-62.

Richet, Denis. "Autour des origines idéologiques lointaines de la Révolution française." *Annales: Economies, Sociétés, Civilisations.* Vol. 24, 1969: 1-23.

Ross, Trevor. "Copyright and the Invention of Tradition." *Eighteenth-Century Studies.* Vol. 26, no. 1 (Fall 1992): 1-27.

Rousseau, Jean-Jacques. *The Confessions of Jean-Jacques Rousseau.* Trans. J. M. Cohen. London: Penguin Books, 1953.

———. *Essai sur l'origine des langues où il est parlé de la mélodie et de l'imitation musicale.* Paris: Gallimard, 1990.

———. *Oeuvres complètes.* Ed. B. Gagnebin and M. Raymond. 4 vols. Paris: Gallimard, Bibliothèque de la Pléiade, 1959.

———. *Reveries of the Solitary Walker.* Trans. Peter France. London: Penguin Books, 1979.

———. *On the Social Contract with Geneva Manuscript and Political Economy.* Ed. Roger D. Masters. Trans. Judith R. Masters. New York: St. Martin's Press, 1978.

———. *The Social Contract and Discourse on the Origin of Inequality.* Ed. and trans. Lester G. Crocker. New York: Simon and Schuster, 1967.

Sade, Donatien-Alphonse-François, Marquis de. *Justine ou les malheurs de la vertu.* Paris: Livre de poche, 1973.

Saint-Amand, Pierre. *Diderot Le Labyrinthe de la relation.* Paris: Vrin, 1984.

Schwartz, Joel. *The Sexual Politics of Jean-Jacques Rousseau.* Chicago: University of Chicago Press, 1984.

Sheriff, Mary D. *Fragonard: Art and Eroticism.* Chicago: University of Chicago Press, 1990.

Shklar, Judith N. *Men and Citizens: A Study of Rousseau's Social Theory.* Cambridge: Cambridge University Press, 1969.

Simon-Ingram, Julia. "Expanding the Social Contract: Rousseau, Gender and the Problem of Judgment." *Comparative Literature.* Vol. 43, no. 2 (Spring 1991):134-49.

———. "The Theatrics of Dialogue: Diderot and the Problem of Representation." *Compendious Conversations: The Method of Dialogue in the Early Enlightenment.* Ed. Kevin L. Cope. Frankfurt: Lang International, 1991: 357-67.

Snyders, *La Pédagogie en France aux XVIIe et XVIIIe siècles.* Paris: Presses Universitaires de France, 1965.

Spengemann, William C. *The Forms of Autobiography: Episodes in the History of a Literary Genre*. New Haven: Yale University Press, 1980.

Starobinski, Jean. "L'Incipit du 'Neveu de Rameau.'" *La Nouvelle Revue Française*. 1er déc. 1981 (347): 42-64.

———. *Jean-Jacques Rousseau: La Transparence et l'obstacle*. Paris: Gallimard, 1971.

———. "Sur l'emploi du chiasme dans 'Le Neveu de Rameau.'" *Revue de Métaphysique et de Morale*. 1984 Apr.-June. Vol. 2: 182-96.

Talmon, J.L. *The Origins of Totalitarian Democracy*. New York: Frederick A. Praeger, 1960.

Taylor, George V. "Noncapitalist Wealth and the Origins of the French Revolution." *American Historical Review*. Vol. 72, 1967: 77-103.

Timasheff, N.S. "Totalitarianism, Despotism, Dictatorship." *Totalitarianism*. Ed. Carl J. Friedrich. Cambridge: Harvard University Press, 1954: 39-47.

Trachtenberg, Zev M. *Making Citizens: Rousseau's Political Theory of Culture*. London: Routledge, 1993.

Trilling, Lionel. *Sincerity and Authenticity*. Cambridge: Harvard University Press, 1971.

Undank, Jack. *Diderot: Inside, Outside, and In-Between*. Madison: Coda Press, 1979.

Vartanian, Aram. *Diderot and Descartes*. Princeton: Princeton University Press, 1953.

———. "Diderot and Maupertuis." *Revue internationale de philosophie*. 1984. Vol. 38(1-2): 46-66.

Warner, Michael. *The Letters of the Republic: Publication and the Public Sphere in Eighteenth-Century America*. Cambridge: Harvard University Press, 1990.

Weber, Max. *Economy and Society. An Outline of Interpretive Sociology*. Ed. Guenther Roth and Claus Wittich. Berkeley: University of California Press, 1978.

———. *From Max Weber: Essays in Sociology*. Trans. and ed. H.H. Gerth and C. Wright Mills. New York: Oxford University Press, 1946.

———. *The Protestant Ethic and the Spirit of Capitalism*. Trans. Talcott Parsons. New York: Charles Scribner's Sons, 1958.

Weber, Shierry N. "The Aesthetics of Rousseau's *Pygmalion*." *Jean-Jacques Rousseau*. Ed. Harold Bloom. New York: Chelsea House, 1988.

Weirich, Paul. "Rousseau on Proportional Majority Rule." *Philosophy and Phenomenological Research*. 1986 Sept. Vol. 47(1):111-26.

Young, Iris Marion. "Impartiality and the Civic Public: Some Implications of Feminist Critiques of Moral and Political Theory." *Feminism as Critique*. Ed. Seyla Benhabib and Drucilla Cornell. Minneapolis: University of Minnesota Press, 1987.

Index